WINNING IN HIGH-TECH MARKETS
The Role of General Management

**How Motorola, Corning, and General Electric
have built global leadership through technology**

Joseph Morone
Center for Science and Technology Policy
School of Management
Rensselaer Polytechnic Institute

Harvard Business School Press
Boston, Massachusetts

97 96 95 94 93   5 4 3 2 1

The paper used in this publication meets the requirements of the American National
Standard for Permanence of Paper for Printed Library Materials Z39.49-1984.

Library of Congress Cataloging-in-Publication Data

Morone, Joseph G.
    Winning in high-tech markets : the role of general management /
Joseph Morone.
        p.   cm.
    Includes bibliographical references and index.
    ISBN 0-87584-325-5 (acid-free paper)
    1. High technology industries—United States—Management.
I. Title.
HC110.H53M67 1992
658.8—dc20

                                                                92-15842
                                                                      CIP

CONTENTS

To
Lindsay Jean Evans

Preface

I first met George Fisher, chairman and CEO of Motorola, in April 1990. I was hoping to convince him to participate in the project that culminated in the publication of this book, but I fully expected to hear the usual response that he and his colleagues just did not have the time. His reluctance, however, came from an entirely different source. "Holding us up as a model of success," he explained, "makes me nervous. I'm afraid that once we start reading about ourselves, we'll become complacent, and that is just about the worst thing that could happen to us."

Later, as I learned more about Motorola, I came to understand his reaction. This is a company that is driven by one imperative: do whatever it takes to lead. In the field of mobile and portable communications, Motorola has been the global leader for 40 years. Yet it is still pushing itself to improve, measuring itself against the best competitors in the world and always striving to be better.

As I finish this book, I think back to that first meeting. It is January 1992, and George Bush has just returned from his visit to Japan. The news media are filled with reports about auto industry executives complaining about closed Japanese markets and advocating even more protectionism in our domestic markets. Why do they, and not the George Fishers of this country, receive so much attention? Why do we focus on the firms that have lost their markets and want to insulate themselves from foreign competition rather than those that have built global leadership by meeting the best of the competition head on? We suffer from an abundance of negative role models—the fallen LBO artists of the 1980s; finger-pointing executives who blame everybody but themselves for their failure to compete in global markets; and worst of all, a new generation of populist politicians, whose "America first" rhetoric is tinged with anti-Japanese racism.

But there are also positive role models in this country. In places like Harrisburg, Corning, Waukesha, Schaumburg, and Corvalis, there are American managers who understand what is required to compete successfully in the toughest of short-cycle-time, investment-intensive, high-tech global markets. They have succeeded not because they were protected by the government but because they have been unwavering in their pursuit of technology leadership and

better products at competitive costs. The lesson they teach is as simple as it is inspiring: the United States can succeed in the world's
toughest high-tech markets, against the strongest foreign competitors. But to do so, we must look first to ourselves. We must begin
with our own firms and our own policies. The losers complain about
closed markets; the winners make better products at lower costs and
then use every means at their disposal to compete and succeed
abroad. They too must deal with closed foreign markets, and when
they do, they are in the forefront of those arguing for government
leadership in breaking down the barriers. But they argue even more
vociferously that the first step to succeeding in global markets is
to be better than the competition. The lesson for this country, its
educational system, and its political leadership could not be any
clearer: there is only one way to reassert American economic leadership, and that is through the pursuit of total leadership in every
domain in which we choose to compete.

This book describes in detail how three U.S.-based businesses—
GE Medical, Motorola's family of communications businesses, and
Corning—built and sustained such leadership in global, high-tech
markets.

Method of Inquiry

After an introductory chapter, case studies of these three businesses
are presented. Each case traces the evolution of the most significant
product lines of the business and describes the role senior management played in that development. The case studies are followed by
two additional chapters; the first discusses the implications of the
cases for management practice, the second for government policy.

This inquiry is based on one important methodological assumption. In order to identify managerial practices associated with success,
it is necessary to study them over time. Many studies of "best practice" begin with firms that are successful today, observe the practices
of the firms' current management, and then attribute the former to
the latter. But today's successes are largely the result of yesterday's
practices, just as today's practices will result in tomorrow's successes
and failures. Current management might be departing from the practices of its predecessors, and we might be observing not best practice,
but rather the early steps in the demise of what used to be a successful firm. The only way to avoid this trap is to study managerial practices as they evolve with the business. For this reason, the three case
studies in this book are historical in nature. Each traces the evolution
of today's general managerial practice across a span of decades.

Of course, the historical case study is subject to its own limitations. The most significant are the problems of selective recollection and revisionism. I have attempted to minimize these difficulties by basing each case study on three independent streams of information: internal company documents, written at the time of the events described in the cases; publicly available documents, also from the time of the events; and interviews with participants in the events. I interviewed at least two participants for each period of time examined. Another classic weakness of the case method is limited generalizability. The only way to minimize this problem is to structure the sample of cases in such a way that the differences among the cases are maximized. If we find similarities in general managerial practices in companies as entirely different as those studied here, there is reason to believe that the applicability of those practices extends beyond these particular cases.

The final limitation of this kind of study is that it requires access to detailed information about the companies being studied. This book would not have been possible without the goodwill of senior management at Motorola, Corning, and GE Medical Systems. I am indebted to George Fisher; John Trani, senior vice president of GE Medical Systems; and Dave Duke, vice chairman, Corning Incorporated, for granting me permission to conduct these studies. I am also indebted to three people who went out of their way to help me put together the cases: Bill Weisz from Motorola, Bill Prindle from Corning, and Bobby Bowen from GE Medical. These three introduced me to many of their colleagues who graciously met with me and discussed the managerial practices of their businesses. For the Motorola case, I am especially grateful to John Mitchell, Marty Cooper, and Jack Germain; for the Corning case, Bill Armistead, Forrest Behm, Dick Dulude, Jack Hutchins, Tom MacAvoy, Al Michaelsen, Bill Dumbaugh, and Ted Kozlowski; and for the GE Medical case, Morry Blumenfeld, Lonnie Edelheit, Art Glenn, Red Redington, Charles Reed, Walt Robb, and George Wise.

The larger study on which this book is based was funded by the Sloan Foundation and the Lehigh Center for Innovation Management Studies. For those of us who do our research at the intersection of management and technology, these two groups are a salvation. There is nowhere else to turn to for support, and it is no coincidence that their research agendas are heavily influenced by current and past managers of technology. I also wish to acknowledge my intellectual debt to Dick Rosenbloom of the Harvard Business School. Many of the arguments in this book grow out of his earlier work, and at important junctures in this project, he offered what in hindsight has proved to be sage advice. Thanks also to Roland Schmitt, president of Rensselaer and my former boss at GE, for introducing me to these firms; Bob Hawkins, my dean, for his patience and support; Al Paulson of Rensselaer and Bruce Guile of the National Academy of Engineering for their encouragement and insights; Vicki Burns and Jan Smith for their skillful and patient secretarial help; and my many students, especially Steve Walsh, Gary Lynn, Damian Saccocio, John Brandolini, Sherri Naughton, and Peter Theis. Finally, I had one unfair advantage in writing this book. My wife, Lindsay Evans, edited each version of this manuscript, helped hone the arguments, and at critical moments, reminded me that if I were to practice what I preached in this manuscript, good enough was not nearly good enough.

WINNING IN HIGH-TECH MARKETS

CHAPTER 1

TECHNOLOGY AND COMPETITIVE ADVANTAGE

It began with black and white televisions in the late 1960s. The consumer electronics industry, created and dominated by firms epitomizing U.S. industrial might, was swept away by competitors that first offered low-cost, low-end products; then, a growing array of better-quality products at comparable costs; and finally, a broad range of higher-value and sometimes radically new products. It happened again in the steel, automotive, and machine tool industries. Now it is occurring in high technology. U.S. firms are being outperformed in the fast-growing, dynamic, technology-intensive industries that they themselves pioneered. In semiconductors, Japanese firms controlled 80 percent of the world market for memory chips in 1988 and had eclipsed U.S. industry in most critical areas of technology.[1] In electronics more generally, four of the five largest producers in 1990, and six out of the top ten, were Japanese (see Figure 1.1). IBM was still number one, but it was followed in dollar value of electronics-related sales by Matsushita, NEC, Toshiba, Hitachi, Philips, Siemens, Fujitsu, and Sony.[2] More revealing than dollar volume are the underlying technology trends. According to a 1990 study prepared by the Council on Competitiveness, in such key areas of electronics-related technology as optoelectronic components, packaging and interconnections, display, hardcopy (i.e., printing), and optical information storage, U.S. industry was either "weak" relative to Japanese competitors, or "losing badly."[3] This study reaffirmed the conclusion of several previous studies, perhaps the most notable of which was the Japanese government's own assessment of the relative strength of U.S. and Japanese technology.[4]

In factory automation, a similar tale has unfolded. In the business heralded by U.S. industry in the early 1980s as the vehicle for industrial rejuvenation, most of the leading U.S. competitors had succumbed by the end of the decade. And in advanced materials, a 1988 report by the Office of Technology Assessment found that U.S. companies in the field of ceramics believed by a two-to-one margin that Japan was the world leader. The battle seemed over before it

1

Figure 1.1
Electronics Companies, Global Leaders

Company	1989 Electronics Sales ($ million)
IBM Corp.	62,710
Matsushita Electric Industrial Co.	31,319
NEC Corp.	24,957
Toshiba Corp.	22,674
Hitachi Corp.	22,055
Philips NV	21,594
Siemens AG	19,825
Fujitsu Ltd.	18,477
Sony Corp.	16,904
General Motors Corp.	16,880

had even begun.[5] By the end of the 1980s, there were growing indications that this pattern was repeating itself in other areas of advanced materials such as high-temperature superconductors.[6]

The decline of U.S. industrial performance in high-technology industries raises a host of questions. How could U.S. firms have lost so much ground so quickly in such important industries? How could technology-rich firms, in a technology-rich society, be so outperformed in technology-intensive markets? Is it already too late, or are there steps that can be taken by U.S. industry and government to reverse the slide? These questions lead to a more fundamental concern: Why are some firms better than others at building and sustaining advantage on the basis of technology? In virtually every competitive environment, and in virtually every region of the globe, it is possible to find competitors that are better than their counterparts at recognizing and seizing on the strategic implications of technology. Why have Sony, Matsushita, and JVC been more adept than their U.S. and European counterparts in making strategic use of technology in consumer electronics? Why has Toshiba been more adept in semiconductor memories, Canon and Sharp in fax and digital imagery, Fanuc in factory automation, and Kyocera in advanced materials?

As many examples as there are of technology-intensive industries in which U.S. firms have lost their lead, there are numerous instances of precisely the reverse pattern—similar industries in which U.S. firms have been, and continue to be, leaders on the basis of technology. Merck has been more adept at building advantage on technology than many of its counterparts in the pharmaceutical industry. Union Carbide, Dow Chemical, and GE Plastics have been more adept in their sectors of the chemical industry, as have Hewlett-Packard in computer peripherals, Intel in microprocessors, AMP in electronic connectors, Nucor in steelmaking, and Microsoft in software. What accounts for their success? Why are some firms—foreign or domestic—better at building advantage on the basis of technology than others?

Many factors contribute to the firm-to-firm variation in ability to make strategic use of technology. Japanese electronics companies, for example, enjoy a number of structural advantages that have contributed to their dramatic success. Differences in U.S. and Japanese macroeconomic conditions, as well as government trade and technology policies have also played a role. As important as these external factors are, however, this book focuses on the role that internal management plays in building and sustaining advantage on the basis of technology. A debt-laden economy, and financial and political environments relentlessly oriented toward the near term, cannot help U.S. firms in global competition. But there are enough U.S. firms that succeed in technology-intensive industries despite these handicaps, and enough foreign firms that fail despite their more supportive environments, that one cannot help but conclude that success in these industries, as in any other industry, begins with actions taken inside the firm.

Once we examine the actions of the individual firm, it quickly becomes apparent that differences in how firms manage their technical functions—manufacturing, engineering and R&D—help account for the variation in ability to make effective use of technology. But these differences lead inevitably to the larger question of why some firms manage their technical functions more effectively than others. The answer lies primarily with the behavior and practices of general management—the people with profit and loss responsibility who set the tone, objectives, and directions of the firm. The premise of this book is that to understand why some firms are better than others at building advantage on the basis of technology, and to understand why so many U.S. firms have failed to compete effectively in high-tech markets, we must look first and foremost within the firm, at the top. We must examine the behavior and practices of general management.

A second premise of this book is that an effective way to develop an understanding of the role general management plays in building advantage on the basis of technology is to study U.S. firms that have succeeded in the same high-technology markets where many of their counterparts have failed. For there are U.S. firms, a small number to be sure, that compete effectively in precisely those industries where Japanese firms have thrived. They are led by managers who have built and sustained global market leadership on the basis of technology leadership—despite the structural advantages enjoyed by their Japanese counterparts and despite the structural disadvantages created by the political, financial, and economic environment in the United States. This book is about these general managers and their practices. It explores how three U.S. businesses have built and sustained leadership in high-technology industries: Corning Incorporated in high-performance glass and ceramics such as optical fibers and liquid crystal display glass; GE Medical Systems in diagnostic imaging equipment; and Motorola in mobile and portable communications. Each firm is a global leader in fast-growing, dynamic, short-cycle-time, multibillion-dollar markets. Each has built its position on the basis of technology leadership. And each exhibits a pattern of general managerial practice that is as striking in its similarity to that of the two others as it is in its divergence from conventional U.S. practice.

Why Some Firms Make Better Use of Technology Than Others

Contemporary scholarship offers two broad explanations for differences among firms in their ability to make effective use of technology. One focuses on factors external to the firm, such as macroeconomic conditions, government policy, and industry structure, and helps account for cross-national variations. The other, which focuses on internal variables, maintains that if firms vary in their ability to exploit technology, the reasons have to do with how they manage R&D, engineering, and manufacturing. These two approaches are complementary, and together they go a long way toward explaining why some firms are more adept at building advantage on the basis of technology than others. But both are incomplete without consideration of a third factor—the role of general management.

External Sources of Variation

The most comprehensive framework for analyzing the myriad external conditions that influence a firm's ability to compete in technology-intensive, global markets is provided by Michael Porter in *The Competitive Advantage of Nations*.[7] Porter describes four interdependent clusters of external conditions: "factor conditions," the richness of a nation's endowment in what economists call factors of production—human resources, physical resources, knowledge resources, capital resources, and infrastructure; "demand conditions," the sophistication, size, and nature of the domestic market for a firm's products; "related and supporting industries," the competitive strength of the network of domestic firms that supply or complement the firm (e.g., software suppliers complement computer manufacturers); and "firm strategy, structure, and rivalry," patterns of managerial practice, industrial structure (e.g., degree of concentration and vertical integration) and interfirm rivalry that are characteristic of the nation in which the firm is based.

One of these external factors in particular has become the focus of considerable attention in the debate over whether and why U.S. firms have had difficulty competing in technology-intensive markets. It is a profound difference in the *structure* of U.S. and Japanese industry. While this is by no means the only important difference between U.S. and Japanese industry,[8] it is arguably the most significant. It illustrates both that external factors can influence the ability of firms to compete on the basis of technology and that such factors by themselves are insufficient to account for why some firms are more adept than others at building and sustaining advantage on the basis of technology.

Industry Structure. Charles Ferguson, Clyde Prestowitz, Carl Kester, Robert Zielinski and Nigel Holloway, and others have shown that Japanese firms are, in a number of important respects, structured differently from their U.S. counterparts.[9] The differences have been most clearly documented for the electronics industry, where perhaps the most striking dissimilarity between U.S. and Japanese firms is the relatively high degree of vertical integration in the Japanese firms. A Council on Competitiveness analysis reports that

> participants at each level of the vertically disintegrated U.S. electronics industry face large, well-financed, diversified industrial firms whose extended family of companies often include OEM business, component manufacturing, raw materials supply and manufacturing equipment production capability.[10]

The laptop computer industry exemplifies this pattern, although the same could be said of consumer electronics or imaging (i.e., facsimile machines, printers, copiers, cameras, and so forth). The laptop computer market, $7.5 billion in 1990, was expected to triple in volume by 1993, in the process growing from roughly one-fifth to one-third of the overall personal computer market. As of 1991, the leading suppliers of laptop computers were Toshiba, NEC, Tandy, Zenith Data (acquired in 1990 by Bull of France), and Compaq.[11] The two U.S. firms, Tandy and Compaq, are primarily personal computer makers. In 1990, Compaq had total revenues of $3.6 billion and Tandy $4.5 billion. The two Japanese firms, Toshiba and NEC, are several times larger. Toshiba's total electronics-related sales (70 percent of total sales) were $22.7 billion, and NEC's were $25 billion. Both are horizontally integrated into other fields of electronics. Toshiba competes in, among other things, telecommunications, medical equipment, and consumer electronics; NEC competes in telecommunications, mobile communications, mainframe computers, and facsimile machines. Both are also vertically integrated. NEC and Toshiba are the world's top two semiconductor manufacturers and are also leaders in the development of the liquid crystal displays and batteries that are critical components in the laptop computer business. This combination of both horizontal and vertical integration gives the Japanese firms significant economies of scale and scope.[12]

Reinforcing the differences in degree of integration are the fundamental variations in the ownership structure of U.S. and Japanese firms. Many, if not most, of the major Japanese competitors in high-technology markets are members of a network or association of firms called a keiretsu. NEC, for example, is part of the Sumitomo Group, one of Japan's major keiretsu.[13] The Sumitomo Group is comprised of 20 firms—most of them large and highly integrated in their own right—from a diverse set of industries including construction, cement and glass, mining, machinery, chemicals, real estate, and financial services. Each member of a group typically owns a few percent of the total stock of each other member firm; in total, between 15 and 30 percent of each company in the group is owned by other members. The result is a complex set of relationships, ranging from financial support, to sharing of information, to close buyer-supplier relations. In 1987, for example, trade among firms within the Sumitomo group accounted for 14 percent of those firms' total trade. Marie Anchordoguy reports that "most computers used by Sumitomo group companies today . . . are from NEC, the group's computer maker."[14] There is no counterpart to this kind of interrelationship among U.S. firms. As Prestowitz explains, a group in the United States comparable to the Sumitomo Group would include the likes of "Chase Manhattan Bank, Inland Steel, Pittsburgh Plate Glass, Reynolds Aluminum, IBM and the Du Pont Company."[15]

This high degree of integration in Japan's industrial structure is connected to a pattern of corporate ownership that is strikingly different from that found in the United States. About 70 percent of the outstanding stock of publicly held Japanese firms is owned by other corporations and financial institutions. Most of this stock is not actively traded; that is, the majority of owners of major Japanese firms are "stable shareholders," who use stock ownership, in Kester's words, "to cement business relationships among companies and serve as indicators of mutual long-term commitments," rather than as financial investments. "A decision to sell equity held under these arrangements would be seen as tantamount to a permanent repudiation of the relationship."[16] In the United States, of course, ownership has precisely the opposite character. The predominant motivation is financial gain; buying and selling, sometimes in the space of minutes, and often in large volumes by institutional investors seeking to maximize short-term returns, is the rule.[17]

These differences in ownership structure are of particular significance in the competition for high-technology markets, where long time horizons and high levels of capital and R&D investment are prerequisites for success. Stable ownership leads to "patient capital." It places less emphasis on short-term returns and more on long-term survival and growth, less on return on investment as the primary measure of success, and more on market share. In high-technology industries, where more than one dollar of capital investment is often required to produce every dollar of annual sales, and where a decade of business development is often required before breakeven is achieved, patient capital can be all-important. Many observers attribute the virtual absence of U.S. firms in the critical liquid crystal display (LCD) market—which is well over a billion dollars in size, growing at over 35 percent per year, and of fundamental importance to almost every field of electronics[18]—to the lack of patient capital among large U.S. corporations. It certainly was not for lack of creativity: LCD technology was developed in the United States.

Differences in industry and ownership structure thus help explain the disappointing performance of U.S. firms relative to their Japanese competitors in high-technology industries. But in a sense, these structural differences only highlight the question of why some firms make better strategic use of technology than others. For there is ample evidence that U.S. firms can outperform their Japanese counterparts in precisely those markets where these differences clearly favor the Japanese. The cases in this book concern three such firms—global leaders in their markets despite the high levels of integration of Japanese firms, the benefits of keiretsu membership, and the advantages of stable ownership. The success of these firms in the face of such disadvantages can only mean that there are other factors at work that help account for differences in a firm's ability to build advantage on the basis of technology.

Internal Sources of Variation

Technology management. The factors internal to the firm that help account for variations in ability to compete on the basis of technology are the subject of a body of scholarship that gained widespread currency during the 1980s. Before its newfound popularity, the study of the "management of technology" concentrated on the R&D function—on the factors associated with successful R&D projects, how to organize R&D operations, and how to manage and motivate scientists and engineers.[19] Now a broader view prevails.[20] Manufacturing and process technology, and the entire new-product development process, are being studied. Moreover, the focus has shifted from a sometimes exclusive concern with internally generated technology to a more balanced concern with both internally and externally developed technology and with strategies for acquiring the latter.[21]

By the end of the 1980s, this broader view had swept through the management and economics literature, and universities throughout the country were scrambling to establish MOT (management of technology) programs and concentrations. We now have a more detailed understanding of successful technology management practices and of the organizational requirements for achieving them. The uses and limits of programmable automation, along with the need to simplify operations, improve quality by "doing it right the first time," and accelerate new product development and customer response time, have all been well documented.[22]

One of the most interesting developments has been the growing realization that technology management practices vary considerably among firms, and that some practices are more clearly associated with commercial success than others. The more that is learned about technology management, the more apparent it becomes that some firms are more adept at managing their technical functions than others, and that these differences translate to competitive advantage. Harold Edmondson and Steven Wheelwright, for example, argue that with regard to manufacturing practices, U.S. firms fall into three broad groups: firms seeking local, quick fixes for near-time manufacturing problems; the largest group—firms committed to catching up to the best manufacturing practices by adopting tools such as just in time, total quality control, and programmable automation; and the third group, which employs many of tools of the second group and strives not to catch up, but to "develop distinctive competencies in manufacturing that provide a competitive advantage in the marketplace."[23] Only "a handful of such firms"—Edmondson and Wheelwright cite Hewlett-Packard and Chaparral Steel—appear to be operating at this third level.

Perhaps the most dramatic example of differences among firms in their technology management practices and the competitive impact made by these differences comes from the auto industry. James Womack, Daniel Jones, and Daniel Roos, in *The Machine That Changed the World*, report that Japanese car makers take an average of 46.2 months to develop a new car, compared to 60.4 months for American car makers. Moreover, they require an average of 16.8 man-hours to assemble a vehicle, compared to 25.1 man-hours for American car makers; they produce an average of 60 defects per 100 vehicles produced, compared to 82.3 defects for American car makers; and they devote 4.1 percent of the space in their assembly facilities to repair, compared to 12.9 percent for their American counterparts.[24]

While evidence of such differences helps explain why some firms are better than others at building advantage on the basis of technology, it raises a closely related question. Why do some firms have more superior technology management practices than others? Why are only a handful of U.S. firms striving to become world-class manufacturers? Why are Japanese car manufacturers so far ahead of U.S. manufacturers in speed of new product development, productivity, and quality? The search for answers to these questions leads inevitably to general management and the role it plays in the process of building and sustaining advantage on the basis of technology. Robert Hayes and Ramchandran Jaikumar, for example, write that the pursuit of world-class manufacturing capability requires nothing short of

> . . . profound reform in the modern corporation. At one level, reform means changes in cost accounting and performance measurement procedures, human resource management, and capital budgeting. At the next level, it means new organizational structures that can accommodate more interactive and cooperative working relationships. At a still higher level, reform means that top officers must cultivate new skills and managerial styles. It may well require a new generation of executives.[25]

Technology strategy. Although contemporary studies of management of technology point to the significance of general management, they shed little light on exactly what is required of general management in order to successfully build and sustain competitive advantage on the basis of technology. Within the management of technology field, the body of scholarship that comes closest focuses on "technology strategy." A technology strategy specifies the firm's "technological goals and the principal technological means for achieving both those technological goals and the business goals of the organization."[26]

The significance of a technology strategy is that it explicitly links the management of a firm's technology functions to its larger business strategy. From the technology strategy perspective, technology must be planned and managed so that it is consistent with, and supportive of, the overall objectives of the firm. Developing a technology strategy and ensuring its consistency with the company's business strategy are the central concerns of the chief technical officer. The primary measure of success of those activities is not the scientific elegance of the research performed or the uniqueness of the technology developed, but their utility to the firm. This is what Alan Kantrow meant when he said that it is "plain common sense" to view a company's technology strategy "within the context of its general business orientation,"[27] and what Porter intended when he argued that while technology strategy is a "potentially powerful vehicle" for pursuing competitive advantage, the particular form that technology strategy takes should depend on the general business strategy being pursued by the firm. "Depending on which generic [competitive] strategy is being followed, the character of the technological strategy will be different."[28]

Contemporary thought about technology strategy places decisions about company technology in the context of company strategy, but it stops short of treating company strategy itself—and the closely associated decision-making practices of general management—as a variable in the process of building, or failing to build, advantage on the basis of technology. This implies that business strategy is separate from company technology, and that technology is solely a means to the goals set out in business strategy. But business strategy is itself variable, therefore we need to consider the possibility that differences in business strategy are associated with differences in the ability of firms to exploit technology. Surely what distinguishes the innovative firm from one less innovative is not just that it is more efficient in applying technology in support of its business strategy, but that its business strategy itself is conducive to recognizing, seizing upon, and exploiting technology. It is one thing to make technology strategy consistent with business strategy, and quite another to develop and implement a business strategy that promotes successful exploitation of technology. While the former might be construed as good technology management practice, only the latter can lead to a genuinely strategic use of technology—to the building of competitive advantage on the basis of technology.[29]

The demise of the U.S. consumer electronics industry illustrates this point well. Many observers attribute the Japanese success to superior technology management practices. But the few careful analyses of this industry offer a more fundamental explanation. Richard Rosenbloom and William Abernathy concluded that by the late 1960s and 1970s, U.S. firms considered television a mature business, one in which technology no longer offered much leverage, whereas the Japanese firms saw it as a high-technology growth business.[30] This difference in business strategy led to different time horizons, investment strategies, and approaches to new product and process development—in short, entirely different technology strategies. The Japanese firms did indeed enjoy a clear technology advantage by the mid-1980s, but that advantage was built over the course of decades and was the product of business strategies that were strikingly different from those pursued by their technology- and resource-rich U.S. counterparts.

The same pattern can be found in the closely related history of the videocassette recorder. Rosenbloom and Michael Cusumano conclude that the firms that succeeded in the decades-long struggle to bring the VCR to market proceeded by means of "learning by trying," that is, by innovating over an extended period of time through a gradual series of incremental product improvements. This sounds like a lesson in technology strategy until one digs a bit deeper. The winners were able to pursue such a technology strategy because of

> clarity of focus and the consistency of strategic management . . . Strategic consistency, then, differentiated the successful VCR pioneers from the others. Leadership provided by general managers was essential to achieving consistent direction over a lengthy period of development. At Sony, top managers explicitly and consistently guided the direction of VCR development efforts. At Ampex, top management direction was sporadic and inconsistent over time; engineers on their own failed to develop a fruitful direction for technical development.[31]

The point here is not that differences in technology management and strategy are unimportant, but that if we seek to understand why some firms are more adept at exploiting technology than others, we also need to consider general managerial practice as an important variable. After all, the most striking feature of the failure of U.S. firms to compete effectively in high-tech industries is that many of those firms possessed superior technological capabilities. The examples extend well beyond consumer electronics, where RCA had the most advanced technological capabilities by far in the 1960s and 1970s. Xerox, by virtue of the R&D performed at its Palo Alto Research Center (PARC), had a decade's technological lead in the field of personal computing, yet it never came even remotely close to exploiting it commercially.[32] GE spent hundreds of millions of dollars automating its factories in the early 1980s, and tens of millions a year in R&D related to factory automation, yet it was thoroughly outperformed in the factory automation business by the much smaller Fanuc. And there is no lack of technological strength to explain the failure of U.S. firms to enter and establish leadership in fields such as flat panel displays and electronic imaging. Explaining these commercial failures must begin with the strategic steps—the actions of general management—taken by Japanese firms and not taken by their technology-rich U.S. counterparts to lay the foundations for future business success.

Toward a General Managerial Perspective on Technology

To understand why some firms make better strategic use of technology than others, we therefore need to examine not only variations in external conditions and in technology strategy and management but variations in the general management of the firm as well. We need to identify, analyze, and understand the general managerial practices associated with building and sustaining advantage on the basis of technology. In short, we need a behavioral model of the role general management plays with respect to technology in firms that are adept at competing on the basis of technology.

This book examines this role of general management in three U.S. businesses that have been especially good at building advantage on the basis of technology. The analysis is pursued from three distinct, though clearly related, perspectives. For each firm we first explore general management's business strategies; then, its technology strategies for implementing those business strategies; and finally, the decision-making style underlying the formulation and implementation of business and technology strategies.

Business Strategy and Technology

The formulation and implementation of strategy is an ongoing process, continuously adapting to the firm's changing capabilities, experiences, markets, and competition.[33] How does this evolving process influence, and how is it influenced by, the equally dynamic process of technology development? A small number of studies have explored at least some of the dimensions of this question. In one way or another, each points to a relationship between strategic focus and consistency on the one hand, and successful exploitation of technology on the other. We have already cited Rosenbloom and Cusumano's study of the evolution of the VCR, which emphasized the "clarity of focus and the consistency of strategic management" displayed by Sony, Matsushita, and JVC. Modesto Maidique and Hayes described a similar relationship in their study of successful high-tech firms:

> Even a superficial analysis of the most successful high-technology firms leads one to conclude that they are highly focused. With few exceptions, the leaders in high-technology fields, such as computers, aerospace, electronic instruments, and duplicating machines, realize the great bulk of their sales either from a single product line or from a closely related set of product lines. IBM, Boeing, Intel, and Genentech confine themselves almost entirely to computer products, commercial aircraft, integrated circuits, and genetic engineering, respectively.[34]

This suggests that business strategies with certain attributes—strategic consistency and focus in particular—are conducive to, if not necessary for, successful exploitation of technology. This leads to a number of interesting questions. First, can this relationship be generalized? Second, are other attributes of business strategy, in addition to focus and consistency, also associated with the successful exploitation of technology? Third, how do we distinguish between strategic consistency and focus that lead to successful exploitation of technology and strategic consistency and focus that is blind to new opportunities?

Finally, the history of the VCR is in large measure a description of what we might call "strategy pull"; general management knew that it wanted to develop video technology for the consumer market, and it pulled technology development in that direction. But do businesses that make strategic use of technology also exhibit a tendency toward "technology push"—toward the shaping of business strategy in response to technology developments? How does technological opportunity (or risk) shape business strategy? Is it possible that some, or even many, of the opportunities pursued by the successful exploiters of technology were identified, championed, and perhaps even forced on reluctant and skeptical general managers by technology groups within the company?

Each case in this book will ask the following questions about the relationship between business strategy and technology:

1. Can we identify attributes of business strategy that tend
   to be associated with, or are conducive to, the strategic
   use of technology?

2. How does business strategy influence technology development?

3. How, in turn, does technology influence business strategy in such businesses?

Technology Strategy and General Management

A related but distinct set of questions that help illuminate the role of general management in the process of building advantage on the basis of technology center around technology strategy. What role does general management see for technology in the implementation of its business strategy? Does it explicitly use technology as a source of sustainable competitive advantage? If so, does it pursue a deliberate technology strategy? When we examine businesses that have been adept at making strategic use of technology, do we find an orientation among their general managers toward technology leadership as opposed to fast following, radical innovation as opposed to incremental, or product technology improvements as opposed to process? Do they explicitly pursue learning curves, and if so, what is their motivation? Do they think about life cycles and the threat of technological maturation and displacement, and if so, how do they protect against them? In short, we would like to shed light on how general management views these basic precepts and concepts of contemporary scholarship about technology strategy and management.

Consider, for example, the notion of technology leadership as opposed to fast following.[35] Two of the most frequently cited examples of fast followership are IBM's PC and GE's CT (computerized tomography, an X-ray-based medical imaging technology).[36] After the fact, these appear to be cases of successful fast following. But what were the strategic considerations at IBM and GE at the time the key decisions were made? Was general management at IBM and GE deliberately watching developments at Apple and EMI (the early market leaders), waiting for the right time to enter the fray (in other words, pursuing a fast followership strategy)? Or were they simply slower to recognize that a major opportunity (or threat) existed, and, once they did, moved as quickly as possible before it was too late? After the fact, it does not matter; IBM and GE behaved as if they were fast followers. If, however, the goal is to understand the role general management plays in the process of building advantage on the basis of technology, the difference is important. It is necessary to understand the intended strategy of general management in these cases—to understand whether and how considerations of fast following figured in their strategic decision making, rather than how their actions might be characterized after the fact.

This book will therefore explore three aspects of the relationship between general management and technology strategy. We must ask the following about businesses that have been adept at building advantage on the basis of technology:

1. Can a general managerial posture toward technology be discerned? That is, what is general management's view of the impact of technology on its business and business strategy?

2. Can the elements of a technology strategy be discerned—for example, a particular orientation toward pursuing radical or leapfrog innovations as opposed to incremental innovations, or toward pursuing manufacturing technology improvements as opposed to product technology improvements?

3. In particular, can a particular orientation toward technology leadership—toward pioneering new markets, developing superior products, and pursuing learning curve and cost leadership—be discerned?

Decision Making and Technology

A third set of issues that illuminates the role of general management concerns the decision-making style of general managers as they face the often risky and uncertain problems involved in building and sustaining competitive advantage. Should general management support an ambitious and costly development program that might lead to an entirely new line of business? How many programs can it afford to support, and how does it go about deciding which ones to support? Should it proceed with the scale-up of a promising but still uncertain new business opportunity that will require tens of millions of dollars at the least but is still years away from breakeven? How long should it continue to nurture such opportunities, and how does it balance the demands for resources for longer-term prospects against the more immediate needs of existing businesses?

Contemporary scholarship on decision making offers more confusion than insight on these issues. It suffers from a schism of long duration, with normative models that prescribe how decision makers should behave on one side and behavioral models that describe how successful decision makers actually behave on the other. Normative models of decision making, for both the public and private sector, suggest that decisions should be made on the basis of comprehensive, quantitative analysis. The decision maker should scan a wide range of options, calculate the consequences of each, evaluate those consequences, and then select an option that satisfies an appropriate decision rule. In some circumstances, this will be to maximize expected value; in others, minimize expected loss; in still others, maximize the minimum benefit. The dominant rule for private sector managers is that investment decisions be made so as to maximize net present value.

The works of Charles Lindblom, James March, Henry Mintzberg, J. Brian Quinn, and Herbert Simon, however, suggest that in practice the conditions needed to pursue, let alone achieve, the standards of the normative models rarely if ever prevail in real decision-making contexts.[37] What is far more common in both private and public sector decision making is that the alternatives facing decision makers are at best "dimly perceived";[38] knowledge about the consequences of those alternatives is incomplete; the time and resources required to generate information needed for decisions are rarely available; and decision-making objectives and values are themselves ambiguous and often in conflict.

Empirically based studies of decision making suggest that successful decision makers employ decision strategies fundamentally different from those recommended by the normative literature. These studies all suggest that successful decision makers exhibit an underlying strategy of "learning from experience" or "learning by doing." According to Quinn, the approaches used by successful decision makers "frequently bear little resemblance to the rational-analytical systems so often touted in the planning literature." Successful managers in large organizations, he argues, rely on

> . . . much more evolutionary practices than this model usually implies. Their approach might at first seem to be disjointed or muddling, but on closer analysis the rationale behind their incremental approach to strategy formulation was so powerful that it perhaps provides a normative model for most strategic decisions.[39]

Mintzberg, in his empirical studies of decision making, reached a similar conclusion, and went so far as to argue that his findings "put into question virtually every conventional belief about how strategies are supposed to form in organizations." The key to successful strategic decision making in his view is not "foresight, but a capacity and willingness to learn" from experience. This stands in sharp contrast to the more conventional approach where decision makers "retreat to their offices and mire themselves in detached analysis instead of getting out in the field and learning."[40]

The conflict between normative and empirical models of decision making reaches a head in building and sustaining advantage on the basis of technology. In addition to the usual difficulties that face general management in competitive markets, technology intensity adds a layer of complexity. The only certainty in the uncertain process of developing new product and process technology is that the unexpected lies ahead. The path to successful technology development is strewn with surprises, partial successes, and failures. The markets for products still under development are equally uncertain; often, they literally do not exist and cannot be explored until early generations of the product have been developed and introduced. Moreover, the threat that a new technological approach will displace one's own is always present, as are questions about how fast the competition is proceeding and how well its products and processes will perform. Added to the high degrees of uncertainty are the high rates of R&D spending and investment usually required to remain competitive in high-technology markets.

The manner in which general managers deal with these uncertainties is thus fundamental to building advantage on the basis of technology, for it may well be that some styles of decision making under these conditions are more conducive to building such advantage than others. A central part of this investigation is therefore to explore the decision-making style of general managers in firms that have competed successfully in technology-intensive markets.

1. In the face of uncertainty, how have those general managers gone about evaluating new product and business opportunities? How and why have they decided to pursue some opportunities and forgo others? What decision rules do they employ, and what time horizons do they exhibit?

2. More generally, which of the two general models of decision making discussed above more accurately describes the style of decision making that they actually employ?

The Cases

This three-pronged (business strategy, technology strategy, and the decision-making style underlying them) investigation into general management's role in building advantage on the basis of technology is based on detailed, historical case studies of three U.S. businesses that have successfully competed on a worldwide basis in high-tech markets targeted by Japanese firms. The cases have been drawn deliberately from those high-technology industries where the United States has had the most difficulty in competing and where the Japanese successes have been most conspicuous. The point is not to harp on U.S. failures but rather to seek understanding of what is required for success. If our goal is to discern patterns of general managerial practice that are conducive to building advantage on the basis of technology, where better to look than at businesses that thrive in the very markets where so many of their counterparts have failed?

Unfortunately, there are not many U.S. successes from which to choose. Many of the U.S. firms that are widely recognized for their ability to compete on the basis of technology—such as 3M, Merck, and Procter & Gamble—compete in markets on which the Japanese have not focused. When we limit consideration to markets targeted by Japanese industry, we find no more than a half-dozen U.S. firms that have clearly been successful (by such typical standards as market share and relative profitability) over an extended period of time: Hewlett-Packard in desktop printers, Intel in microprocessors, AMP in electrical and electronic connectors, Corning in specialty glass and ceramics, GE Medical Systems in diagnostic imaging equipment, and Motorola in communications. This book explores how three of these six outstanding high-tech competitors—Corning, GE Medical, and Motorola Communications—have built global leadership in precisely the kind of high-technology markets in which other U.S. firms have had trouble competing.

> Corning Incorporated produces a wide array of specialty glass and ceramic products, ranging from ceramic substrates for automotive catalytic converters to telescope mirrors. Since the late 1960s, Corning has almost completely transformed itself from a $500 million manufacturer in mostly maturing markets (television bulbs, light bulb envelopes, passive electronic components) to a $3 billion (not including the joint ventures in which it holds equity) leader in a number of dynamic, fast-growing high-tech markets. Several of the markets it leads are marked by a strong Japanese presence and by many of the characteristics of the semiconductor market (capital- and R&D-intensive, learning curve-driven, commodity-like). The optical fiber market, which Corning pioneered in the 1970s and leads in the 1990s, was targeted

by Japan's Ministry of International Trade and Industry (MITI) and NTT (Japan's equivalent of AT&T) in the late 1970s. And it is virtually the only glass manufacturer in the world capable of supplying the high-performance glass needed by LCD manufacturers, which are none other than Japan's large, vertically integrated electronics giants. Ironically, these Japanese LCD firms are as dependent on Corning's high-performance glass as the U.S. computer manufacturers are on the Japanese LCDs.

GE Medical Systems produces high-performance, highly differentiated medical diagnostic imaging equipment. In 1973, it was a $200 million X-ray equipment manufacturer with a declining market share and less than $1.5 million in profits. It was ending nearly a decade of a decidedly unsuccessful effort to diversify from X-ray equipment into broad-based medical equipment and was a candidate for divestiture by its parent company. Less than 20 years later, it had grown to more than $2 billion in sales. Against competition such as Toshiba, Hitachi, Siemens, and Philips, it built itself into the world's leading supplier of diagnostic imaging equipment, particularly computerized tomography (CT) and magnetic resonance (MR) imaging systems.

Motorola is the global leader in mobile and portable communications markets—mobile and portable radios, pagers, cellular telephones, portable data equipment, and the like. Even though these are primarily industrial markets, they resemble consumer electronics (a business Motorola exited in the mid-1970s) in a number of respects. Among the primary competitors have been the large, vertically integrated Japanese electronics companies, such as Matsushita and NEC, which in the late 1970s and early 1980s attacked the low end of Motorola's markets in much the same way they had attacked consumer electronics a decade earlier. Manufacturing and quality are critical sources of advantage in these markets, and cycle time is short and getting shorter. Motorola has succeeded in building and sustaining global leadership in virtually every segment of the mobile and portable communication market despite these similarities to consumer electronics. Along the way, it has grown from a fledgling mobile radio operation in the late 1940s to a $5 billion, still rapidly growing collection of businesses.

While these three businesses are similar in that they have competed successfully in global high-tech markets, they differ from each other in a number of respects, the most prominent of which are relative size, degree of diversification of parent company, degree of influence of founding family, ownership structure, type of products, and type of production environment. See Figure 1.2 for a summary of these differences.

GE is of course the largest parent company in the sample, and the most diversified. Corning is the smallest and also highly diversified. Motorola is intermediate in size and relatively undiversified. Members of the founding families still play prominent roles in the general management of Motorola and Corning. The recently retired chairman of Motorola, Robert Galvin, is the son of founder Paul Galvin, and Christopher, Robert's son, is now a member of the corporate executive office. The family influence is even stronger in Corning, where chairman and CEO James Houghton is the great-great-grandson of the company's founder. James's brother, Amory, was his predecessor, serving as CEO from 1966 to 1983. In contrast, there is no family influence, and no tradition of such influence, in GE.

As for ownership structure, GE's and Corning's is comprised of relatively low percentages of institutional investors, whereas Motorola's exhibits a relatively high level. Our businesses also differ in the nature of the technology environment in which they usually operate. Corning is primarily a components manufacturer, whereas Motorola Communications is a manufacturer of relatively small, inexpensive systems, and GE Medical of relatively large, expensive electronics systems. The production environments of Motorola Communications and GE Medical are primarily assembly operations, whereas Corning's is primarily a materials processing operation.

This diversity makes it unlikely that the successes of our cases can be attributed to a structural or cultural feature that the firms happen to share. If very different U.S. businesses are succeeding in markets where many others are having a hard time competing, the managerial practices of those businesses are the most likely source of their success. Moreover, given how different they are from each other, any similarities we find in technology-related, general managerial practices become especially noteworthy.

Figure 1.2
Diversity Of Cases

	Degree of Diversification	Size	Family Influence	% Institutional Investors	Product Type	Production Environment
Corning	high	$3B*	high	52%	component	materials processing
GE	high	$60B	none	49%	large system	fabrication/ assembly
Motorola	low	$11B	medium	69%	small system	fabrication/ assembly

*Does not include sales from equity JVs.

Notes

1. National Advisory Committee on Semiconductors, "A Strategic Industry at Risk: A Report to the President and the Congress," Washington, DC, November 1989.
2. "Business Roundup," *IEEE Spectrum*, vol. 28 (January 1991), p. 80.
3. Council on Competitiveness, "Gaining New Ground: Technology Priorities for America's Future," Washington, DC, February 1991, p. 9; National Science Foundation, "The Semiconductor Industry: Report of a Federal Interagency Staff Working Group," Washington, DC, November 16, 1987.
4. Ministry of International Trade and Industry, "Trends and Future Tasks in Industrial Technology," White Paper, 1988. See also, George Gamota and Wendy Frieman, *Gaining Ground: Japan's Strides in Science and Technology* (Cambridge, MA: Ballinger, 1988).
5. U.S. Congress, Office of Technology Assessment, *Advanced Materials by Design*, OTA-E351, Washington, DC: U.S. Government Printing Office, 1988, p. 21.
6. See, for example, The Committee to Advise the President on High Temperature Superconductivity, "High Temperature Superconductivity: Perseverance and Cooperation," Executive Office of the President, Office of Science and Technology Policy, 1988.
7. Michael E. Porter, *The Competitive Advantage of Nations* (New York: Free Press, 1990).
8. A complete account would surely have to examine differences in the cost of capital and in government policy. For a discussion of the former, see Joseph Morone and Albert Paulson, "Cost of Capital, the Managerial Perspective," *California Management Review*, vol. 33 (Summer 1991), pp. 9–32; for a discussion of policy differences, see Jeffery E. Garten, "Japan and Germany: American Concerns," *Foreign Affairs*, vol. 68 (Winter 1989/1990), p. 86.
9. Charles H. Ferguson, "Computers and the Coming of the U.S. Keiretsu," *Harvard Business Review*, vol. 68 (July–August 1990), pp. 55–70; W. Carl Kester, *Japanese Takeovers: The Global Contest for Corporate Control* (Boston: Harvard Business School Press, 1991); Clyde V. Prestowitz, Jr., *Trading Places: How We Allowed Japan to Take the Lead* (New York: Basic Books, 1988); Robert Zielinski and Nigel Holloway, *Unequal Equities: Power and Risk in Japan's Stock Market* (New York: Kodansha International, 1991).
10. Council on Competitiveness, "A Strategic Assessment of National Technology Priorities and U.S. Competitiveness: Sectoral Profile— Electronic Components, Equipment, Semiconductors and Related Devices," Washington, DC, March 1990, p. 8.
11. Deidre Depke et al., "Laptops Take Off," *Business Week*, March 18, 1991, pp. 118–124.
12. For a more detailed treatment of this issue, see Ferguson, "Computers and the Coming of the U.S. Keiretsu"; also, C.K. Prahalad and Gary Hamel, "The Core Competence of the Corporation," *Harvard Business Review*, vol. 68 (May–June 1990), pp. 79–91.

13. For a concise description of keiretsu, see Marie Anchordoguy, "A Brief History of Japan's Keiretsu," *Harvard Business Review*, vol. 68 (July–August 1990), pp. 58–59; for more detail, see Kester, *Japanese Takeovers: The Global Contest for Corporate Control*; Prestowitz, *Trading Places: How We Allowed Japan to Take the Lead*; and Zielinski and Holloway, *Unequal Equities: Power and Risk in Japan's Stock Market*.

14. Anchordoguy, "A Brief History of Japan's Keiretsu," p. 59.

15. Prestowitz, *Trading Places*, p. 160.

16. W. Carl Kester, "Governance, Contracting, and Investment Time Horizons," Working Paper 92003, Harvard Business School, July 19, 1991, p. 25.

17. This kind of trading also occurs in Japan, but for the stock of major corporations, it is limited to the roughly 30 percent not held by stable shareholders.

18. For an analysis of the LCD market, see H. Wakabayashi, "The Expanding Liquid Crystal Display Market," Nomura Securities International, April 1990.

19. For a comprehensive review of this literature, see Edward B. Roberts, "Managing Invention and Innovation: What We've Learned," *Research-Technology Management*, vol. 31 (January/February 1988), pp. 11–29.

20. See, for example, National Research Council, *Management of Technology: The Hidden Competitive Advantage* (Washington, DC: National Academy Press, 1987).

21. E.g., Mel Horwitch, ed., *Technology in the Modern Corporation* (New York: Pergamon Press, 1986).

22. E.g., Robert H. Hayes, Steven C. Wheelwright, and Kim B. Clark, *Dynamic Manufacturing* (New York: Free Press, 1988).

23. Harold E. Edmondson and Steven C. Wheelwright, "Outstanding Manufacturing in the Coming Decade," *California Management Review*, vol. 31 (Summer 1989), pp. 70–90.

24. James P. Womack, Daniel T. Jones, and Daniel Roos, *The Machine That Changed the World* (New York: Rawson Associates, 1990), pp. 92, 118.

25. Robert H. Hayes and Ramchandran Jaikumar, "Manufacturing's Crisis: New Technologies, Obsolete Organizations," *Harvard Business Review*, vol. 66 (September–October 1988), p. 79.

26. Paul S. Adler, "Technology Strategy: A Guide to the Literatures," in Richard S. Rosenbloom, ed., *Research in Technological Innovation, Management and Policy*, vol. 4 (Greenwich, CT: JAI Press, 1989), p. 26.

27. Alan Kantrow, "The Strategy-Technology Connection," *Harvard Business Review*, vol. 58 (July–August 1980), p. 21.

28. Michael E. Porter, "The Technological Dimension of Competitive Strategy," in Richard S. Rosenbloom, ed., *Research on Technological Innovation, Management and Policy* (Greenwich, CT: JAI Press, 1983), p. 10.

29. This argument is developed in Joseph Morone, "Strategic Use of Technology," *California Management Review*, vol. 31 (Summer 1989), pp. 91–110.

30. Richard S. Rosenbloom and William J. Abernathy, "The Climate for Innovation in Industry: The Role of Management Attitudes and Practices in Consumer Electronics," *Research Policy*, vol. 11 (1982), pp. 209–225.

31. Richard S. Rosenbloom and Michael A. Cusumano, "Technological Pioneering and Competitive Advantage: The Birth of the VCR Industry," in Michael L. Tushman and William L. Moore, eds., *Readings in the Management of Innovation*, 2d ed. (Cambridge, MA: Ballinger, 1988), p. 16.
32. Douglas K. Smith and Robert C. Alexander, *Fumbling the Future: How Xerox Invented, Then Ignored, The First Personal Computer* (New York: William Morrow, 1988).
33. Much of contemporary thinking about business strategy is based on Michael E. Porter, *Competitive Strategy; Techniques for Analyzing Industries and Competitors* (New York: Free Press, 1980).
34. Rosenbloom and Cusumano, "Technological Pioneering and Competitive Advantage: The Birth of the VCR Industry"; Modesto A. Maidique and Robert B. Hayes, "The Art of High Technology Management," *Sloan Management Review*, vol. 25 (Winter 1984), p. 19.
35. E.g., Christopher Freeman, *The Economics of Industrial Innovation* (Cambridge, MA: MIT Press, 1982); Porter, "Technological Dimension of Competitive Strategy."
36. E.g., David J. Teece, "Profiting from Technological Innovation: Implications for Integration, Collaboration, Licensing and Public Policy," in Tushman and Moore, eds., *Readings in the Management of Innovation*, pp. 621–647.
37. David Braybrooke and Charles E. Lindblom, *A Strategy of Decision* (New York: Free Press, 1970); James G. March and Herbert A. Simon, *Organizations* (New York: Wiley, 1965); James G. March and Johan P. Olsen, *Ambiguity and Choice in Organizations* (Bergen, Norway: Universitetsforlaget, 1976); Henry Mintzberg et al., "The Structure of Unstructured Decision Processes," *Administrative Science Quarterly*, vol. 21 (June 1976), pp. 246–275; J. Brian Quinn, *Strategies for Change* (Homewood, IL: Irwin, 1980); Herbert A. Simon, *Administrative Behavior* (New York: Free Press, 1976).
38. Richard R. Nelson and Sidney G. Winter, *An Evolutionary Theory of Economic Change* (Cambridge, MA: The Belknap Press of Harvard University Press, 1982), p. 171.
39. J. Brian Quinn, "Managing Strategies Incrementally," *Omega*, vol. 10, no. 6 (1982), p. 613.
40. Henry Mintzberg and Alexandra McHugh, "Strategy Formulation in an Adhocracy," *Administrative Science Quarterly*, vol. 30 (June 1985), pp. 193–194.

PART I

CASES

CHAPTER 2

GE MEDICAL SYSTEMS

In 1974, GE Medical Systems (GEMS) was in trouble.[1] Although it was the leading domestic producer of X-ray equipment, its share of the U.S. market was dropping rapidly. Net income, which had peaked at $5 million (on $167 million in sales) in 1971, had dropped to $1.3 million (on $215 million in sales) the previous year. Foreign sales were negligible. In its own estimation, GEMS' product line was aging, suffered from large product gaps, and was of lower quality than that of its two primary competitors—Siemens and Philips—and of comparable quality but more expensive than Picker, its third major competitor. Manufacturing was "a disaster," with a 16-month lag between order and product availability in a business where half that was closer to the norm.

Fifteen years later, GEMS had grown to roughly ten times its 1974 size and was the number one supplier of medical diagnostic imaging equipment in the world. Among such competitors as Johnson & Johnson, Siemens, Philips, Toshiba, and Hitachi, and in a rapidly changing, uncertain market, GEMS had transformed itself from a maturing business with a doubtful future into a global leader. It built its position on the basis of product technology leadership in two of the new diagnostic imaging modalities that had emerged during the course of that decade and a half—computerized tomography and magnetic resonance.

History

Background

For most of its history, which can be traced back to the earliest days of GE, GEMS was a producer of X-ray equipment and film.[2] Although it was the leading domestic supplier, it was an insignificant business by GE's standards. In 1962, for example, the General Electric X-ray Department (GEXD), as GEMS was then called, had sales of $55 million and net income of slightly less than $1 million—this at a time when total GE sales and income were $5 billion and $256 million, respectively.

During the second half of the 1960s, GEXD began a decade-long

27

effort to diversify its position in the medical business beyond its narrow focus on X-ray equipment and film. GEXD became General Electric Medical Systems. It established the strategic objective of becoming "the number one international multiline medical equipment company" and launched a series of attempts to develop product lines such as heart monitors, pacemakers, artificial lungs, and blood gas analyzers.

Unfortunately for GEMS, diversification was an unmitigated failure. Not only did the new business development fail, but by the early 1970s, the formerly successful X-ray business was running into serious difficulties. Although sales had grown to $215 million in 1973 from just $60 million a decade earlier, earnings had begun to plummet and market share was eroding. In late 1973, Jack Welch (GE's current CEO) became vice president of GE's Components and Materials Group, of which Medical Systems was a part. One of Welch's first actions was to replace the general manager of GEMS with Walter Robb, who had been general manager of GE Silicones.

The challenge facing Robb when he took over the business was to bring about what would be called in the late 1980s a "turnaround" of GEMS. Over the course of 1974, Robb devised and began to implement a new strategic direction for the business: rather than continue to diversify, GEMS would return to its core business—X-ray equipment. Instead of spreading its resources across a variety of new medical equipment ventures, GEMS would divest itself of the new businesses and focus on revitalizing the traditional X-ray line and reestablishing it as a cost-effective and profitable, albeit maturing, business. Product development plans were completely revised, pared down from 4.8 percent to 4.1 percent of sales and targeted at improving and filling the gaps in the basic X-ray product line. Manufacturing was overhauled, cost reduction and quality improvement programs were put into place, plans for expansion were developed, and engineering, product development, and product line management were reorganized. As Robb later described, "We had no choice but to 'circle the wagons' and rely on our one remaining strength—our sales and service organization—to get orders for what we could make. We had to buy time to get the product upgrades completed."[3]

Computerized Tomography

It was against this backdrop of restructuring and refocusing that GEMS' experience with computerized tomography began.[4] CT or "CAT scanning" is an X-ray-based technology that produces detailed images of cross sections of anatomy. In conventional radiography,

X-rays penetrate the body and expose photographic film placed behind it. Since dense structures within the body absorb more of the X-rays than less dense parts, a two-dimensional image or shadow of the more dense structures is created on the film. In contrast, in CT imaging, a single "slice" or cross section of the body is exposed to X-ray beams from hundreds of different angles. A computer then constructs these hundreds of exposures into a cross-sectional image of that one slice of the body. Whereas the more conventional approach does not distinguish effectively among adjacent organs or structures, CT does. It produces detailed images of tissue deep within the head and body and thus offers a view of internal organs that in the past could only be accomplished with exploratory surgery. George Wise, an historian of science at GE's Corporate Research & Development Center (CRD), describes the advantages of CT as they were seen in 1974:

> As doctors began to try out the machine, they found that it had one big overriding merit. It could detect much smaller density differences than could a conventional X-ray. A slight difference in density between a brain tumor and normal brain material might not cast an X-ray shadow. But computed tomography would reveal the tumor's existence and map its location. CAT had, doctors learned, "phenomenal" diagnostic accuracy for head tumors. Certain types that were missed one-third of the time by conventional systems were missed only five percent of the time by CAT. A patient who had a persistent headache now had a much better chance of finding out if it had been caused by an operable, life-threatening tumor. CAT could save his life.[5]

CT first came to the attention of GEMS in 1971, when EMI, the British company that pioneered the technology, proposed that GEMS become the North American distributor of its new product. GEMS declined, even though it was still attempting to diversify, because the market for CT seemed minuscule. GEMS estimated a demand of no more than 50 units over the next five years, at roughly $400,000 to $500,000 per unit. Looking back on this period, Robb describes the reasons for GEMS' lack of interest:

> From our point of view, CT violated every tenet of the [business]. Its resolution was only one-tenth that of a good film; it was very slow and inefficient, requiring as much as forty-five minutes of equipment time to scan the entire brain; it required the physician to view the anatomy in an alien

way—cross sections rather than projections; and it was relatively expensive. What we all missed was that even with all
of CT's disadvantages, it still provided substantially better
diagnostic information in the head than any other technique.
In an era of tremendous concerns over patient safety and
comfort and malpractice suits, CT had a crucial advantage.[6]

A CT program emerges. As Robb turned to the task of putting the
core business back in order, it became increasingly apparent that
GEMS' early analysis of the CT market had been badly off the mark.
Sales of EMI systems were taking off, a number of other companies
had announced their intention of entering the market, and EMI itself
planned to introduce a substantially faster system for whole body
applications (as opposed to its initial system which was limited to
scans of the head). Perhaps most tellingly, CT sales were beginning
to eat into expected sales of X-ray equipment. At the same time, two
separate groups within GE were becoming increasingly concerned
about GEMS' inaction on CT. One of them was the executive board
of the Component and Materials Group (to which GEMS belonged),
an internal advisory committee that reported to the vice president of
the group, Jack Welch. A key member of that board was Dr. Charles
Reed, former head of the group and a key figure in the history of
another GE business built on the basis of technology—GE Plastics.[7]
Early in 1974, Reed began to urge Welch to respond to what Reed
was convinced was "a revolution." "We were fiddling while Rome
burned," Reed recalls. Simultaneously, GE's Corporate Research &
Development Center also began to promote action on CT. In response
to a corporate technology study that had identified medical technology as an important growth area, CRD began to invest a significant
portion of its resources (7 percent of its 1973 budget, compared to 3
percent in 1968) in the general area of medical research. A number
of groups at the lab soon became aware of the rapid developments
in CT technology.

The combination of all these factors led GEMS to conclude by
spring 1974 that one way or another, it would have to get into the
CT business. As one manager at CRD noted at the time, GEMS'
attitude recently changed from "too small a market to be interesting"
to "we have got to get into this business." This change came about
when they realized that sales of the EMI head scanner (at $350,000
each) were going to be more like 1,900 units over the next five years,
instead of the originally predicted 50 units. But while it was clear that
GEMS would have to respond to the "CT revolution," it was not at
all clear how this could be done. As late as autumn 1974, while CT

was recognized as "#1 on the list of needed technological programs," GEMS still had no plan in place for pursuing it.

One approach to the CT market that was proposed during this period was to enter the market quickly with a product similar to the head scanner already being offered by EMI. Explained Robb,

> Our in-house engineering team, in a manner that must have been an exact duplicate of what happened at many other companies, came up with a proposal to essentially copy EMI's technology with lots of little improvements. Frankly, it was hard to turn this proposal down since we knew it would get us into the market quickly, and with a competitive product.[8]

But Robb did turn the proposal down, making it clear that in his view, a "me-too" product would not overcome EMI's lead. "They would have been in production by the time we were only completing a working prototype." At CRD, advocates of the me-too approach argued that GEMS' advantage in CT would derive from having "the best X-ray sales and service organization in the U.S.A.," along with the "biggest market share of X-ray equipment." But Robb found this unconvincing. Lonnie Edelheit, a key contributor to the development of GE's CT system and general manager of GEMS' CT business in the early 1980s, remembers that "Walt Robb kept pushing for a breakthrough; the rest of us were willing to get into the CT business by reproducing what was already there." Bobby Bowen, then manager of CT engineering and now vice president and general manager of the advanced technology division, also remembers that "Walt had a fundamental view that in order to be successful, really successful, you had to have something fundamentally different and better, preferably technology."

The search for "something fundamentally different and better" was led by CRD. EMI's CT system was limited to applications involving head scanning and took four and a half minutes to complete a single scan. Roland Redington, the manager and leader of the CRD effort, recalled years later, "Everyone knew that you wanted to go faster . . . and do whole bodies. The question was how to do it." By June 1974, CRD had settled on a possible approach, one that had been proposed by researchers at Massachusetts General Hospital and the Varian Corporation at about that time and "had been in the air from the beginning as an obvious alternative to EMI's method."[9] The EMI "pencil beam" system used an X-ray tube to focus on a single detector, and the patient was placed between the tube and the detector. The image was computed by gradually transversing both the tube and the detector across the patient's body, taking many individual X-ray measurements at many points. CRD, and as it turned out many other research groups and firms, pursued the "fan beam" method. In this approach, the X-ray tube emitted an array of beams in a pattern the shape of a flat unfolded fan. These beams were absorbed by a corresponding array of detectors. With each X-ray pulse, information about a much broader area of the anatomy was collected, which meant that much less movement of the tube-detector system was required to compute a complete "slice" of the body. This, in turn, meant that the fan beam was inherently faster than the pencil beam system.

The fan beam was promising, but it was also much riskier than the already proven pencil beam. A manager at CRD reported to the manager of engineering of GEMS that "At this time, the fan beam is just a concept. . . . However, it is a decidedly attractive one." As Wise (the CRD historian) describes, the manager

> went on to explain the [potential for a] proprietary position it offered GE, and its greater speed and mechanical simplicity. But it presented problems, too. To use it, you would have to put together a bank of 160 or more individual detectors, all uniformly accurate and stable. And you would have to invent a new mathematical method of reconstructing the picture, analogous to but more sophisticated than the one Hounsfield [EMI] used.[10]

The initial approach—fast, whole-body scanning. The reduction of scanning time was generally recognized as a logical next step in CT technology, as was the development of systems that could scan whole bodies, rather than just heads. In mid-1974, the National Institutes of Health (NIH) issued a request for proposals to develop a ten-second (at the time considered very ambitious) whole-body scanner. At this stage, GEMS had still not budgeted any funds for CT development; whatever work was going on at CRD was being funded by CRD itself. CRD and GEMS considered the NIH proposal an opportunity to obtain substantial development funds, and so in late summer 1974 they submitted a joint proposal with the Mayo Clinic to develop a fan beam-based, whole-body scanner. The proposal was rejected by NIH in favor of a system developed by a small company called American Science and Engineering, which used yet another approach to higher-speed scanning: a complete ring of fixed detectors, instead of the fan beam array of detectors that had to be gradually rotated.

From whole-body to breast scanning. GEMS "fell into inaction on

CT" after being turned down by NIH, but CRD persisted—still using its own funds for development. Earlier in the year, a radiologist from the Mayo Clinic had urged the group at CRD to begin working on a system that would scan for breast tumors. After the NIH rejection, the CRD team decided to turn its attention in this direction. The "work could be carried out jointly with Mayo, and would cost less and offer a lower degree of technical challenge than the whole-body scanner."[11] After a few months of study, the group concluded that it was feasible to develop this kind of machine, although by as late as December of that year, it rated the pencil beam, rather than the fan beam, "our first choice because of its simplicity." The group had still not met the requirements of the fan beam approach for an array of reliable, stable detectors and for a means of reconstructing an image out of the accumulated data. By the end of 1974, then, CRD's intention was to develop, without any financial support from GEMS, what was in effect a me-too system—albeit one with a new application.

This changed quickly and dramatically. A consultant from the State University of New York at Buffalo demonstrated a solution to the reconstruction problem, and a group at CRD completed experiments that indicated a vacuum tube detector invented by a small company called Xonics would satisfy the requirements for stability and reliability. A fan beam system for breast scanning now seemed feasible. The group showed its results to Robb early in 1975 and he responded enthusiastically. He agreed that this system was indeed worth pursuing and immediately authorized establishment of, and financial support for, a joint GEMS/CRD crash program. The objective was to develop a CT system for scanning breasts in ten seconds, deliver it to the Mayo Clinic for clinical evaluation by October of that year, and, if possible, display it at the November meeting of the Radiological Society of North America, the major trade show in the X-ray business.

From breast scanning back to whole body. A few months after its January 1975 inception, the crash CT development effort was already being substantially changed. Reactions by radiologists to the expected performance of the breast scanner were leading GEMS to the "preliminary conclusion that a well-defined market does not exist for a breast scanner." At the same time, it was beginning to appear that GEMS was falling behind in whole-body scanning. EMI had announced it was developing a 20-second body scanner, and the images produced by a prototype of the system were said to be "spectacular." Ohio Nuclear (later known as Technicare) was also making rapid strides in the marketplace with a CT system that was essentially a copy of the EMI system and was also developing an 18-second whole-body scanner. Moreover, a number of other companies, including Siemens, Acta (acquired in mid-1975 by Pfizer), Artronis, Philips, Syntex, Searle, and Varian, were working on systems that would "leapfrog" the EMI pencil beam system. Perhaps most important, the market for CT was taking off even more rapidly than had been predicted only a few months earlier.

These developments led Robb and Jack Welch to conclude that the crash project to develop the breast scanner would have to be supplemented with a second, simultaneous crash project to develop a whole-body scanner. Red Redington recalls:

> The big opportunity was clearly whole body. The market moved really fast. It also was clear that our approach was going to work. We hadn't yet demonstrated an image [with the breast scanner], but it was clear that the technology was going to work. When Robb and Welch proposed the acceleration, we accepted with pleasure. We had always viewed the breast scanner as a step along the path toward developing the whole-body scanner. But it had been our plan to run the development sequentially.[12]

Now the two projects would run in parallel. Completion of the prototype breast scanner was still scheduled for October, at which time it would be shipped to the Mayo clinic for clinical testing. The whole-body scanner would be announced at the November meeting of the Radiological Society of North America (RSNA), and a prototype was scheduled for completion by January of the following year. Simultaneously, to establish an immediate presence in the head-scanning market, GEMS negotiated a licensing agreement with a small company called Neuroscan that had developed a head scanner similar to EMI's.

In June 1975, GEMS had a three-pronged (head, breast, body) CT development program in place. It projected $7.5 million in sales for 1976 from 4 breast scanners ($400,000 each), 1 whole-body scanner ($550,000), and 15 Neuroscan head scanners ($350,000 each). Sales were projected to grow to between $50 and $60 million by 1980, or about 15 percent of the $375 million CT market that GEMS projected for that year.

These projections were highly uncertain, as GEMS well knew. By November 1975, the total potential market for CT was still unknown, with estimates ranging between 2,000 and 6,000 units. It was "too early for realistic assessment" of the market for body scanners, and there was still some doubt as to whether the 1975 market was the peak for CT or just a beginning. Despite this uncertainty, one trend was clear: both the market and the technology were continuing to develop faster than anticipated. Whereas in June GEMS had estimated that the total market for 1975 would reach $80 million, by November it was projecting a $125 million market, and by the end of the year the actual size reached $150 million.

Crisis. The three-pronged program seemed well on its way to success by early 1976. Arrangements for licensing the head scanner from Neuroscan were concluded; the prototype of the breast scanner had been completed on schedule and was undergoing clinical trials at the Mayo Clinic; and the whole-body scanner had been announced at the RSNA meeting late in 1975. Several other companies announced similar systems, but GEMS' system was expected to complete a scan in 4.5 seconds. This was much faster than the systems then available from EMI and Ohio Nuclear, which took 80 and 150 seconds, respectively, and faster than the other systems they were developing, which would require roughly 20 seconds. From a clinical perspective, speed of imaging was an important factor, particularly for whole-body scanning during which patients were required to hold their breath. The only system announced at the show that was competitive with GEMS' in speed was Varian's, also fan beam based and expected to require 6 seconds to complete an image. The response to GEMS' product announcement was far more enthusiastic than anticipated; 65 orders were booked during the next four months, before GEMS had produced a single whole-body image! (As recently as June 1975, GEMS had projected total sales of 20 units, 15 of which were to be for the licensed head scanners.)

Success, however, proved elusive. Clinical trials conducted in late 1975 and early 1976 with the breast scanner showed that it was no better than conventional mammography at detecting breast tumors, and it was much more expensive. Meanwhile, Neuroscan ran into development problems with its head scanner. In May 1976, GEMS reported that the problems were damaging its product image in the marketplace, and that the anticipated sales of the licensed head scanner were not materializing. But the most significant problems arose from the whole-body scanner. The prototype was completed and shipped to the University of California–San Francisco Medical Center for clinical evaluations in April 1976. By then it was clear that the GEMS body scanner was indeed faster than anything on the market. But two significant deficiencies had also shown up: the scanner produced spurious circular or ring-shaped images that were artifacts of the system rather than representations of features in the objects being imaged. And, while the images it produced of bodies were of comparable quality to EMI's—even with the unwanted rings —

head images taken with the same system were clearly inferior. Moreover, it had become apparent by then that buyers of CT systems would not purchase body scanners if they could not also be used for head scanning.

Once the system was shipped for clinical evaluations, and knowledge of its limitations began to spread in the market, new orders, according to Robb, "slowed to a trickle, and during one month, we had more cancellations than orders." To make matters worse, there was considerable concern that the problems were intrinsic to the fan beam approach and might not be correctable. Other companies using the fan beam had uncovered similar difficulties. A few months earlier, Geoffery Hounsfield, the EMI scientist (and later, Nobel Laureate) who invented CT, claimed that the fan beam system would never produce images without rings; and when the consulting firm Booz-Allen & Hamilton examined the issue at GEMS' request, it recommended, according to Red Redington "that we abandon our approach and go do a 'me too,' [using] some sort of a fixed detector system."

GEMS persisted with the fan beam, however, and after what Robb calls "months of brain-wracking efforts" and historian Wise calls a "long, slow period of problem solving," the GEMS whole-body system was gradually improved. The most significant changes in the system were new detectors, manufactured to much tighter tolerances than the original arrays, and revisions in the software associated with acquiring and reconstructing the imaging data. Lonnie Edelheit recalls:

> The worst day of my life was understanding the nature of the ring problem. The best day was figuring out how to beat it. For a long time it looked like Hounsfield was right. We were in a lot of trouble . . . It took an invention—a lucky invention—to get us through it. We figured out a way in software to take the rings out.

The first product—CT7800—and renewed crisis. In November 1976, one year after announcing its fast body scanner, GEMS began to ship the first systems. Despite all the difficulties, in the end 1976 was a successful year for the GEMS CT effort. Even with cancellations earlier in the year, 84 orders were booked, representing a 20 percent market share. But GEMS' troubles were not yet over. Its body scanner was indeed faster than anything on the market, but while the system now produced "credible" head images and enabled GEMS to regain lost orders, the new 7800 was not the technology leader Robb had envisioned. "At this point, we were still just equal to the [pencil beam] machines in terms of overall image quality." And while GEMS was struggling to make its leapfrog product comparable to already established technology, its competitors seemed to be succeeding in developing a new generation of technology. A new class of CT systems, offered by American Science and Engineering and announced by EMI and Ohio Nuclear, offered the potential for "remarkably good images" at prices roughly comparable to the 7800. GEMS suddenly was falling behind in the technology race, and "once again, orders began to be cancelled."[13]

At the same time, the market for CT machines suddenly and unexpectedly collapsed. Demand in the U.S. market, which dominated world demand for CT, dropped from 420 units in 1976 to 220 in 1977, and even lower to 154 in 1978. This decline was the direct result of stricter enforcement by the Carter administration of a 1974 law requiring a "Certificate of Need" from the Department of Health, Education and Welfare (now Health and Human Services) before a hospital supported by federal Medicare/Medicaid payments could acquire a piece of equipment costing more than $100,000. The downturn occurred just as a flurry of new competitors were entering the market. Pfizer, Siemens, Philips, Hitachi, and Searle had all entered in 1976, followed by Toshiba, Picker, CGR, and several others in 1977. Moreover, the market leaders, EMI and Ohio Nuclear, had been building up capacity, and GEMS, according to Robb, "had just occupied a large, new factory exclusively devoted to CT production, and large orders had been placed for long lead time components such as computers, data acquisition systems, and so forth."

As a result, when GEMS finally launched its CT whole-body scanner, instead of leapfrogging into a leadership position in a booming market, it found itself falling behind in a market that was suffering from a combination of overcapacity and sharply declining demand. Furthermore, there was no question in early 1977 that the 7800 was not a leadership product. Bobby Bowen recalls that "AS&E was the key competitor. Their product was better than the 7800, even after we tried to improve it; the 7800 wasn't working out, we were in deep trouble, and everyone recognized that we needed a major product upgrade."

The 8800. Because of these difficulties, Robb was "frankly beginning to wonder if we had made the right decision [i.e., to pursue the fan beam]." Welch in particular had begun to ask whether it might not be time to acknowledge that GEMS had followed the wrong path and to shift to the technical approach employed by the competition. At his urging, Robb assembled a group of outside experts for advice on the question of competing technical approaches.

Product development continued throughout this period. In fact, GEMS had begun to develop an improved product even as the 7800 was being introduced. The earlier efforts had focused on improving, but not changing, the original design of the detector. Now, product development went one step further and was aimed at developing an entirely new detector system that would increase the number of individual detectors from 301 to 523 within the same overall fan length. The panel of outside experts concluded that if the new detector proved to be as big an improvement as GEMS hoped, then GEMS should persist with the fan beam. Otherwise, it should shift to the approach being used by the competition.

This conclusion "bought us the time we needed." By mid-1977, the new detector system was completed and it was producing dramatic increases in resolution and image quality. This "was just what the radiologists and radiation physicists were waiting for. Now, the resolution was so good that even the differences between white and gray matter in the brain could be seen on the CT scan."[14] Figure 2.1 is an excerpt from a 1978 strategic plan describing GEMS' view of its competitive standing once the 8800 was introduced.[15]

GEMS announced the development of the new detector in mid-1977 and followed this with an announcement that it would offer a new CT System, the 8800, incorporating the new detector and other system improvements. With the 8800, GEMS finally had its leadership product.

Orders for the new system began to arrive in the fall of 1977, and the first 8800s were shipped the following spring. After taking $46 million in orders in 1977, $103 million in orders were received in 1978. GEMS' domestic market share, on the basis of this new product, leapt from 21 percent to 60 percent—and this while the market was still shrinking (see Figure 2.2).[16] The product finally broke even in 1978, registering $2 million in operating income. Just as GEMS had repeatedly underestimated the rate at which the CT market would grow, so too had it greatly underestimated its ultimate success. "Against budget, these results represented 250% of orders, 175% of sales, and a $7 million swing in net income against a $5 million budgeted loss."[17]

The market for CT was still depressed when GE introduced the 8800. But in hindsight, it appears that the market slump worked to GEMS' advantage. The slowdown hit just when GEMS' product position was weakest. Orders that would have been placed with competitors were delayed, and by the time the market began to rebound, GEMS had established its superior product position.

Product enhancements and "continuum." The highly successful introduction of the 8800 was followed by a series of both incremental and more substantial product enhancements, a process that continues to this day. Underlying these enhancements was a philosophy of product upgrades that began when GEMS was preparing to announce the 8800 and has since become a hallmark of the business. GEMS faced a marketing dilemma: the 8800 would not be ready for shipment for months; if the 8800 was announced in advance, orders for the 7800 would virtually cease. On the other hand, if it did not announce the 8800 in advance, its competitive position would continue to slip, and orders that would have waited for the 8800 might be won by competitors. GEMS resolved the dilemma by devising a new policy, called "continuum," which was conceived and named by Jack Welch: every CT product enhancement would be compatible with earlier CT systems so that current GEMS customers could upgrade their existing systems to take advantage of the new developments. Thus, the 8800 was designed in such a way that a customer who had already ordered a 7800 could upgrade to an 8800 by replacing the 7800 detector array and data acquisition system and by adding a high-speed array processor. Given the pace at which the technology was changing, continuum became an attractive marketing device, in effect protecting the customer against the very real threat of rapid obsolescence.

The first significant enhancement for the 8800 was announced in March 1978, at about the time the first 8800s were being shipped. "Scoutview" gave the 8800 the capacity to produce conventional X-ray images for identifying the parts of the body to be scanned. Other enhancements of the 8800 included a higher heat capacity X-ray tube designed specifically for CT, a new target imaging computer that provided improved spatial resolution, and application studies that were important for defining new uses and therefore expanding the market for CT. The net effect of these and other improvements was to ensure that for several years, the CT8800 remained the "gold standard" in CT equipment, as is demonstrated by the high market share that GEMS continued to enjoy in the early 1980s.

The 9800. While upgrades to the 8800 were being developed, GEMS was also preparing for the next generation CT machine. By May 1978, Art Glenn, general manager of the CT business, had already begun to plan what eventually became the 9800. In his view, even though the market might not be as large as it had been, it was still being driven by technological change, and in order to maintain its leadership, GEMS would have to continue to push the development of CT. In the CT business, he argued in one of his strategic plans, "Innovation [is the] only long-term share-gain strategy for

Figure 2.1
GE's Competitive Position in CT

Competitor	Technology	Performance	Flexibility	How Do the Competitiors Measure Up Today			
				Reliability	Throughput	Upgradability	Overall
General Electric	• Proven Xenon • Highest Image Quality	• Established 120 Installations • 1-Year Field Experience	• Limited • Major Task to Add Features	• 96% Uptime • 5-Year Detector Warranty	• No Mobile Patient Couch • Good But Not an Advantage	• Easily Upgradable • No Gantry Changes	+
Ohio Nuclear (2000 Series)	• Unproven • Many Problems with 2020 • High-Cost System	• Only a Few Installations • No Performance History for 2020 Series	• Much Software Flexibility • Versatile Hardware Architecture	• Excellent with Delta 50 • Many Problems with 2000	• 5 Patients per Hour • Mobile Patient Couch	• Requires Gantry Change • High Cost	◯
Pfizer	• Purchased Rights to AS&E Design • Still Unproven	• Few Installations • Mediocre Perfomance	• Versatile Architecture	• Mediocre to Poor But Improving Rapidly	• Unknown	• None Except to Add Microdose	◯

EMI (7000 Series)	• Unproven • No Images to Show • Still Behind Competitors	• Good on 5005 • Still Behind Competitors • None Yet on 7000	• Minimal	• Mediocre on 5060 & 1000 Series • Unknown on 7000	• Low • Upgrading Required to Increase	• Change Out of Equipment	◯
Siemens	• Instant Reconstuction • Poor Image Quality	• No History with Fast Scan • Only 2–3 Prototype Installations	• Unknown	• Unknown	• High	• None	◯

Conclusions

- GE The Current Leader in Image Quality
- System Meets Today's Requirements

Issues

- Will Present GE Systems Meet Tomorrow's Needs?

Figure 2.2
CT—Total Market and GEMS' Share

	1975	1976	1977	1978	1979	1980	1981	1982
U.S. Market:								
Unit orders	290	420	220	154	170	290	550	550
GEMS:								
Worldwide Orders $m	8.1	83.6	45	103	119	204	340	398
% share, U.S. market	5.5	35.7	21.5	60	48	55	68	56

competitors . . . [and] technology will fuel continued innovation."[18] Indeed, soon after the 8800 was shipped, competitors began announcing their intentions to introduce a new generation of products that would surpass the CT8800 in both speed and resolution. Of particular concern were the possible new products of EMI, Technicare (formerly Ohio Nuclear), Pfizer (which had acquired American Science and Engineering), and Siemens. The competitive situation was summarized by Glenn in the 1978 strategic plan for the CT business: "GE current leader in image quality; [8800] system meets today's requirements . . . [but] limited in future market. Competitors better positioned to address future needs due to more recent system design."

Accordingly, GEMS' CT strategy was to "continue 8800 enhancements to maintain order rate [and simultaneously, to] develop Century Series to . . . maintain technology leadership." The Century Series, or 9800, would be more than twice as fast as the 8800, have better resolution, and, given the projections of competitive products, would indeed preserve GEMS' product leadership. Development of the 9800 began quietly (in order not to detract from sales of the 8800) in 1979. "At that time, there was no announcement date committed, but the plan was to be prepared to respond to competitors as the GE [i.e., 8800] market share began to erode."[19]

The 9800 was introduced at the end of 1981. While it had originally been envisioned as a head-imaging unit only, by the time it was introduced, the 9800 was a body imager. Two versions were offered—a higher-priced high-resolution system and a lower-priced low-resolution system. Over the course of the 1980s, the 9800 gradually displaced the 8800; as it did, it was upgraded following the continuum philosophy. One of the first important areas of upgrading was the speed with which the 9800 reconstructed the overall images. (The system scanned in 2 seconds, but it took roughly 60 seconds to construct the final image.) A new version of the 9800 was introduced in 1984 that cut reconstruction time to 15 seconds. Subsequent enhancements included improved X-ray tubes, solid state detectors that led to significantly better resolution, and a variety of new applications for CT systems.

Multiple tiers. At the time the 9800 was introduced, it was becoming apparent that the CT market was dividing into premium, medium-priced, and low-end segments. The original market had now become the premium segment, comprised of systems costing $700,000 or more. This was still by far the largest segment, and GEMS, with its combination of the 9800 and 8800, was the overwhelming share leader. GEMS did not participate in either of the other two segments, but it was clear that in the long run, and especially in foreign markets, the medium- and low-priced segments would become increasingly important. By the middle 1980s, with the 9800 series firmly entrenched in the premium market, GEMS was also well on its way to establishing a strong position in the medium- and low-priced segments, although it got there in a largely unforeseen and unplanned fashion. The critical step was a joint venture with a Japanese firm, Yokogawa Electric Works (YEW). Prior to 1982, YEW served as GEMS' distributor of the 7800 and 8800 in Japan. But YEW soon found that these systems were not suitable for the Japanese market and proposed a version of the 8800 that was. Out of this suggestion grew a joint venture between GEMS and YEW—YMS (Yokogawa Medical Systems). Engineering and manufacturing in the joint venture would be performed by YEW, and GEMS would contribute its CT8800 technology. Initially, GEMS owned 51 percent of the equity in the joint venture; later it raised its share to 75 percent.

Once the joint venture was established, YMS undertook development of a lower-cost, "defeatured," compact CT system that would be suitable for the international market. This system was called the CT9000, and it became "a very important machine in Japan and Europe." The 9000 was followed in 1985 by the CT Max, which was also successful in international markets. And by 1987, YMS was producing two new products—one aimed at the medium-range market, the other at the lower end of the market.

Robb refers to YMS as "the Yokogawa miracle." YMS was not "good at the high end, but they were terrific at low cost—much better than Milwaukee [i.e., GEMS]," which suffered from a "continuous creep" of features and price. Though not originally planned this way, what had emerged by the mid-1980s was a continuously improving, multitiered product line, in which the high-performance, high-priced products were produced by GEMS, and the lower-performance, lower-priced products were produced by YMS. The combination of GEMS' strength in the premium market and YMS' at the lower end gave and continues to give GEMS a leading share of the global market for CT.

Magnetic Resonance Imaging

While the CT product line was being continuously broadened and enhanced, GEMS was also developing a second major product line— magnetic resonance imaging (MR).[20] MR is based on a fundamentally different technology than CT. With MR, the patient is placed in a magnetic field, which causes certain nuclei within the body to align with the field. Radio frequency waves are then applied to the field, knocking the nuclei out of alignment with the field. In the process, the nuclei absorb energy; when the radio frequency is removed, the nuclei release the absorbed energy and realign themselves with the field. The released energy in effect produces a signal, the strength and duration of which varies depending upon the density and other characteristics of the tissue being examined. The image is computed on the basis of these varying signals and allows the detection of variations in body tissue—such as the difference between a healthy or diseased heart, brain, or spine—that often cannot be detected using CT imaging. A second major potential application of MR involves not the imaging of organs, but spectroscopy—that is, the imaging of the chemical composition of tissue. This is a completely different function from anything possible with CT.

Strategic context. In late 1973, when he was taking over the business and CT was new in the marketplace, Robb defined GEMS as primarily an X-ray equipment manufacturer and his task as refocusing the business back on X-ray. But the unexpected growth of CT had transformed GEMS' market from a maturing, cost-oriented, stable environment to a rapidly changing, performance- and technology-oriented, dynamic one. By the second half of the decade, Robb no longer viewed GEMS as simply an X-ray equipment business; now it was a diagnostic imaging equipment business. GEMS' product offerings still included X-ray equipment, which still represented the largest single fraction of sales, but new diagnostic imaging modalities were expected to represent a more substantial fraction of GEMS' future business.

Thereafter, every new diagnostic imaging technology became a new product opportunity for GEMS. The CT project was soon followed by efforts in ultrasound and nuclear imaging. According to a strategic planning document from late 1976, GEMS is "in a catch-up position in nuclear and ultrasound—but is using acquisitions for entrée and development programs for new technology leadership." Nuclear imaging grew into a moderately successful business, but, despite repeated efforts over the course of the next decade, GEMS was never able to build a profitable business in ultrasound until it began to market a product developed by YMS. Another major attempt at the development of a new diagnostic imaging product came in the early 1980s with digital X-ray. Robb wrote at the time, "Though the full impact of digitizing X-ray data is still not fully known, I believe there is potential for it to produce as big a revolution in the diagnostic imaging field as occurred with CT back in the early 1970s."[21] The excitement was due to the possibility that digital X-ray could be used as a noninvasive alternative to catheter-based methods for exploring the vascular system, which would lead to the widespread use of X-ray to screen patients for vascular disease. In the early 1980s, product development support for digital X-ray was as high a priority as the continued development of CT, but the technology proved a disappointment, since it was never as useful diagnostically as had been hoped.

Once the strategic focus on diagnostic imaging equipment had been established, there was no ambiguity about whether to pursue the potential new diagnostic imaging modalities that arose from time to time. Robb and Welch, in Redington's words, were "actively looking for ways to do another CT." If there were doubts about a new diagnostic imaging opportunity, they tended to be about timing and how to balance these new opportunities with continued exploitation of already established product lines. As Robb explained in a speech in 1981,

> It's true that a terrific market did develop almost overnight for CT, and that ultrasound also suddenly became a hot product. And it's true that we are also looking for a huge market for digital X-ray systems and, perhaps, NMR eventually. But what we must not overlook is the simple fact that when each of these modalities appeared, they gained market share only at the expense of older, established modalities. CT hurt X-ray and nuclear, as did ultrasound. Digital X-ray will undoubtedly have a tremendously negative impact on X-ray as well. And some expect NMR to [do the same to CT].[22]

MR spectroscopy. In 1977, an MR image of a human wrist was featured on the cover of the British science journal, *Nature*. CRD had been aware of MR for several years prior to this, but the actual publication of an image led Redington to "start taking this seriously.

It was in the midst of CT, but you're always looking around." By 1979, Redington's group at CRD was convinced that MR would be an important new imaging modality for GEMS and proposed to develop an MR imaging system. Robb, however, was not interested, believing that MR would require much more research before it could be used as a practical diagnostic imaging technology. EMI, the early leader in CT technology, had by this time demonstrated MR-based images, but they were of "awful quality" and nobody at GEMS gave MR serious consideration as a new imaging modality.

In addition to imaging, it was also believed at the time that MR might be used for spectroscopy or chemical analyses of the body. When Robb rejected the CRD proposal to develop an MR imaging system, Redington turned to this second area of application. In Redington's opinion, if Robb had accepted the proposal to develop an MR imaging system, GEMS would have been first to market. But once GEMS turned down the proposal and it became clear that any development of MR would have to be supported by CRD rather than GEMS funds, the project had to take on more of a research orientation. And if it was oriented more toward research than product development, "I [Redington] felt very strongly that we had to do something that we could brag about. . . . It couldn't just be an imaging program—there wasn't enough [research] bang there," since other research groups had already demonstrated MR images. CRD therefore turned to the development of MR spectroscopy. At the time, GEMS believed this was the correct decision, since its CT business had identified MR spectroscopy as an important potential complement to CT imaging in the future.

This shift to spectroscopy meant that CRD would have to use a much more powerful magnet than would have been necessary for MR imaging, a factor that proved critical to GEMS' ultimate success in MR. It was generally believed at this time that it was not possible to do MR imaging with the high-field magnet required for spectroscopy. Therefore, in summer 1980, when CRD ordered a 1.5 Tesla superconducting magnet (as opposed to the resistive magnet with field strength of .5 Tesla or less that was sufficient for imaging), there was no question that the objective was now spectroscopy. It would take a year before the magnet could be delivered, however, so in the interim, Redington again proposed to Robb that his group work on MR imaging. This time, however, his reason was that "if you are going to do spectroscopy, you have to localize the system; you have to know where the signal is coming from." A low-field, resistive magnet was required for this task and Robb agreed to supply the $100,000 required to purchase it.

In fall 1980, CRD began to work on MR imaging—but only as a step toward MR spectroscopy. GEMS did not consider MR imaging an important new business opportunity; digital X-ray and more advanced CT technology were still the two development priorities. MR was promising as a potential avenue toward spectroscopy, and as such, a potential complement to CT some time in the longer-term future. Robb stated in a speech in 1981, "Though we are still in the research stages with NMR technology, there is no doubt that General Electric will be at the forefront of NMR when and if it becomes a viable medical diagnostic tool."[23]

From spectroscopy to imaging. The picture once again changed dramatically in the middle of 1981. The market for MR imaging was growing more rapidly than GEMS had anticipated. More than 30 firms were actively engaged in development, and there was "tremendous enthusiasm in the market." Firms such as Picker, Technicare (which had been acquired by Johnson & Johnson), Diasonics, Philips, and Siemens were all known to be developing MR imaging systems, and the quality of images demonstrated by at least some of the systems in clinical trials was substantially better than GEMS had anticipated. Moreover, many of these firms were aggressively pursuing MR precisely because they saw it as a vehicle for overcoming the seemingly insurmountable advantage that GEMS had built in CT. Thus, what GEMS had thought of as a long-term opportunity to develop a complement to CT (MR spectroscopy) was beginning to be a near-term threat to CT (MR imaging).

In response to these developments GEMS had no choice but to modify its strategy and establish a plan to enter the MR imaging market. By early 1982, GEMS had devised its strategy: GEMS would begin to work on a premium MR imaging system, which would require a .5 Tesla superconducting magnet. A CT-like crash program was started with a product to be announced in December of the following year, and shipments to commence at the beginning of 1984. In essence, the approach established in early 1982 was the one CRD had proposed in 1979. The difference was that now, as had occurred a decade earlier with CT, GEMS found itself behind the competition—a full year behind in the opinion of outside observers.[24] Moreover, it was clear to Robb that the product at which GEMS was aiming would not provide the kind of market leadership that GEMS had achieved with CT.

Right now, our images are comparable to what other companies are currently demonstrating, and are made on what could be a lower-cost unit than most firms are proposing. . . .

Hence, in the area of NMR hydrogen imaging, we have the
opportunity to be very competitive should this forthcoming
year's clinical research prove the technology to be medically
useful.[25]

The one chance for differentiation continued to be the CRD work on
spectroscopy, not the crash project on imaging.

Product development was thus initiated. A team was assembled
at GEMS, CRD began to transfer its imaging know-how to the team,
and the development of a superconducting magnet was initiated at
CRD. Initially, GEMS purchased its magnets from an outside vendor,
Oxford Instruments, which was, along with Intermagnetics General,
a small firm in Schenectady, New York, the only source of superconducting magnets. Since GEMS had decided to pursue the high-
image-quality end of the MR market, necessitating a superconducting
magnet, and since the magnet would account for roughly half the
total system cost, a critical part of GEMS' new MR strategy was the
internal development of a magnet manufacturing capability, thereby
ensuring future cost leverage. This option was available to GEMS
because, as a result of efforts during the 1970s to develop superconducting generators for GE's electrical power generation business,
CRD had world-class expertise in the areas of technology required
for development of superconducting magnets.

The leapfrog strategy. When CRD finally received the 1.5 Tesla
superconducting magnet it had ordered a year earlier, GEMS requested that it downgrade the magnet to .5T and focus its efforts
on imaging at this lower field, rather than continue to put primary
emphasis on spectroscopy. At the time, no one believed it possible
to do imaging at the higher-field strength. But once the 1.5T magnet
was in place in late 1982, Redington's group—which now included
some of the world's leading scientists in MR imagery—decided to try
to make images at full-field strength despite GEMS' request and the
conventional wisdom. They found that not only was this possible,
but the quality of head images was dramatically superior to anything
done at the lower-field strengths that were being used by GEMS and
its competitors.

Suddenly, GEMS once again had its basis for differentiation—a
system that produced better head images and was also capable in the
long run of doing spectroscopy. GEMS was the only competitor in
the field that had so far demonstrated imaging at high-field strength.
Moreover, it was also preparing to develop its own superconducting
magnet manufacturing capability. This combination offered the po-

tential for a strong leadership position, and GEMS quickly revised its strategy.

The 1.5T system would take longer to develop than the .5T system that had been proposed originally. GEMS could have proceeded by entering the market quickly with a .5T system, but Robb chose instead to wait. In his view, the lower-field system simply did not offer sufficient basis for differentiation. The risk in waiting was that potential customers might invest in the lower-field systems that were already being introduced by GEMS' competitors. Therefore, GEMS did everything it could to "freeze the market." As Redington describes,

> Milwaukee [i.e., GEMS] gave us a lovely charter. Blow smoke; develop as fast as you can; publish everything you do; and keep people waiting for whatever it is that GE will do next, so that they don't spend their money on someone else's machine.

This strategy would not have worked if GEMS had not been demonstrating clearly superior images. But it was, and by the time it formally announced its high-field product in late 1983, it had already received nearly 50 orders (at over $1 million per machine). By then, GEMS had also announced it would invest $31 million to develop its own superconducting magnets and to convert what had been a facility for GE's mobile communications business into a magnet manufacturing plant. It was also investing an additional $25 million to construct an MR system assembly facility, and $8 million more to acquire Nicolet's MR imaging business, which was focused on even higher-field systems (for research applications) than the one GEMS had announced. By fall 1984 when GEMS began to ship its MR product (Signa), it had already invested over $100 million in the development of the product and the magnet manufacturing capability. (Signa is a registered trademark of GE Medical Systems.)

Crisis, again. Unexpectedly, however, by the time GEMS began to ship Signa, the market seemed far less attractive than it had only a year earlier. As had happened with CT, the expected booming market suddenly began to look overcrowded. More than 25 firms had now entered the business, and whereas in mid-1983 estimates for the 1984 worldwide market for MR ranged as high as $500 million, the actual 1984 market was closer to half that size.[26] The federal government had once again introduced new regulations for containing health care costs, which led to a sharp and largely unanticipated slowdown in hospital spending for large equipment. This in turn led to a much more cautious market response to the new MR equipment, which was nearly twice as expensive as CT equipment. The question was not whether MR could perform functions that CT could not, but whether this capability was worth twice as much as the already expensive CT systems. Demand was further depressed by the confusion among potential customers that was generated by conflicting claims made by GEMS and its competitors about the relative value of high-field strengths.

Compounding the problem for GEMS (and its competitors), the regulatory changes and marketplace confusion were also depressing demand for CT. The domestic market, which grew to a peak of $750 million in 1983, shrank to $575 million in 1984, and $500 million in 1985. Suddenly, GEMS was under income pressure. During the development of CT, Robb had been able to support new product development with income from GEMS' X-ray business while still increasing overall earnings. Robb had hoped to do the same with MR, this time using income from the CT business, and cutting back on CT development. Once the CT market and sales began to shrink, however, the pressure on GEMS' bottom line grew, and in order to maintain MR development, he was forced to cut back substantially on support for continued CT and X-ray development.

There had never been any question that developing MR would reduce net income below levels that would otherwise have been attained in the near term (two to three years). But with the unexpected problems in the marketplace and the resulting overcapacity, the pinch was tighter than expected and lasted longer. MR did not become profitable until 1988, five years after the original product announcement and seven years after GEMS embarked on the effort.[27] Throughout this period, however, Robb and his successor, John Trani, with Welch's active support, if not prodding, continued to spend heavily on MR product development (in large measure at the expense of CT).

By the time MR started to produce a positive operating margin in 1988, GE reported that it had spent roughly $300 million on program development, support of CRD, and investment in plant and equipment for MR. By then the market had revived, growing to an estimated $625 million in 1986 and $940 million in 1988, and GEMS was well positioned to reap the rewards. High-field imaging had become "the de facto standard in MRI," and Signa was the clear leader in high-field imaging. As early as 1986, analysts were reporting that GEMS was selling three times the number of MR systems in the United States as its nearest competitors, and by the end of the decade, Signa was praised in an article in *Diagnostic Imaging* (the leading trade journal in the field) as "the dominant product in the MR market."[28] Estimates of Signa's share of the market ranged from 40 to 50 percent, roughly twice that of the nearest competitor's; and in the high-field segment of the market, its share was much larger.

Product evolution—multiple tiers, plus continuum. The MR product line evolved in much the same fashion as CT, with continuous upgrades, application of the continuum philosophy, and introduction of a lower-tier product line. The first upgrades to Signa reached the market in 1985, and as shown in Figure 2.3, they have been and continue to be introduced steadily ever since. A prime example was the Signa Advantage, introduced in 1989. (Signa Advantage is a registered trademark of GE Medical Systems.) By that time, GEMS had sold more than 600 Signa systems. *Diagnostic Imaging* described the introduction as follows:

> Although high-field scanners still outnumber their mid-field counterparts, some potential buyers fear that the equipment could be made obsolete by continuing advances in technology. To counter this concern, GE Medical Systems has become the first major manufacturer to build a modular MR scanner . . . the Signa Advantage. . . . When the company announced the Signa Advantage last month, it told old Signa customers that their systems can be upgraded to the Advantage level. . . . The Signa Advantage features enhancements of four major performance parameters: upgradeability, throughput, image quality and applications.[29]

While this continuum philosophy was being implemented, a lower-priced, lower-performance product line was also being developed. This began in late 1983, around the time GEMS concluded it would need a multitiered product line for CT in order to serve foreign markets and smaller hospitals in this country. This was especially true for MR: by the mid-1980s, a Signa system carried a list price of more than $2 million. According to Art Glenn, manager of the MR program, Jack Welch was once again the instigator. He began pushing Glenn to consider a lower-cost MR system even before GEMS formally announced its Signa line. In December 1983, Glenn's group was investigating possible low-end system configurations, and six months later, it settled on a .5 Tesla, superconducting magnet-based system.

GEMS had initially set out to make its own lower-cost CT systems, but it then turned to a joint venture with Yokogawa Medical Systems. This time, using GEMS' MR technology, YMS would develop the lower-priced, lower-performance system from the start.

Figure 2.3
MR—Continuous Improvement

1984	1985	1986	1987	1988	1989	1990
Product Roll-out (fall 1984)	1.6 Upgrade (spring 1985—40 systems)	2.0 Upgrade (early 1986—130 systems)	3.0 Upgrade (mid-1987—280 systems)	Laser Camera (spring 1988)	Signa Advantage (new generation)	New Options
	1.8 Upgrade (fall 1985—70 systems)	2.5 Upgrade (fall 1986—187 systems)		Performance Plus (mid-1988)	3.3 Upgrade (mid-1989—620 systems)	4.1 Upgrade (spring 1990)
				Cine Plus Package (mid-1988)	New Options	4.5 Upgrade (mid-1990)
				New Surface Coils (fall 1988)		

Source: Adapted from GE Medical Systems, "Signa, High-Performance Roadmap."

This meant that a considerable amount of proprietary technology had to be transferred from GEMS to YMS. Before GEMS was willing to do this, it restructured the terms of its joint venture with YEW and increased its equity share to 75 percent. The MR Max, as the lower-priced system was called, was announced in 1987, four years after the initial planning, and it sold for about 40 percent less than Signa. The market response, according to *Diagnostic Imaging,* "will exceed the company's expectations for 1988,"[30] and by mid-1989, MR Max was described as having the "dominant market share in the mid-field arena" and the "number two system [second to Signa] in the world in terms of sales."[31] By then, GEMS had already introduced a major upgrade, the MR Max Plus. Existing customers of the MR Max were upgraded free of charge.

Discussion

Business Strategy and Technology

Strategic focus. As discussed in Chapter 1, the role of general management in translating technology into competitive advantage can be viewed from three conceptually distinct perspectives: that of general management's business strategy, technology strategy, and decision-making style. When we consider the history of GEMS from the first of these perspectives, we find considerable support for the argument, made by Rosenbloom and others, that businesses that make successful use of technology exhibit a consistent strategic focus that gives direction to technology development.[32]

When Robb took over GEMS in late 1973, he was confronted not only with a financial and operational crisis, but with a business that had been attempting to diversify into a broad-based medical equipment company for nearly a decade. Robb quickly established a much narrower strategic focus—initially, X-ray equipment, and shortly afterward, diagnostic imaging equipment. Diagnostic imaging is still the strategic focus of the business 15 years later. In the second half of the 1970s, GEMS "focused primarily upon the U.S. diagnostic imaging equipment market." By the early 1980s, the goal was to become the worldwide market share leader in diagnostic imaging markets; and by the late 1980s, it was to achieve the number one or number two worldwide share position in sales as well as profitability, in *every* diagnostic imaging modality.[33]

Strategic consistency goes hand in hand with managerial stability, and in the case of GEMS, there is abundant evidence of such stability. Robb headed the business from 1973 until 1986, when he was succeeded by John Trani (who, it should be noted, did *not* come from GEMS but rather from GE's mobile communication business). Robb reported to Jack Welch through most of the 1970s, and also during the 1980s when Welch became CEO. Many of the top management positions reporting to Robb and now Trani are filled by people who grew up within GEMS during the development of CT. A similar stability is apparent at CRD, where throughout this decade and a half, the major R&D efforts were led by Redington. Robb himself had begun his career at CRD, and when he left GEMS in 1986, he returned to CRD as senior vice president.

The impact of strategic focus on technology development. GEMS' consistent focus on diagnostic imaging created a context for technology development. Opportunities that fit within that context were pursued with vigor; those that fell outside were ignored. From the mid-1970s onward, GEMS pursued virtually every emerging diagnostic imaging modality. The CT campaign was followed by the unsuccessful efforts in ultrasound and digital X-ray, MR, and several more recent forays into new approaches to diagnostic imaging. The continuous improvement of CT and MR once they had been successfully introduced into the marketplace also reflects the influence of the strategic focus on technology development. The CT 7800 was introduced by GEMS in 1976, and since then, the technology has been continuously improved and broadened. The only time resources were diverted from CT was at the height of the development of MR, and this was the result not of a deviation from the strategic focus, but rather of its continued pursuit.

While the strategic focus channeled and concentrated technology development activities, however, the history of GEMS also reveals an important example of "technology push." CRD began to advocate MR imaging three years before GEMS actually decided to pursue it. GEMS was able to leapfrog the competition only because CRD persisted despite the lack of enthusiasm and financial support from GEMS. On the other hand, MR was by no means a pure case of technology push. By the time CRD began to examine MR, the focus on diagnostic imaging was well established. Redington and his associates became interested in MR precisely because they saw the potential significance of this new diagnostic imaging modality for the business. CRD's work on MR was motivated, in Redington's words, by "a business driver. We were trying to develop coverage for the business." At the time, GEMS was preoccupied with CT and so there was certainly no business pull involved. Redington remembers that his group examined MR nonetheless because "you are always looking around." The important point is that the looking around occurred in areas of direct relevance to diagnostic imaging. This was indeed technology push, but it was operating within the confines of the strategic focus—within the strategic focus of GEMS, but beyond its field of view. As we shall see, a similar pattern appears in the histories of Motorola and Corning, which suggests that successful exploitation of technology may require not just the driving of technology by consistent, stable strategic focus, but a technology push that operates within the confines of that focus.

Technology Strategy

The role of general management in the process of building and sustaining advantage on the basis of technology can also be illuminated by examining the history of GEMS from a technology strategy perspective. Did GEMS management exhibit, either implicitly or explicitly, the elements of a technology strategy?

Product leadership. Perhaps the single, most striking feature of this 15-year history is the deliberate and persistent pursuit of technology leadership by the general manager of the business, Walt Robb. Robb could not have been more explicit about his concern for leadership:

> If you can be number one, no matter whether that market turns out to be $200 million or $1 billion, you have reason for confidence. If you have to spend $50 million to be number one in a $200 million market, that's much better than skimping, spending $10 to $20 million, and being a loser in a $1 billion market. Big companies ought to have a big advantage in this game. But you have to be willing to take a shot and let it run. You won't get there if you are not willing to spend the money.

This concern with leadership first reveals itself at the outset of GEMS' experience with CT, when Robb rejected his engineering group's proposal for a quick entry into the CT business with what he described as a me-too product. Ironically, it was the technical groups—at GEMS and also at CRD—that initially proposed to enter the market with a product equivalent to the competition's, and to rely on GE's marketing strength as its source of advantage. Robb, on the other hand, resisted these calls, urged his engineering management to turn to CRD, and pushed CRD to strive for a product that would give the business an "unfair advantage." Once the feasibility of this kind of approach was demonstrated in January 1975, Robb moved quickly to establish a crash development program.

A similar pattern can be seen in MR. Once it became clear that GEMS would have to respond to developments in MR imaging, the issue for Robb became not whether it could enter the market with a high-quality product, but whether it could enter the market with a clearly superior product that would enable GEMS to leapfrog the competition. In ultrasound, too, even though GEMS did not ultimately succeed, Robb and Welch were deliberately seeking "another CT." Indeed, Robb regrets not having pursued the opportunity for product leadership in ultrasound more aggressively. He believes GEMS and CRD had the basis for a breakthrough, but at CRD's urging, GEMS turned the concept over to an outside company for development, and "they blew it." "I didn't fight it [going outside] at the time, because there was some sense that you didn't want to distract from CT; but in retrospect, we should have gone with it." Conversely, in digital X-ray, "it is not clear that the technology was available at the time for a leapfrog. We wanted to believe there was one there, and that clearly affected our judgment."

Robb sees the pursuit of product leadership as the key to GEMS' transformation into a global success. When he began his tenure at GEMS, "We didn't even think in terms of world share." GEMS had less than 10 percent of the global market for X-ray equipment, and Welch made it clear to Robb that part of his assignment was to determine whether the business was even worth retaining. But, "Once the CT program came along, Jack stopped talking that way. Had we taken the incremental approach, we might have sold the business" and would never have built GEMS into a world leader.

This view of GEMS as a pursuer of technology leadership is somewhat inconsistent with past descriptions that characterize GEMS as a fast follower. For example, Teece, in his seminal piece, "Profiting from Technological Innovation," argues that once EMI succeeded in bringing the new CT technology to market, GEMS developed a competitive CT system, "borrowing ideas from EMI's scanner," and then used its superior marketing and service strength to outperform the original innovator in the marketplace.[34] Ironically, this is precisely the approach Robb rejected in 1974, and much of the history of GEMS' experience in CT is the struggle to develop a superior product based on a different technological approach—one that EMI had rejected as unworkable.

No doubt GEMS' marketing strengths helped enormously in its struggle for leadership, but what is equally clear from this history is that while such "complementary assets" may have been necessary for success, they were not sufficient. Until GEMS was able to introduce the 8800, which was superior to any system then on the market, it was in serious difficulty in the marketplace. Its 21 percent share in

1977 was no doubt due more to its marketing strengths than its product. But its ability to achieve a 60 percent share the following year—at a time when the overall market was shrinking—only came with success in bringing a superior product to market. Distribution and marketing then solidified GEMS' advantage. According to Bobby Bowen, "A world-class distribution system keeps you alive when you are in trouble, but you've got to have the product. Our distribution is very so-so with products that are so-so . . . good products and good distribution reinforce each other. When you don't have both, you don't have the reinforcement."

Another interesting feature of this pursuit of product leadership is that GEMS was not first to market in either CT or MR. But there is no evidence to suggest that GEMS was deliberately pursuing a fast-follower strategy. Rather, in both instances, GEMS appears to have misjudged the importance of the new technologies and the rapidity with which the markets for them would grow. As several of his former managers attested, Robb was "amazingly risk averse for someone who took enormous risks with technology." In both instances, he was reluctant to move rapidly into the new technology area, skeptical that it was as important a development as it appeared to its early followers. Moreover, in the view of Bobby Bowen,

> We have never invested in the kind of way that would allow you to start in front. It is only recently that we have begun to spend what I would call risk money. There is not an obvious thing to follow at the moment. So now we do a lot more basic and exploratory work, to figure out where to spend the big money. . . . But in the past we came from behind and stayed in front. We didn't allocate resources that allowed you to get out in front first.

Once it became clear that CT and MR posed serious threats to the X-ray business, GEMS moved aggressively to establish its leadership position. Fast followership implies that later entrants wait until a dominant design has appeared before leaping into the fray with a competitive and largely imitative product. In this case, the pioneers appeared to have demonstrated the viability of the technology and the presence of a market for it, but the follower—GEMS—leapfrogged the pioneers, becoming a pioneer in its own right. At a minimum, this suggests that the conventional notions of pioneering and fast following may be obscuring a useful distinction: time of market entry and technology leadership. As shown in Figure 2.4, a firm may be first to market with new technology and in this sense a pioneer;

Figure 2.4
Technology Leadership and Early Market Entry

		MARKET ENTRY	
		Lead	Follow
TECHNOLOGY	Lead	Pioneer	GEMS
PERFORMANCE	Follow	EMI	Fast Follower

but it may quickly end up a technological laggard. Conversely, a firm might be sluggish in reaching the market but become a technological leader once it actually does get there.

This case also raises interesting questions about the notion of dominant designs. The case for fast following is often based on the argument that in the early, turbulent stages of the product life cycle, before there is a dominant design, there are limited benefits to being the innovator since competing technological approaches rapidly eclipse one another. This argument has the weight of both logic and history on its side, but it suffers from one limitation. Exactly when the dominant design emerges becomes apparent only in hindsight. It could be argued today that GEMS established the dominant design in CT with the fan beam. But from 1973 through 1975, most would have argued that the EMI approach was the dominant design; similarly, in 1982, most observers would have argued that low-field MR was the dominant design. Our notions of dominant designs and the relative merits of fast following may be more useful to the historical analyst than to the actual decision maker who, in the midst of the technological fray, struggles with the problem of how and when to enter a rapidly growing, dynamic market that is at once both a threat to his business and an opportunity for growth.

Incremental technology improvement and product leadership. Once GEMS established product leadership with the CT 8800 and MR Signa, that leadership was reinforced and sustained by continuous improvements. As Robb describes:

> We knew there was a lot of room for improvement—even before we realized there was a crisis and that we *had* to develop the 8800. And we continued with the 9800 and the solid state detector. Until 1985 [when the CT market crashed at the same time that demand for MR systems stalled] we never really cut back on CT, at least not significantly. We were moving as fast as technology would allow.

The same thing happened with MR. Within five years of Signa's introduction, GEMS had introduced four major product upgrades (all of them backward compatible). In addition to the periodic introduction of new generations of equipment, GEMS introduced countless smaller, more application-specific product enhancements, all consistent with the continuum logic of forward compatibility (see Figure 2.3). Morry Blumenfeld, Signa product general manager, describes this process:

> We are very explicitly driven to stay ahead. Very explicitly. . . . This goes back to CT. We applied in MR very early and in a very deliberate way what we learned in CT—to get the market you've got to be the one who, in essence, defines what the applications are, and brings those up to snuff. We know what we want to do. We know exactly now [summer 1990] where we would like the product to be in 1992, 1993, and 1994. Well, it gets hazier in 1994, but certainly we know where we want the product to be three years from now. We see so many ways of improving things.

From a strategic perspective, this stream of continuous product improvements complements GEMS' more radical product developments. The 8800 and Signa enabled GEMS to establish its competitive advantage; the subsequent incremental and generational (e.g., 9800, Signa Advantage) improvements enabled it to maintain that advantage over time. But while incremental innovations complemented the more radical product innovations, they also worked against each other. The development of major new product lines usually conflicted with the incremental improvement of existing product lines. The focus on X-ray in the early 1970s made the initial CRD interest in CT seem a distraction. Similarly, the initial CRD interest in MR seemed a bother to an organization that was doing everything it could to bring CT to market. But the problem went much further than mere distraction. Each new product line threatened to cannibalize sales from existing lines, which led to an understandable resistance to the new product possibilities. Moreover, the development of each major new product line required a disproportionate amount of resources. CT could only be funded by cutting back on X-ray development. Later, when Glenn was pushing to develop the 9800, he did not receive as much funding as he believed necessary to fully exploit the opportunity because GEMS was beginning to pursue digital X-ray. And at the height of MR development, support for CT and X-ray was "KOed by Walt."

How did GEMS balance the pursuit of product line improvements with that of entirely new product lines? There does not appear to be any simple formula. What is clear is that the responsibility for mediating the conflict lies squarely with the general manager. As

Bobby Bowen describes it, ultimately, the trade-offs in resource allocation among products were made by Robb, based on his

> feeling about where the industry was going, and where the growth was going to be and not going to be. . . . In X-ray, which Walt thought wasn't going anywhere . . . he invested what he thought was a reasonable amount to keep it going, but he had the feeling that in the long haul it was never going to be a big deal. Then digital came along, and he thought that might change the rules, so he invested a lot of money. . . . So Walt used his vision of things to make his resource allocations . . . and you wind up starving things that you judge don't deserve to be nurtured.

Decision Making and Technology

As discussed in Chapter 1, contemporary scholarship on decision making offers two competing models: a more analytic approach, in which general managerial decision making is driven by the results of model-based projections of future results, and a more experience-based approach, in which decision making is driven by a combination of strategic considerations and learning from experience. GEMS' history offers considerable support for the second experience-based model.

High uncertainty. General managerial decision making in this case is heavily influenced by the high degree of uncertainty. The road to leadership in diagnostic imaging was strewn with technological and market surprises. Initially, GEMS failed to forecast the rapid development of the market for CT. It responded in January 1975 with its crash effort to develop a breast scanner, but by mid-year, the market and competitors had moved so much more rapidly toward whole-body scanning than GEMS had anticipated that it had to completely revise its approach. At year's end, the market was still moving faster than expected, and GEMS was beginning to worry that its whole-body scanner would be late to market. During 1976, GEMS was further surprised by market demands for body scanners that could also do head scanning. Then, it was jolted by a series of unexpected technological setbacks: its body scanner produced ring artifacts; the breast scanner did not demonstrate significant benefits; and the licensed head scanner failed in the marketplace. The unwanted surprises continued the following year. Competitors began promising better systems at comparable prices, raising serious doubts about the wisdom of the fan beam approach; and the market collapsed just as GEMS was expanding capacity. History seemed to repeat itself with MR. GEMS was once again surprised by the speed at which the market developed, then unexpectedly uncovered a source of differentiation in high-field imaging, and later, was badly surprised by the sudden collapse of the market.

It is this unrelentingly uncertain and unpredictable nature of new business development in high-tech markets that makes the conventional, analytic style of decision making problematic. The projections of future financial performance on which this style of decision making is based are predicated on assumptions about the future size and rate of growth of the market, the pace and degree of success of technology development, the progress made by competitors and competing technologies, and the impact of such exogenous variables as government regulations. But of course it was precisely these factors that proved to be so thoroughly unpredictable for GEMS. Robb could not help but be well aware of the uncertain nature of his enterprise and thus of the dubious validity of model-based projections of future performance. In his words, in this kind of environment, "you can't make financial models that can be relied on. You can make the numbers come out any way you want."

Learning by doing. Instead of basing their decision making on financial models, Robb and his associates approached the development of their new businesses in a serial, iterative fashion. Each step in the effort to develop CT and MR led to new and often unanticipated lessons about the market and technology, which led GEMS to adjust its approach—which in turn led to new experiences, further adjustment, and so on. Thus, once it became clear that CT was a major new business opportunity, as well as a threat to the core business, Robb began to urge CRD to develop a basis for product leadership. Once CRD demonstrated the feasibility of the fan beam concept, Robb responded with the crash mammography project. As it became apparent that the market for whole-body scanning was becoming much more important than it had seemed a few months earlier, the crash project was enlarged to include whole-body scanning and the licensed head scanner. When GEMS discovered that the market was demanding body scanners that also could do head scans, and that its body scanner produced the undesirable ring artifacts, it pushed ahead with a painstaking effort to improve the product. And when the resulting 7800 proved to be mediocre, and competitors began to promise better systems at comparable prices, GEMS reacted with yet another effort to improve the product, this time amid growing doubts that the fan beam approach would ever prove successful. The result of this last effort was the dramatically better detector system, which once developed, led to the 8800. Bobby Bowen describes this serial, iterative, disappointment-laden decision process in this way:

> Several cases have been written about the history of CT, but they don't describe anything that I recognize. They tend to project what ought to have been rather than was. There is a tendency to assume that a lot more occurred by planning than what actually occurred. . . . In fact, one thing tended to follow from the next. There were a lot of curves on the road that we hadn't anticipated. We took things as they came. A lot of people think of product development as involving a lot of planning, but I think the key is learning, and an organization's ability to learn.

Persistence and the strategic context. In order to learn from experience, however, a business must also be willing and able to persist. Robb explains:

> Anytime you have a product that is a quantum change, you are going to have crises. So many times, it would be easy to back off. . . . But you *make* it work. If you ever start giving in on a schedule, then you'll give in again on the next one. You just never give in. You just *have* to make it one way or another.

What was it about CT and MR that merited such persistence? Why did Robb feel that he could never give in, despite the seemingly endless string of setbacks? The answer leads back to the context for technology development created by strategic focus. CT and MR could not have been more strategically relevant for GEMS. Failure in these new markets would have been tantamount to failure of the business. Each adjustment to each new setback, each crash effort to solve each new crises was propelled by a sense of strategic urgency. "We really didn't have any choice" but to persist, Robb believes. If the 8800 had not proved successful, "we would have shifted to the fourth generation [the approach being introduced by competitors]." If GEMS had come out with a me-too product in the beginning, instead of pursuing the leapfrog fan beam approach, and it had failed, "we would have realized this, and by 1979, we would have come out with another system—as long as the company [i.e., Welch] had been willing to stick with it." Persistence in technology development was thus fueled by the strategic imperative to lead in diagnostic imaging.

Notes

1. This case study would not have been possible without the permission generously granted by John Trani, senior vice president, GE Medical

Systems, and without the help generously provided by Bobby Bowen, vice president and general manager, Advanced Technology Division, and Morry Blumenfeld, Signa Product general manager, GE Medical Systems; Lonnie Edelheit, R&D manager, GE Corporate R&D; Arthur Glenn, vice president and general manager, Communications and Strategic Systems Division, GE Aerospace; Roland Redington, retired, Corporate R&D; Charles Reed, former senior executive in various GE positions; Walter Robb, senior vice president, GE Corporate R&D; and George Wise, GE Corporate R&D.

2. The information for this section is drawn from an interview with George Wise, GE Corporate R&D, and the following unpublished, internal GE documents: GE Medical Systems Business Division, *EB Session 1*, June 1975, and *EB Session 2*, November 1975; C. M. McFarland et al., Components and Materials Group, "Internal Technology Study," 1969; Peter Stewart, "A Program for General Electric's Future Business in Medicine," Report of the Corporate Medical Study Team, December 1967; Walter Robb, "1980 Belleair Presentation"; and George Wise, "The Biggest Hit of Them All."

3. From Robb, "1980 Belleair Presentation."

4. The information for this section is drawn from interviews with Bobby Bowen, Morry Blumenfeld, Arthur Glenn, Roland Redington, Charles Reed, Walter Robb, and George Wise. Information is also drawn from the following unpublished internal documents: GE Medical Systems Strategic Plans—*EB-I, EB-II*, 1975; *EB-I, EB-II*, Session D—Components and Materials Group, 1976; *EB-1*, 1979; CT Programs, S-1, 1980; Arthur Glenn, "GE CT Story—Beginning Through 1983"; various memos and project reports from the historical files of George Wise, Corporate R&D; George Wise, "The Biggest Hit of Them All"; and speeches by Walter Robb— MSD-80-12, MSO-82-5, MSD-81-63, "1980 Belleair Presentation," NY Security Analysts Presentation, September 20, 1983.

   Also see K. Dummling, "10 Years Computed Tomography—A Retrospective View, *Electromedica*, vol. 52 (January 1984), pp. 13–27.

5. Wise, "The Biggest Hit of Them All," p. 4.

6. Robb, "MSD-81–63," p. 8.

7. From Joseph Morone, "GE Plastics," working paper, Rensselaer School of Management, 1990.

8. Robb, "MSO-82–5," pp. 5–6.

9. Wise, "The Biggest Hit of Them All," p. 11.

10. Ibid., p. 12.

11. Ibid.

12. Redington interview.

13. Robb, "MSD 80-12," p. 9.

14. Ibid., p. 10.

15. From Glenn, "GE CT Story—Beginning Through 1983," Figure 5, p. 6.

16. Ibid., Figure 12.

17. Ibid., p. 6.

18. "CT Programs, S-1," internal document, 1980, p. 23.

19. Glenn, "GE CT Story—Beginning Through 1983," p. 6.

20. The information for this section is drawn from interviews with Bobby Bowen, Morry Blumenfeld, Arthur Glenn, Roland Redington, Walter Robb, and George Wise.

    Background information was drawn from numerous issues of *Diagnostic Imaging*, 1983–1990.

21. Robb, "MSD-81-67," internal document, p. 15.

22. Robb, "MSD-81-65," internal document, p. 4.

23. Robb, "MSD-81-67," internal document, p. 22.

24. Rhonda Bramner, "Track of the CAT, Scanning a Hot New Medical Technology," *Barron's*, September 20, 1982, p. 20.

25. Robb, "MSO-82-16," pp. 15–16."

26. "World Business," *The Economist*, January 26, 1985, p. 70; Joseph E. Erchinger, "MRI Suffers Identity Crisis as Market Issues Go Unresolved," *Diagnostic Imaging* (April 1984), p. 42. The new regulations involved creation of standard cost categories called diagnostic related groups (DRGs).

27. GE Company, *Annual Report, 1988*, p. 8.

28. Gary M. Stephenson and Greg Freiherr, "Demand by Smaller Hospitals Recharges MR Scanner Market," *Diagnostic Imaging* (August 1989), p. 53.

29. Stephenson and Freiherr, "Demand by Smaller Hospitals Recharges MR Scanner Market," p. 53.

30. Thomas Hodapp, "Imaging Industry's Growth Boom Should Hit Its Peak in 1989," *Diagnostic Imaging* (December 1988), p. 68.

31. Stephenson and Freiherr, "Demand by Smaller Hospitals Recharges MR Scanner Market," p. 55.

32. Richard S. Rosenbloom and Michael A. Cusumano, "Technological Pioneering and Competitive Advantage: The Birth of the VCR Industry," in Michael L. Tushman and William L. Moore, eds., *Readings in the Management of Innovation*, 2d ed. (Cambridge, MA: Ballinger, 1988), pp. 3–22. See discussion in Chapter 1.

33. Some of GEMS' competitors also seem to have defined their focus as diagnostic imaging, but many others did not. Siemens, for example, which throughout this period has been GEMS' main competitor for worldwide share leadership, pursued a broader approach to the market not dissimilar to GEMS' prior to Robb's tenure. By the early 1980s, GEMS reported that Siemens was "increasingly dependent on non-DI [diagnostic imaging] products" such as hearing aids and pacemakers. Other competitors, such as Johnson & Johnson and Pfizer, which made unsuccessful forays into the diagnostic imaging market, had considerably broader interests in medical equipment than GEMS. On the other hand, smaller competitors focused on one or a few individual segments within the overall diagnostic imaging market.

34. D. J. Teece, "Profiting from Technological Innovation: Implications for Integration, Collaboration, Licensing and Public Policy," in Tushman and Moore, eds., *Readings in the Management of Innovation*, pp. 621–647.

CHAPTER 3

MOTOROLA—COMMUNICATIONS

The story of Motorola's communications business is a story of American competitiveness.[1] Subject to the same global competitive pressures that overwhelmed the U.S. consumer electronics industry, faced with rivalry from the likes of NEC and Matsushita, Motorola stands as not only the sole surviving major U.S. manufacturer in its markets but as the world's leader. It accounts for roughly one-third of the rapidly growing, $4.5 billion cellular telephone equipment market; well over half of the $4 billion two-way radio market; and a reported 80 percent in the United States and a major share in Japan and Europe of the more than $1 billion paging market.[2]

In 1947, Motorola Communications (COMM[3]) was a small component of a $50 million company specializing in consumer electronics—televisions, stereos, and radios for the car and home. Forty-five years later, it had grown into a $5 billion family of businesses that accounted for half of Motorola's total revenue and more than three-quarters of its profit (see Figure 3.1).[4] Growth showed no signs of slowing, as several ambitious new communications business development efforts were launched in 1990. Among the most prominent are a joint venture with IBM called Ardis, which provides a nation-wide network of portable data communications; a system for creating wireless local area networks (LANs) capable of speeds comparable to today's cable-based LANs; and Iridium, a worldwide, satellite-based cellular telephone system that, with the use of a handset small enough to "fit in an overcoat pocket," would "allow the user to make and receive calls from the North Pole to Antarctica."[5]

This nearly half-century of growth was and continues to be driven by a philosophy of technological leadership that was originally formulated by Dan Noble, the first general manager of the business, and then passed on through successive generations of management to today's leadership. Bill Weisz began his career at Motorola in 1948 as a product engineer under Noble, rose through the ranks of COMM management in the 1950s and 1960s, and served in the chief executive office of Motorola as president, COO, and eventually CEO through the 1970s and 1980s. He described this leadership philosophy in a series of memos written in the mid-1960s while he was COMM's

Figure 3.1
Motorola Communications, Financial History
($ millions)

	Communications Sector*		Cellular Telephones**	
	Sales	Operating Income	Sales	Operating Income
1971	305			
1972	365			
1973	469			
1974	586			
1975	621			
1976	659			
1977	824	131		
1978	965	111		
1979	1,127	149		
1980	1,253	156		
1981	1,443	165		
1982	1,527	139		
1983	1,620	92		
1984	1,864	194	180	(50)
1985	2,016	235	295	(19)
1986	2,204	244	347	23
1987	2,459	255	475	75
1988	3,017	326	655	115
1989	3,310	302	1,300	350
1990	3,560	225	2,000	360

*Figures for Communications Sector are from annual reports and 10-K forms. The sales figures for 1971–1975 were reported in the 1975 annual report. Prior to 1975, the company did not report sector sales. It began reporting Communications Sector income in 1978.

**Figures for Cellular Telephones are the author's estimates; Motorola separated this business from the Communications Sector in the mid-1980s and combined it with a money-losing computer operation to form the General Systems Sector. The company reports sales and income for the General Systems Sector as a whole, not for Cellular Telephones alone.

general manager. The objective of the Communications Division, he wrote to COMM's managers, was to be the "worldwide leader" in its field by providing products that were "orders of magnitude better" than the competition's:

> It has always been our philosophy to remain years ahead in technological art and in product at the market place. I would like to see us always two years ahead of our nearest competitors. By being ahead, I mean employing state-of-the-art techniques in product that we are actually selling when our competitors are only thinking about them . . . THIS BASIC PHILOSOPHY IS MANDATORY.[6]

Twenty-five years later, a new generation of management was, if anything, even more ambitious in its pursuit of leadership. By the early 1990s, leadership had come to mean being not just the best in one's industry, but the "best in class"—better than the world's best—in every process or function in the organization, from R&D to customer service.

This 45-year pursuit of leadership falls into three distinct, though closely related, patterns:

1. Continual efforts to create new businesses by pioneering new classes of products;
2. Continual efforts to grow existing businesses by enhancing, broadening and renewing existing product lines; and
3. Continual efforts, especially since the late 1970s, to improve quality and shorten cycle times.

The history of COMM, and the role played by general management in that history, can be traced by following the evolution of each of these patterns.

Creating New Businesses

Motorola introduced its first mobile radios (two-way radios for vehicles) in the late 1930s. These were simple, AM systems sold to police departments. At the time, Dan Noble was a professor at the University of Connecticut, where he had developed a prototype of an FM mobile radio system for the Connecticut State Police. Paul Galvin, Motorola's founder, convinced Noble to join the company in 1940, and immediately after the war, Noble turned his attention to Motorola's mobile radio business. From the outset, Noble insisted that the new business be organized separately from Motorola's car radio business in order to ensure that the attempt to develop mobile radio not be subordinated to the larger and more immediate demands of the already established business.

John Mitchell, like Bill Weisz, began his career at Motorola working as a design engineer in this new communications business. He worked his way through the management ranks of COMM, served as its general manager in the late 1960s and early 1970s, and then joined Weisz and Chairman Bob Galvin in the chief executive office, where he eventually became president and chief operating officer. Mitchell explains that from the beginning, the mobile radio business was marked by two features that not only set it apart from the competition but helped to set the mold for Motorola's future communications businesses. First, it had a dedicated sales force, unlike its primary competitors—RCA and GE—which sold their two-way radios through their consumer electronics businesses. "This meant that our field distribution people began to understand the customer—the railroad business, forestry, the police, the fire business." And as they began to understand the customer, they began to direct the product development effort toward new products tailored for specific customers. The sales organization, Weisz describes, was led by Homer Marrs.

> He used to insist that we know the customers better than they know themselves. He and his organization dragged us into these markets kicking and screaming. They knew the customer demand, and they would wander into our factories and labs, bring in potential customers, and cajole us into developing the new products.

The result was that very early on, COMM began to grow by addition—by adding new products tailored to specific new markets. Mitchell explains:

> What's unique about railroads? A locomotive is 64 volts, not 12, and they want to change the radio as they go through each section of country. When they pull into the station and change the crew, they change radios, since the next section of line is on a different frequency. So you need a plug-in radio.

Police and fire departments operated in a very different fashion, as did taxi companies and other organizations that operated fleets of vehicles, and COMM varied its products accordingly.

Second, in each of its market segments, COMM strove to offer the best-performing products and to be first to market with them. And in those instances when COMM was not first, superior distribution kept it competitive until it could respond. "Bill Weisz was always screaming about being first to market. My [Mitchell's] attitude was that if we don't make it first, when we do get there, we're going to kill them." Thus, during the 1940s and 1950s when radios were still being built with vacuum tubes, COMM "built more reserve gain in the system so our equipment would keep performing." This made the systems more expensive, but since COMM dealt directly with the customer, it had significantly lower distribution costs that offset the higher product costs. Whereas competitors' products "would begin to fade in six months, in a year and a half, ours would still be cooking away." At the same time that COMM was selling better performing vacuum tube-based products, it was also developing transistorized systems. It required ten years of development, but by the end of the 1950s, COMM introduced the first fully transistorized mobile radio. By then, COMM was well established as the "pre-eminent" mobile radio business.

From Mobile Radios to Portable

While the mobile radio business was growing rapidly during the post-war decade, a portable radio business was also taking root in COMM. Just as the practices that led to mobile radio's success set a pattern followed by future COMM businesses, the way in which the new portable radio business was established and nurtured was also re-peated often in the future. As Mitchell explains:

> We grew by horizontal development. We couldn't sell more and more mobiles so we had to make portables, and then we had to make pagers, and then we had to make telephone units, railroad units, mountain top repeaters, motorcycle radios—anything that moved, that had a two-way radio on it, or anything that was remote talking—we would make it. Our latest is the Iridium satellite system. It's a very natural extension of this same mentality that says, drive for perfor-mance even if it costs more, and find some other way to get costs out of the system, or charge higher prices.

COMM introduced its first line of commercial, portable two-way radios—called the "Handie-Talkie radio"—in 1947, roughly ten years after it introduced its first mobile radios. (A portable two-way radio called the "Walkie-Talkie" had been developed for the military dur-ing World War II.) Unlike mobile radios, which are designed for use in vehicles, portable radios are designed to be carried by individuals. Bill Weisz was a member of the team that designed this first portable radio line. It had limited use and low power, and required large batteries, but it turned out to be the first step in what would become an important and enduring new business for COMM. By 1954, a second-generation portable—the H Series, featuring a fold-out chas-sis for easy access—was introduced, this one designed by a team led by John Mitchell. This was the first portable radio to use transistors, making it lighter and smaller than the first generation, and it had 20 times the power output. The first fully transistorized portable radio—the HT200—was introduced in 1960, long before anything comparable. It was with the introduction of this still smaller, lighter, and more reliable portable that the business began to take off.

From Portable to Paging

During the course of the 1950s, as successive generations of portable radios were being developed, several new product line possibilities were pursued by COMM. In 1953, Noble had separated two new business units from the growing two-way radio business—microwave communications and power line controls. By the late 1950s, the array of new COMM product lines had grown to include closed-circuit television, power voice speakers and megaphones, precision test and measurement equipment, radio-controlled traffic light systems, and aircraft navigation and communication equipment.

Some of these ventures were quickly abandoned; others like the closed-circuit television line lasted into the 1970s, but, with one important exception, none was especially successful. That exception was paging, although during the 1950s its success was anything but apparent. Like the portable radio business before it and several new COMM businesses after it, the paging business went through what John Mitchell refers to as a "pre-emergent state," which lasted for almost a decade. This period began in 1955, when a small new-product development group managed by Bill Weisz introduced COMM's first pager. Like the first portables, these were fragile, "kludgie," and of limited practical use. They operated on low frequencies and were intended for use within a single building since Weisz's group expected private paging—that is, paging systems for individual companies and government agencies—to comprise the bulk of the market. (This kind of private system then dominated the mobile radio market.) Moreover, for private systems operating at low frequency, Motorola would not need to go through the sometimes painful process of winning Federal Communications Commission (FCC) approval for use of the required frequencies.

COMM installed its first paging systems at an AC Spark Plug plant in Flint, Michigan, a Motorola facility, and at Mount Sinai Hospital in Chicago. This was a pioneering effort and it showed. Installation was problematic, since the low-frequency system required that "a hell of a lot of wire" be laid around each building—wire that was frequently cut or moved accidentally by people working in the building. There was a good deal of interference on these low frequencies, and the paging receivers themselves were so fragile that they usually broke when dropped.

By the time these first trouble-filled systems were installed, Noble had placed Weisz at the head of a new business unit within COMM called Portable Products. Since pagers are portable devices, the fledgling paging effort was included in the new unit. Weisz recalls this era:

> If you go back to the handful of people in the portable radio business, we had a view of communications—the idea was to communicate with the person, not the vehicle. We had this view that portables would take over the world. Transmitters [needed for two-way portable communications] at this stage were heavy and big, whereas a paging device would be smaller. For us, paging was just a step toward more convenient, smaller, lighter, two-way communication with the individual. There was no fancy marketing at this stage. When you are pioneering in something the world doesn't even know it wants, you have to have a belief that the world is going to want what you have, and that it will start falling over its feet to get it.

In the late 1950s, the world was hardly falling over itself to get COMM's low-frequency pagers, but even with all the difficulties, the group gained enough experience with its early pagers to reinforce their belief that they were moving in the right direction. Mitchell recalls,

> If you went to Mount Sinai Hospital and tried to take back the first pagers that they were bitterly complaining about, they wouldn't give them to you. It was a concept they didn't want to give up, just like the first garage opener or water softener or electric window. Once you tried it, if it didn't work, you wanted to get it fixed, not throw it away. You wanted a better one that was reliable.

Therefore, the group persisted. In 1961, it introduced a second-generation, low-frequency pager that was significantly smaller and lighter than the first. More important, in the late 1950s, it began to develop a VHF pager, which would require FCC authorization but would eliminate the need for wiring buildings. It would also be usable on a citywide basis, rather than just indoors, since the higher-frequency radio signals penetrate buildings and vehicles. Moreover, Weisz and his associates already had experience using VHF frequencies with their portable and mobile radio businesses, and so they were building on a growing base of expertise.

The first VHF pager was designed by a team led by John Mitchell and introduced in 1960. It created the possibility for paging networks of up to several thousand users on a single two-way radio channel with a citywide range (roughly 15 to 30 miles). But development of this new kind of pager represented only the start of the battle. The market for paging, and, even more important, the infrastructure for creating and serving that market, also had to be developed. The private market for pagers was expanding more slowly than expected. The alternative to the private market was subscriber paging, whereby the paging equipment would be sold, not directly to the end-user but to intermediaries—either the telephone companies or Radio Common Carriers (RCCs)[7]—which would operate a paging system as a subscriber-based service business.

In 1960, the phone companies were not especially interested in paging, and the RCCs were relatively young and undeveloped. So not only did the portable products unit have to create a demand for the new paging equipment by RCCs, in many instances, it had to develop the RCCs themselves. Indeed, it went so far as to provide financing for a number of them, which at the time represented a real financial gamble. Simultaneously, considerable effort went into convincing the FCC to allow the RCCs to use the frequencies that the FCC had allocated to them for mobile communications for paging.

Creating the RCC market for paging and winning regulatory approval proved to be a chicken-egg problem. As Weisz recalls, the new "product wouldn't do you any good without the operator infrastructure and government approvals," but on the other hand, "we couldn't get the operator infrastructure and government approvals without the product." The solution was to keep advancing the product—to make it smaller and lighter, to increase its reliability and durability, to improve its range, and to reduce the infrastructure or operating costs (most notably, by increasing the number of pagers that could be supported by a given level of fixed equipment). Improvements in paging technology continued unabated after the first VHF system was introduced in 1960. Four years later, and ten years after the introduction of the first low-frequency pager, the business introduced its second-generation VHF pagers—PageBoy I. This new pager was 20 percent smaller and 26 percent lighter than its predecessor, offered an 80 percent increase in range, was significantly more durable, and sold for $245, or 27 percent less than the earlier system.[8] With hindsight, it can be said that PageBoy I brought COMM's paging business out of its "pre-emergent" state. As Weisz put it:

> The first VHF was too big, too heavy, but it was another step in the right direction. All the versions up to the PageBoy were steps along the way. Each sold a bit more, each did a

bit better, each taught us more about the marketplace. Within this view of a world of portable, person-to-person communications, the business developed step by step.

From Paging to Cellular Telephones

Another product line developed by COMM in the 1950s was the mobile telephone. It, too, went through a long pre-emergent state. Phones were large and bulky, calls had to be placed through an operator, and the systems could handle only a very limited number of users. In the early 1960s, AT&T decided to develop an improved mobile telephone service (IMTS) that would be fully automatic and nationwide. The two primary contenders to develop the equipment for IMTS, under contract to AT&T, were COMM and General Electric. COMM won the contract, developed the system, and introduced both an initial, manual version in 1962 and the fully automatic version in 1963. The system was developed by a group in the mobile radio business led by Marty Cooper (who would also lead the development of COMM's cellular telephone system). Cooper recalls that the "product we came out with was so good, and so reliable, that there just wasn't any competition." By the mid-1960s, Motorola owned a 98 percent share of the IMTS equipment market.

The mobile telephone line was made a separate business unit during the mid-1960s. Cooper, who had gone on to become operations manager of portable products, was reunited with the telephone business in 1970 when he was named head of a new division that included the telephone line. By this time, the situation in the telephone business had changed rather dramatically. Harris Corporation had taken advantage of what Cooper believes was Motorola complacency and seemingly overnight had gained 30 percent of the market. As Cooper recalls:

> We lived with that first IMTS product. We came out with a higher frequency band, but otherwise just let it drift along. . . . All the guys who had built the business and made the customer contacts were now managers, and because there had been no competition, they thought that all they needed were order takers. We had to hustle for a period of years to recover that situation.

But changes more significant than an erosion of market share were also taking place. As mobile telephone services grew in popularity, they began to reach the limits of the amount of radio frequency allocated to them by the FCC. In large cities, the few available channels were overloaded, which led to poor performance (users had a difficult time completing calls) and narrow limits on the number of users who could subscribe to the systems. In New York City, for example, "customers could wait many years or even indefinitely to obtain the service."[9]

In response, the FCC proposed in 1968 to assign a 115Mhz block of frequencies—most of it at 800 to 900 Mhz, the high end of the UHF band—to mobile and portable radio systems.[10] The FCC also requested proposals regarding how this additional spectrum could be used most efficiently. A long debate resulted about which technologies to use at these frequencies and about how the frequencies should be divided among AT&T, the RCCs, and private mobile radio systems.

Initially, the FCC proposed to prohibit the RCCs from using the new frequencies and to allocate 70 of the 115Mhz exclusively to AT&T, which intended to use them for cellular telephone systems. The concept of cellular telephone systems had been developed by AT&T's Bell Laboratories. Conventional mobile telephone systems employed a single high-power transmitter that connected individual mobile phone users with the normal, wire-based telephone system. The area covered by the transmitter might be as large as 50 miles. Each user within that area would be assigned a radio frequency channel for use with his or her mobile telephone. In the cellular system proposed by AT&T, the large area would be broken into several smaller areas, each using a lower-power transmitter with a range of up to 10 miles. Each user within the cell would again be assigned a radio channel, but as the user traveled from one cell into another, the channel that was being used would now be available to others still within that cell. Thus, for a given geographic area and a fixed number of available channels, many more users could be served. The cellular concept "promised a thousandfold increase in the availability" of mobile telephone services—if a system for rapidly switching users from one channel to the next and for reassigning channels back to other users could be developed. By 1970, such a system appeared to be technologically possible.[11]

Motorola responded to the FCC by arguing that RCCs should not be excluded from the new spectrum and by offering its own ideas on how to use the spectrum more efficiently. In May 1970, however, the FCC announced that it intended to proceed with its AT&T-oriented reallocation plan, and it gave all parties until July 1972 to respond to this proposal. The issue for Motorola thus became a matter of trying "to convince the FCC that someone other than AT&T

could provide a viable MTS [mobile telephone system] service." John Mitchell, then general manager of COMM, recalls:

> We were trying to figure out [in early 1972] how to convince the commission that there was some other authority besides Bell Lab. Bell had just made a proposal to put the first cellular mobile radio system in Philadelphia. Marty [i.e., Cooper, now manager of the division that included COMM's mobile telephone business] argued that we had to come out with a portable cellular system that would go much further in applying radiotelephone than mobile. There are a hell of a lot more people than there are autos, and when you park your car and leave, you can't use your mobile radio, but you can take your portable with you.

Cooper was expressing the same philosophy that had driven the development of pagers and before that, portable radios. As Mitchell recalls, "We all grew up in the portable radio business, so we were convinced that portables would outgrow mobiles." This view of person-to-person communications dated back to the earliest days of COMM. But in those days, it was shared by only a handful of young engineers in a small business unit. By the late 1960s, those young engineers had become COMM's senior management, and they were so imbued with the portable communications vision that, as Weisz put it, "You had to be stupid not to see it." So whereas in the 1950s, COMM was a mobile radio business that was also exploring a wide range of other communication businesses, by the late 1960s, mobile and portable commnications had become the primary focal points. At the same time, John Mitchell, then the general manager, was in Cooper's words, "infusing COMM with the mobile and portable religion."

Thus, when Cooper came to the new division that contained the mobile telephone business in 1970, "I had made up my mind that cellular was going to be a portable business." By this time, R&D in COMM had been decentralized among the individual business units. There remained, however, a central research department that was independent of the business units. Cooper made the research department his "adjunct," persuading it to do the R&D necessary to support his division's product line. Two years before the decision was made to respond to the FCC with a proposal for a portable cellular system, he began working with the research department to develop the technology base that would eventually be needed for a portable cellular phone system.

We had an antenna group in the research department, and I would say, "We're going to have a portable at 900 Mhz; can you build an antenna that works at 900Mhz? I don't yet know exactly what it's for, but we'll need an antenna that works on a box this size." Or, I would say, "We're going to need a synthesizer for a lot of channels, which I know cellular is going to need. Start working on it." And so the research department was developing the base technology for cellular . . . and then in 1972, when we had to respond really fast to the FCC, we were able to put together a proposal for a portable cellular system in a matter of weeks.

By mid-1972, COMM had proposed a portable cellular system to the FCC and commenced development of an initial version. By 1973, the system had been tried out in field tests in Chicago, New York, and Washington.

The portable cellular concept enabled Motorola to establish its position in cellular communications with the FCC, but COMM's cellular telephone business was only beginning its pre-emergent stage in 1973. The regulatory proceedings continued through the rest of the decade; it was not until December 1983 that the FCC granted the first commercial license to American Radio Telephone Systems, an RCC, to operate a Motorola cellular system. Throughout this period, COMM continued to develop the technology. Like the first portables and pagers, the first cellular phones that it demonstrated in 1973 were "big, kludgie, and very expensive." By 1976, Cooper's group had developed a second generation that was "just about the right size," and by the end of the decade, an even better version had been developed. By the time the first sales were recorded in 1984, COMM had invested 15 years and $150 million in development. "This was a dedicated effort," Cooper recalls, "over a 15-year period with no revenues, or trivial revenues."

Not surprisingly, as the development project continued to drain COMM resources year after year with no return, it met with considerable internal resistance. According to Cooper:

There were any number of times that it would have been killed had it not been protected by Mitchell. John believed in portable. He had confidence in me. And he believed that you had to spend on R&D if you were going to survive in the future. This is the essence of Motorola, the essence of why we stayed in that business and why people didn't kick me out of the company any number of times.

The internal doubts were matched by external skepticism. "Nobody believed us," Mitchell explains, "especially the competition. They didn't believe the world was waiting for a portable. They believed the world was waiting for a mobile phone, because that's what AT&T was developing." But because of COMM's experience with the previous demonstrations, and because of its earlier experience with portable radios and pagers, "we *knew* we had a concept that would sell."

The tough issue through the decade of development, then, was not whether to continue the effort but how much to invest in it. "What did it take to do the next mobile, the next portable, the next switch? Can we afford to do it at this pace or half this pace?" AT&T was also working on the technology, and it could afford to invest much more than Motorola. But, ironically, this worked to COMM's advantage, for AT&T contracted out a good deal of its development work—much of it to COMM! In 1977, the FCC granted licenses to American Radio Telephone Systems to install and demonstrate a Motorola mobile and portable cellular system in the Baltimore/Washington, DC area and to Illinois Bell Telephone Company to install an AT&T mobile cellular system in Chicago. Motorola turned out to be the largest supplier of mobile telephones for the AT&T demonstration. Mitchell explains:

> They never developed the first- and second-generation mobile; they bought it. . . . They tried to enter the business themselves, but they never succeeded. They never caught up because they didn't get in the first two generations. When they were ready to go to market and when they looked at what they had developed and what was already coming out on the market, they saw they were a generation behind, five to seven years behind.

Meanwhile, having worked its way through the development of three generations of equipment, COMM was ready for commercialization by the end of the decade. When the FCC finally granted the first commercial license in December 1983, COMM was well positioned. In less than a year, it had introduced a complete line of cellular products, including seven mobile phones and two portables, and had quickly established itself as the leading worldwide supplier of cellular equipment. The business lost $50 million on $200 million in sales in 1984 (on top of the $150 million that it had already spent on development), but by 1990, it was estimated to be generating $2 billion in revenue and "well over half" of Motorola's profits (see Figure 3.1).[12]

From Voice to Data

Mobile and portable data. The process of "horizontal development" did not end with cellular telephones. By the late 1970s, as COMM was developing its third generation of pre-emergent cellular equipment, it was also launching a new mobile and portable communications business. This business would manufacture equipment for communication of data rather than voice. Again, the business went through a long preliminary state, during which it had to not only pioneer the technology but develop the market and associated infrastructure as well. The driving force behind this persistence in the face of the market and technology uncertainties was again the mobile and portable religion. As Mitchell predicted in 1982 when he was president of the company, "There will be a whole generation that won't be able to operate in business without access to a computer, and they'll want access to that computer on the move."[13]

The data communications business was an outgrowth of work by COMM's mobile radio business that stretched back to the early 1970s. Police departments, fire departments, and railroads were among mobile radio's oldest and most important customers. After receiving FCC approval in 1970, the business began to look for ways to introduce what at the time it called "mobile printers for hard copy readout in vehicles."[14] By the mid-1970s, the business was selling vehicle-based (i.e., mobile) data entry terminals that policemen could use to gain access to national criminal computer files from their vehicles and to "relay printed messages to the dispatcher or directly to the computer from the vehicle."[15] The first hand-held or portable version of these systems (RDX 1000 Portable Data System) was introduced in 1978. Then, in 1982, COMM brought out the PCX portable data communications system, which provided two-way data communications between a 28-ounce, hand-held computer terminal and host computers. The hand-held terminal was battery powered and provided the capability for wireless, radio-based data communications between users in the field (for example, sales or maintenance personnel) and host computers (in an office, for example) on a citywide basis.

The first major customer for the PCX was IBM, which wanted to use it in its field service operation. By 1983, COMM was installing the first version of the PCX system for IBM in Chicago. By 1985, a separate, portable data products division had been established within COMM. This division introduced a mobile version of the data terminal, conducted pilot tests of systems for field service and sales groups of several companies, and installed the system for IBM throughout the country (by 1990, 22,000 units were in use by IBM in 400 cities).[16] In the most significant departure from past Motorola practice, the division installed its own network, which it intended to maintain and operate as a service business for organizations that did not have enough users to justify their own private data communication network. The business continued to grow through the second half of the decade. It introduced a new portable hand-held terminal, capable of transmitting data at rates faster (19,200 bits per second) than any comparable product on the market. It continued to expand its own network and to sell new private systems, the most visible being a system for Federal Express that helped couriers keep track of customer packages and documents.

This decade of business development culminated in 1990 with the creation of Ardis (Advanced Nationwide Data Service), a joint venture with IBM that would offer nationwide portable and mobile data communication. This joint venture combined Motorola's data communication network with the network it had developed for IBM. It was comprised of more than 1,100 radio base stations and was capable of providing coverage for virtually all of the metropolitan United States.[17] Customers such as New York Life Insurance and Sears, Roebuck, which were among the first to announce plans to test the new service, would pay a monthly subscriber fee that at least at the outset of the business was expected to range between $100 and $150 per month.

Even after a decade of development, the business was still in its infancy. As the president and CEO of Ardis admitted when the business was announced, the volume of radio-based data communications "is very low today, almost unmeasurable if you're talking about two-way interactive data." But in common with the other new businesses that had successfully grown out of COMM, the potential market, though still undeveloped, was quite large. By 1990, there were an "estimated 10 million 'mobile professionals' in the United States."[18]

Wireless LANs. While data communications was still growing in the mid-1980s, COMM became involved in developing another data communications business. This one grew out of its cellular telephone business, which had been separated from the rest of COMM in 1985. In 1986, the business had begun to develop the technology for wireless communications among computers within buildings (i.e., wireless local area networks). Five years of R&D and "tens and tens of millions of dollars" later, the new technology was introduced.[19] While it was not the first wireless LAN technology, it was based on a fundamentally different approach than any earlier technology, operating at much higher frequencies (18,000 to 19,000Mhz as opposed to 900Mhz). The new system transmitted data 7.5 times faster than the leading wireless LAN, and in its initial version, appeared to be competitive in speed with state-of-the-art wire-based LANs. (The technology was reported to have already been tested at speeds three to six times faster than wire-based LANs, which would mean 50 to 100 megabits per second compared to 16 megabits per second.) Thus the new technology had the potential to displace traditional local area network technology, which required costly installation and often reconfiguration of wires and cables. On the other hand, like each of the earlier horizontal expansions, the market and technology uncertainties facing the new business were significant, and no doubt a long pre-emergent stage lay ahead. The total U.S. wireless LAN market in 1990 was only about $3 million in size, and estimates of the future potential ranged from 6 percent of all LAN connections by 1992 (or $300 million in sales) to less than 1 percent of all connections by 1995. One analyst described the uncertainties this way:

> Predictions are all over the map because there are mitigating factors, including the fact that the technology is not yet proven, questions surrounding Motorola's ability to market what could be perceived as a LAN product, and psychological resistance to microwaves bouncing around the office.[20]

From Citywide Cellular Telephones to Global Cellular

In mid-1990, Motorola announced the development of yet another mobile/portable communications business. The new enterprise, named Iridium, would be a worldwide, satellite-based cellular telephone system that would enable users anywhere on the earth to make and receive phone calls using a hand-held, portable receiver roughly the size of a cellular telephone. Existing cellular telephone systems operate within areas of relatively high population density. Iridium is intended to cover the large areas of the globe with lower population densities. Users in these areas would place or receive a call with a portable telephone through a network of 77 satellites circling the globe. Every satellite would span 37 cells, each covering an area 400 miles in diameter and capable of handling 336 calls simultaneously. (Capacity could be expanded by adding new frequencies.) The satellites would connect the user either to another portable user or to a local telephone network, from one location anywhere in the world to any other point on the globe.[21]

At the time Iridium was announced, it faced daunting market, technical, financial, and regulatory uncertainties. The investment re-

quired to put the system in place would be massive, an estimated
$2.3 billion, and if all went according to plan, it would be at least a
decade before the system reached breakeven. As John Mitchell described the plan:

> We'll demonstrate the system in 1992. In 1994, we launch
> seven [of the 77] satellites. We launch half of the system in
> 1995, and the rest in 1996. The service will start in 1997, and
> we're going to invest at a constant rate between now [1990]
> and then. . . . It will take four to five years [after the service
> starts] to reach breakeven.

During this decade of development, regulatory approval would have
to be gained in virtually every country in the world—not just in the
United States—which would itself be a long and arduous task. And,
as was the case with each of the earlier horizontal expansions, the
infrastructure that would deliver the communications service created
by the new equipment would also have to be developed. This time,
a global consortium of companies (and perhaps even nations) that
would own and operate the satellite network would have to be pieced
together. So, too, would a network of locally licensed operators based
in every country of the world who would operate the "gateways"
through which the satellite system would be connected to local public
telephone systems in the participating countries.

In creating this network, Motorola once again faced the kind of
chicken-egg problem it had seen so often before in its pioneering
efforts. To convince regulators, potential consortia members, and local operators to participate, it needed to demonstrate the viability of
the technology. But to demonstrate the viability of the technology, it
needed the network. This is why, Mitchell explained,

> We've got to get an operator with a license in every country
> in which we are going to land, and this thing is going to
> cover the world. Instead of waiting out the issuance of li-
> censes in the United States, and then in England, and then
> in Japan, and then around the world, we have to do it simul-
> taneously. We announced early, ahead of demonstration be-
> cause of this. We have to show the world what we can do.
> We had to do the same thing in cellular. In 1973, we started
> demonstrating the portable phone, even though it took until
> 1983 before the service started. Everyone knew it was com-
> ing. They knew what we were demonstrating.

As for its share in the ownership of the network, Motorola announced that it would be willing to invest in as much as 20 percent

of the network (or $400 million). This of course would be independent of the investment that it would be making in developing and demonstrating the system. In addition to owning a portion of the network, Motorola also planned to manufacture and sell the equipment that would be needed for the system—the portable phones, payloads for the satellites, communications links, and related supporting equipment. The satellites themselves would have to be replaced every five to seven years.

> We will have a production line—building about one satellite a month. And you design a second generation while the first one is starting to fly. Starting in about year six, you bring down the first generation and put up replacements that will have new frequencies, new features, enhancements, etc. By then, after you fly that first system, you really understand the market.

The payoffs, which would not be realized for at least a decade, were potentially enormous. Merrill Lynch estimated that the system would generate $700 million in operating income per year (roughly comparable to Motorola's total 1990 pretax income) assuming that Motorola did indeed own 20 percent of the network and the system achieved a worldwide subscribership of five million.[22] (In 1989, there were roughly seven million conventional cellular telephone users worldwide; the number was projected to increase by more than an order of magnitude by the year 2000.)[23]

From Worldwide Cellular Telephone to Personal Communications Networks

At the same time that Motorola was developing Iridium, it was laying the foundation for the converse of Iridium—systems known as "personal communications networks" for short-range portable communications within a single location, such as a building or campus. The system would operate at higher frequencies than current cellular systems (1850 to 1990Mhz versus 800 to 900Mhz), and eventually, it was hoped, would provide the capability for wireless PBXs (private branch exchanges—private telephone systems) using inexpensive, portable handsets. The handsets or phones would initially be wallet-sized, but they would eventually become as small as a wristwatch.[24]

In June 1990, Motorola applied to the FCC for experimental licenses to test the system in Chicago and Atlanta. Earlier, at the end of 1989, it had been selected by the British government together with British Cable and Wireless, NYNEX, and Pacific Telesis as one of the

Figure 3.2
Horizontal Expansion in Mobile and Portable Communications

Mobile Radio					
	Portable Radio				
		Paging			
			Cellular		
				Data	
					"Iridium"
					PCNs
1940	1950	1960	1970	1980	1990

three consortia authorized to build nationwide cellular systems using the personal communications network technology. (The British government was moving considerably faster than the U.S. government in promoting the use of these systems and providing the necessary radio frequency spectrum.) But if Motorola was already laying the groundwork for yet another horizontal expansion, this time the competition would be intense from the outset. Personal communications networks were widely perceived as an important and potentially very large new opportunity in the field of telecommunications. Competition ranged from a small communications company named Millicom that had received FCC permission to test a system in Houston and Orlando to virtually every major telecommunications company in the world, including Ericsson, Northern Telecom, Siemens, Philips, and AT&T.

Whether Motorola would succeed in establishing a leadership position in this new field, just as whether it would succeed in overcoming the hurdles facing Iridium, will only become apparent over the course of the 1990s. Whatever the outcome, personal communication networks are yet another example of an attempt to grow through "horizontal expansion"—through pioneering new technologies and markets in mobile and portable communications (see Figure 3.2).

Growing Existing Businesses

COMM's leadership philosophy applied not only to these repeated efforts to create new businesses but also to a more continuous process of staying ahead once these businesses had been established. The key to sustaining leadership was a process that Bob Galvin, CEO through virtually this entire period, called "renewal." Each product line was continually enhanced and upgraded, and periodically replaced by an entirely new generation of products with new features and fundamentally superior capabilities. In Mitchell's words,

We believe that even our oldest market can still be a growth market. In the police market, we are into our seventh-generation mobile radio, and it is nothing like the fifth or sixth. It is a smaller, more reliable product; it has for the first time security, smartnet, and so forth. . . . In mobile, we went from simple radio to multifrequency radios, to radios that could control big fleets of vehicles . . . to auto scanning, trunked systems, smartnet systems. Along the way, we introduced secure systems, mobile data, private line systems, signalling system expansions. . . . Some of these features took a long time to develop, some less time. Some were features for better sound, some for better coverage capability, but some—like secure, smartnet, trunking—allow customers to reorganize their operations.

Portable radios, pagers, and cellular phones evolved in similar fashion, with each generation smaller, lighter, and better performing than previous generations. Pagers in 1990, for example, weighed less than 3 ounces, compared to the first VHF pagers that weighed 14 ounces. They also offered much higher capacity and were capable of receiving and storing multiple messages from multiple locations in a variety of forms. Similiarly, the fourth-generation portable cellular phone (Micro TAC), introduced in 1989, was one-third the size and weight of the first generation and half the size of the third; and the fifth generation (Micro TAC Lite), introduced in 1991, was less than two-thirds the size and weight of the fourth. At the same time the performance of the various product lines was continually being improved, their breadth—and therefore, the range of market segments they served—was being continually expanded. Thus, by 1976, COMM's mobile and portable radio lines included 4,000 different models. In the cellular business, COMM introduced seven different mobile cellular phone models and two different portable models in mid-1984, a line of cellular convertible telephones (phones that can operate both as mobile and portable devices), a third portable model in February 1985, and a four-model, low-end line of cellular phones called the America Series in January 1986. The same progression can be seen in paging. In 1990, COMM was offering pagers that operated in modes ranging from silent vibration to tone-only, tone and voice, numeric display, and alphanumeric display, compared to the early versions that offered just tone and voice. Different versions of these pagers were offered for four different radio frequency spectra and they came in a variety of different forms, from rectangular shapes to be worn on belts, to a fountain pen shape to be carried in a shirt pocket, to a wristwatch.

Bill Weisz explains the logic behind this continual broadening of product offerings:

> We have never introduced a product that didn't expand the market. There would often be some concern expressed by individual product line managers that new products would cannibalize existing lines, but our philosophy always was— if anybody is going to steal market share from our product lines, it had better be us.

Moreover, the objective was not to offer just a broad line of products, but to offer the broadest product line in the business—to "bracket the competition." This meant serving not only the premium end of the market but the low end as well—from the "Cadillac to the Chevy." Thus the product offerings of each business, in addition to serving a broad range of market segments, usually were structured into several price/performance tiers. And preserving COMM's position in the low-end tier, as we shall see, was just as important as preserving it in the high end.

This philosophy of offering the broadest product line came to be implemented through a decentralized organization. In essence, each product line tier had its own management, with its own profit and loss responsibility. With multiple tiers for each product line, this led to a good deal of internal competition. Mitchell explains:

> As the market developed, we developed more than one product family. The businesses developed into price tiers, and we would have product managers for each tier. They didn't run their own factories or sales department, but they did have design, product marketing and program management. . . . There was a lot of overlap and a lot of fights. By the time we finished beating up on each other internally, the outside competitors had a heck of a time.

Evolution of the Paging Business—An Illustration

PageBoy I. This process of continual enhancement and renewal coupled with continual expansion is well illustrated by the evolution of the paging business. As we have seen, paging, like all the portable communications businesses, went through a decade-long pre-emergent stage. It was only with PageBoy I, introduced in 1964, that the business began to take off. Sales doubled in 1964 and again in 1965, and they increased by 50 percent in 1966.[25]

Actually, PageBoy I was a family of three basic pagers—a tone-only version, offered at both low and VHF frequencies; a tone and voice VHF pager; and a tone-only, high-capacity pager for systems with up to 3,000 subscribers. In the years immediately following PageBoy's introduction, COMM brought out encoders (systems for dispatching paging messages) with greater capacity and a line of pagers that operated at 450Mhz (UHF), which allowed for greater penetration of buildings and vehicles. By the end of the decade, COMM was offering a total of 16 different product variants and was reported to have 80 percent of the market.

PageBoy II. Even with this commanding position and rapid growth, the market for paging was still in its infancy. As Marty Cooper, who was product manager of the portable products business in the second half of the 1960s, recalls, "A large market was not a given; it was evident to us, but it was also evident that the world had not caught on to this yet." PageBoy I, in the opinion of Cooper and his associates, was still too big and too heavy, and therefore development continued. "The drive to get pagers smaller, lighter, and more reliable was so much of a given that we didn't even question it. And it drove us to new technology." For example, in order to develop a better understanding of how to make smaller and lighter batteries, since "nobody was building batteries for portable equipment," a small battery business was acquired. Of more enduring significance, the goal of developing better pagers led to extensive interactions with Motorola's semiconductor business. One of the keys to this interaction was an organization, first established by Dan Noble, called MICARL—Motorola Integrated Circuit Applied Research Lab. In the beginning, MICARL was formally a part of the semiconductor business. It reported to semiconductor management but was funded through contracts from Motorola's equipment businesses, like portable products. Its explicit role was to support the equipment businesses with the technology of the semiconductor business. Over the years, the particular reporting arrangements and management schemes for MICARL varied. But the important point, in Cooper's view, was

> that the Corporation's leadership would not permit MICARL to be used as a resource of semiconductor, and there were many pressures to do so. . . . Finding the right balance was the key. It had to be close to semiconductor, but not theirs. . . . it became an enormous strategic resource, because in essence, we ran MICARL. We [i.e., Weisz, Mitchell, and Cooper] used to go down there and beat these guys over the head to support us.

On the other hand, for obvious reasons, the semiconductor business could not afford to neglect its external customers in favor of the internal equipment businesses. Therefore, Weisz and others always insisted on giving the former as much access to the advanced technology as the latter.

The pursuit of smaller, lighter, and more reliable pagers led in 1971 to the next and fourth major generation of pagers—PageBoy II. (The first was the early, low-frequency pager; the second, the first VHF pager; and the third was PageBoy I). PageBoy II was one-third the size of PageBoy I, came in both tone and tone and voice models, contained 80 components compared to 210 for the earlier model, was offered at a roughly comparable price, and included a number of new features such as message storing. The product was an immediate success, triggering a 51 percent increase in sales in 1971 and another 52 percent in 1972. As late as 1973, no competitor had "come close to it."[26]

The PageBoy II was followed by a low-cost line called PageCom one year later. And two years after that, in 1974, a high-capacity product line was introduced for use in large metropolitan areas. Called MetroPage, this line could handle up to 100,000 subscribers, which represented a hundredfold increase in capacity. As Cooper recalls, "This was a visionary product. Everyone asked, 'Why would anyone want so much capacity?' In fact, we had to create a consortium of RCCs in order to make our first sale."

Product development continued after the PageBoy II with products specifically designed to expand the range of market segments served. The Minitor, for firefighters and emergency medical personnel, and the Director, designed for industrial, energy, and utility market segments, were introduced in 1975. These were followed in 1977 by the Dimension IV, a new generation of UHF frequency pagers, and two, more durable low-end systems, the Metrix (tone only) and the Spirit (tone and voice). By this time, the paging business was offering a total of 80 different models (see Figure 3.3).

Technology roadmaps. General management played a prominent role in this effort to enhance and broaden the individual product lines. Weisz and Mitchell "stuck our noses in the businesses continuously," putting pressure on individual product line management to press for the next generation, for the smaller, lighter, and better-performing product. By the mid-1970s, this general managerial encouragement began to evolve into a more formalized review process, spearheaded by Bob Galvin, then the chairman, in which each business was required to develop what eventually became known as

Figure 3.3
Pagers—Product Enhancement and Renewal

	1955	1960	1965	1970	1975	1980	1985	1990
TONE, TONE & VOICE	1st low frequency / 1st VHF	2d low frequency	PageBoy I Bell Boy (high capacity) 1st UHF 450Mhz	PageBoy II MetroPage (high capacity)				PageBoy III
						Dimension IV Dimension 1000 (900Mhz) Metrix (low end)	BPR Envoy Bravo	Dimension 2000
					PageCom (low end)			
					Minitor Director			Minitor II Director II
NUMERIC						BPR 2000	Sensar (pen) Sensar Bravo Wristwatch	
ALPHA-NUMERIC						Optrix	PMR 2000	

"technology roadmaps." By the 1980s, these had become rather detailed technology and product planning exercises, but in essence, they involve three basic steps.[27] Each business does the following:

1. Projects the future evolution of each product line over the course of the next five to ten years. Projections are built on detailed historical analysis of product life cycles and experience curves, combined with equally detailed competitor analysis. "Once you plot these things," Mitchell explains, "you see that the key next generation should arrive *here*, the selling price has got to be *that*, and the cost to have normal margins has to be *this*."

2. Forecasts the evolution of the technologies required for development of these projected products.

3. Combines the product projections with the technology forecasts. That is, projections of desired future products and the desired timing of these products are placed against forecasts of the technologies needed to develop those products in the time frame desired. In Mitchell's words, "You plot the trends, and then you can say, 'If I'm going to get to this product at that point and cost, I need to do these things now in technology.' "

The philosophy underlying this process is that technology is not developed in the abstract, but rather must be driven by a focus on future products. Research must be product-driven, and in order for product-driven research to be effective, Mitchell argues, the "research program *has* to be looking out a generation or two on a product roadmap." Businesses that are in their pre-emergent state are not subjected to this kind of review. But according to Mitchell, if the business is well established and

> if it has an orderly heritage, where you can almost sit there and rattle off all the generations and who designed them, then you ought to be able to look to the next five to ten years and say you need that radio at that time.

Perhaps more important to senior management than the roadmaps themselves, the process of developing them becomes a vehicle for instilling the leadership philosophy throughout the organization. At least once a year, the chief executive officers review the roadmaps of each organization with the management and key staff of those organizations. These sessions often become a forum for debate about future directions and, in Weisz's words, are "in part, an exercise of forcing the businesses to listen to the leadership philosophy; senior management is constantly hammering away at what we mean by leadership."

Penetrating the Japanese market—pagers for NTT. As the paging product line continued to evolve in the middle and late 1970s, and as the roadmap process was emerging as an integral part of this evolution, a new and, in hindsight, pivotal chapter in the history of COMM was unfolding. Even though COMM was the dominant worldwide supplier of pagers at the time, it was not selling any in Japan. In 1978, Robert Strauss, then the U.S. Special Trade Representative, had begun to urge Japanese officials to open Japan's telecommunications market to U.S. equipment manufacturers. At roughly the same time, a congressional delegation from the House Ways and Means Committee visited Japan as part of an investigation into U.S.-Japanese trade. When the delegation met with officials of Nippon Telephone and Telegraph—then Japan's national telecommunications monopoly and the rough equivalent of AT&T[28]—the delegation was told that the reason NTT was not buying equipment from U.S. manufacturers like Motorola was that no U.S. manufacturers were trying to do business with them.

Jack Germain, who, like Weisz, Mitchell, and Cooper, joined COMM in the 1950s and who led the team that designed the first fully transistorized mobile radio, was then the assistant general manager of COMM. "When we got that message back from our Washington office, we decided to take NTT at their word." An effort to establish COMM as a supplier of pagers to NTT was launched. But if the triggering event was the congressional delegation's visit, the underlying motivation was once again leadership. By 1978, COMM had had enough experience competing with the Japanese in the mobile radio business to know that "they were the coming competitor."

> We felt that if you are going to compete with the Japanese, you have to compete with them in their own backyard. And if you can't compete with them in their backyard, then you are missing something. They are better than you for some reason and if they are better than you for some reason, then at some point in your life, you are going to fail, because that issue is going to come back and hit you in the head.

A four-year campaign to penetrate the Japanese paging market was therefore undertaken. A good deal of politics regarding trade policy was involved. So too was a good deal of learning about Japanese practices, such as those regarding product specifications: "We'd ask, what are the specs, and it would turn out that they don't have specs. They sit down and have a meeting; everyone trusts each other and goes off and does their thing." But much of the reason COMM succeeded in ultimately becoming a leading supplier of pagers in Japan is because of developments within COMM itself.

At Bill Weisz's insistance (Weisz was then chief operating officer of Motorola), a separate entity with its own "strategic budget" was established to pursue the NTT contract. Weisz's logic here was no different from that underlying the longstanding COMM practice of separating nascent activities from established businesses. In this instance, a new pager with entirely different frequencies and signalling had to be developed. As Germain explains, this meant that

> we had to pull resources from already budgeted projects. We had a lot of opposition from lower management; there was a lot of flack about how we weren't making any money, how this was all a loss, how we couldn't afford to do this, and it would disrupt other programs. But you've got to look at the big picture. In any business, there is an investment period, and this was the investment period.

With Weisz's support, Germain overcame the opposition and assembled the required resources, including support from MICARL to develop a microprocessor to handle the signalling in the pager. (This represented the first use of a microprocessor in a pager.) The year 1979 was spent designing a product that would meet NTT requirements, and by February 1980, early prototypes were sent to NTT for review. Agreement was reached to ship 150 pagers for testing and evaluation by September of that year.

This introduced an entirely new challenge: given how politically visible COMM's attempt to penetrate NTT was, it could not afford to fail the field tests. Indeed, it could not afford to have any of the 150 prototypes fail. "Not only would NTT be unhappy, but so would the Japanese government, the U.S. government, and the *Washington Post* too!" At the same time, NTT's standards of reliability (that is, average length of time that the system would operate in the field without failure) were far more stringent than the requirements to which COMM was accustomed. Thus, penetrating the Japanese market meant not only designing and developing a new product, but a product with unprecedented (for COMM) reliability and freedom from defects. "We had eight months to deliver prototypes of a new design, using a new frequency, that was microprocessor-based . . . and that could not fail in the field."

The development effort that ensued became one of the foundations of a corporationwide campaign to dramatically improve quality (see below). According to Germain:

> One of the things we had learned in the paging business, and this I think is probably the beginning of a lot of the quality revolution that took place in Motorola, is that there is a direct correlation between the number of times you fix something in manufacturing and the number of early failures you get in the field—we call them latent defects. If you have trouble making it, you have trouble in the field. If you don't have any trouble making it, you don't have any trouble in the field.

Since in this case, COMM could not afford *any* failures in the field, Germain reasoned, it could not afford to have any failures in manufacturing. The traditional process of assembling a product and then testing and repairing any defects uncovered in testing would not be good enough. The pagers had to be assembled correctly in the first place.

> Now my experience said it couldn't be done. With such a small run and a brand new design, and a very, very limited experience curve, it simply couldn't be done . . . but it was central to our success!

And, indeed, the first attempts to assemble the new pagers without failures in a pilot run of 50 units led to "absolute chaos. None worked; we had all kinds of problems." This of course was normal for a pilot run, and it quickly became clear that the process had not been completely thought through and that problems remained with the design and incoming material as well. This early unsuccessful effort led to a "much bigger push into participative management," which in turn led to a much deeper and more detailed characterization of the process.

> Most processes in the world are not fully characterized. There are many little things that are part of the process that can make or break you, from lighting, to heights of assemblers' chairs, to differences in quality of equipment between assemblers and testers. You get really participative, and all these little things come out of the woodwork, because now we are asking people, "Hey, we want it to be perfect; we don't want any rework; we're going to eliminate testing. It can't get past you unless it is done perfectly." So we changed the whole process.

At the same time that Germain's group was attacking the problem of defects in manufacturing, it was also attacking the reliability issue (i.e., even if the pager is built without defects, how long will it operate in the customer's environment without the need for repair?). The key here was a process called the accelerated life test, which after the NTT project, came to be used throughout COMM. Once a design had been developed and a test unit built, it would undergo a week to ten days of testing during which it would be subjected to an "environment that simulated five years of rugged field use and abuse . . . extreme heat, cold, moisture, and impact."[29] The test results were used to identify weak links in the design, and when correlated with the field history of previous designs, were used to predict frequency of repair. Based on these results, the design would then be revised, the new design would be tested, and so on.

The results of this simultaneous attempt to eliminate defects in manufacturing and improve reliability were eye-opening. The final product run for the prototype units that were to be field tested by NTT was 500 units. The last 200 were assembled without defects, shipped to Japan, and field tested without any failures. By 1982, NTT had ordered 45,000 pagers; by 1984, COMM was shipping 70,000 pagers a year and was designing the next generation of NTT pager; and by the end of the decade, it was a leading supplier of pagers in Japan. Germain, meanwhile, went on to become vice president and corporate director of quality, spearheading a Motorola-wide effort to achieve a thousandfold improvement in quality over the course of the 1980s.

> Out of this whole NTT experience came my favorite expression: it's time to pass around the mirror, so we can all look at the problem—our expectation levels. What you expect to accomplish is what you get. If you never expect perfection, you'll never get it.

The next generation—display pagers. While the NTT effort was under way in the late 1970s and early 1980s, the paging business was also developing an entirely new class of pagers—display pagers. PageBoy II and the many variations of pagers developed during the 1970s were of two basic classes—tone-only and tone and voice. The former delivered a beep or series of beeps, indicating that the user should call a designated phone number; the latter delivered either a beep or an actual voice message. Display pagers, in contrast, transmit written messages. Numeric display pagers transmit phone numbers; alphanumeric display pagers can transmit more complex messages (e.g., "Meet me tonight at 8:00").

COMM introduced its first alphanumeric display pager in 1974. It did not sell well, however, primarily because a convenient way of entering the written message into the paging network had not been developed. COMM tried again in 1981 with a new line of pagers called Optrix. The Optrix was capable of receiving and storing up to four 40-character alphanumeric messages; it was small enough to fit into a shirt pocket and came in display-only, display and tone, and display, tone, and voice versions. The pager was by all accounts a "revolutionary" step forward in paging and was selected by *Fortune* magazine as one of the top ten new products of 1981. Unfortunately, the Optrix ran into a number of obstacles, and its sales were also low. Entering messages continued to be more complicated than it was with traditional pagers. The latter simply used standard touch-tone phones, whereas the new pagers required either computer keyboards or operator assistance. In addition, alphanumeric pagers are spectrally inefficient—that is, they require about ten times as much "air time" as tone-only pagers. This means that for a given capital investment, an operator of a paging system handles significantly less volume if the system offers alphanumeric paging services. This in turn means that subscriber fees for such services are three to four times higher than fees for more conventional services. The receiver itself is also substantially more expensive.

In John Mitchell's opinion, the primary problem was the lack of attention given by the paging business to developing an easy, convenient way to enter the alphanumeric messages. On the other hand, Optrix

> was a whole different concept. And there really was a pre-emergent phase. You could go introduce a new and smaller beeper that vibrated instead of making a noise. But to go to alphanumeric message paging was a big jump, and you had to go through a pre-emergent phase of developing a community of users who wanted to take advantage of it.

And indeed, this new generation of pagers did seem to follow the familiar, decade-long period of pre-emergent development. In 1983, of the roughly 2.8 million pagers in service in the United States, only 5,000 were alphanumeric pagers. By 1987, they represented roughly 1 percent of all pagers in service, 2 percent by 1989, and were expected to reach 4 percent by 1990.[30]

In common with earlier new businesses, enhancement and renewal of the product line continued throughout the decade following its initial introduction. The 1981 version of Optrix was capable of receiving four 40-character messages. By 1983, an enhanced version came out that could receive 80-character messages in addition to a low-frequency model. A silent model that vibrated instead of beeping when a message was received was introduced in 1984, followed in 1985 by a small 16-ounce accessory that worked as both a battery recharger and a printer. Then, in 1986, a second generation of alphanumeric pagers was introduced—the PMR 2000—which, in addition to a printer, battery charger, and input keyboard, offered the ability to store up to 16 messages and a total of 1,984 characters (compared to 160 characters for the original Optrix), as well as a wide variety of options and models. As of 1988, the basic capabilities of the PMR 2000 (not counting its many options and variations) were still far ahead of the competition. Its closest competitors were pagers from Panasonic and Philips that could store up to 1,000 and 512 characters, respectively.[31]

Numeric pagers. George Fisher was vice president and general manager of the paging division when Optrix was introduced. At the time, he expected the market for alphanumeric pagers to develop more quickly than it actually did. "The lesson here is that even though you dominate the marketplace, even though you are the world's leader in a given business, you may not know all there is to know about the market." Indeed, while the paging division was bringing Optrix to market, NEC came out with a simpler version of display paging—the numeric display pager. Numeric display pagers were a compromise between traditional pagers and the new alphanumeric systems. Rather than displaying an entire message, they simply displayed a phone number that the person being paged should call. As a result, they required less frequency space, were easier to use, and were less expensive than alphanumeric devices.

At the time NEC introduced its numeric display pager, COMM had no plans of its own for such a device. But it responded to NEC very quickly and introduced its own display pager, the BPR2000, six to nine months later. Fisher recalls:

> I asked Merle Gilmore [later general manager of the paging division], tell me how you can put together a display pager and invent nothing. And we did it. BPR not only put us in the [numeric display] business but gave us significant market share. It was a highly profitable product.

The introduction in 1981 of the BPR2000 was followed three years later by the addition of new features; in 1986, it was replaced by an entirely new line, the Bravo. The Bravo line was smaller than the

BPR2000, capable of receiving five 24-character messages instead of the two messages that the PR2000 could receive, and it also offered a number of new options.

The threat from the low end. In summer 1982, a year after the introductions of Optrix and the BPR2000, COMM charged that Matsushita and NEC were "dumping" pagers on the U.S. market and filed a formal complaint with the U.S. government's International Trade Commission. The pagers in question were tone-only pagers, which represented the low end of the market. COMM's low-end, tone-only pager was the Metrix, which it had been selling for $150. Matsushita (under the Panasonic brand name) had introduced a comparable pager in late 1981 that was priced at $72 to $90. NEC quickly followed suit. In Fisher's view, this episode and the experience with NTT were the "two most pivotal issues" in the history of the paging business. "There was a time when I lay awake at night thinking we might just get driven out of the business. We were keenly aware of the TV industry—was this it again? That had to go through your mind—is this it again?"

Fisher and his associates quickly reached the conclusion that they could not afford to back away from this segment of the market. Bill Weisz remembers that by this time, Motorola was well aware of the Japanese strategy of attacking the low end of the market and then, having established a foothold, progressively moving against higher segments.

> We had a lot of experience with Japan. We filed a CB [citizens band radios] dumping claim, knew about TV dumping, and watched it in cameras, motorcycles, and cars. We knew the strategy, and we were not going to retreat from products that we were good at. We knew that if you can't compete at the low end, you'd better get out of the whole damn business.

The paging division responded to Matsushita and NEC in three ways. On the legal front, it aggressively pursued the dumping case. In the process, it learned that though dumping is against U.S. trade laws, it is an accepted marketing strategy in Japan. "Pricing many years down an experience curve is not a bad way to gain market share, if you can afford to withstand the pain." But it *is* against U.S. law, and the paging division was using "every tool that we could . . . because what was at stake was the survival of the entire business."

At the same time, the division launched an extensive cost reduction program, which in turn enabled it to sharply reduce prices on the Metrix. And third, it quickly replaced the Metrix with a series of new products that were "better than the Japanese products—in performance, they were at least as good, but they were smaller, with better battery life, less expensive, and on a steeper cost-experience curve." In 1982, the tone-only Metrix was replaced by a tone-only version of the BPR2000. A year later, the BPR2000 tone-only pager was replaced by the Envoy, which became a highly successful product at the low end of the product line for several years. In essence, the Envoy was the BPR tone-only pager in a smaller casing. The Envoy, in turn, was replaced by the Bravo in 1986.

The combination of these steps enabled COMM to preserve its low-end position. Nonetheless, the experience fundamentally changed the nature of the business. Even though COMM won the dumping case, the old price structure was gone forever. "Winning the dumping case just produces stability in the marketplace for a while." Unless the paging division could compete at a fundamentally lower cost level, and unless it could operate on a steeper cost-experience curve than it had in the past, the respite would be brief.

Sensar. In 1983, the same year that COMM was introducing Envoy and continuing to upgrade the new Optrix alphanumeric and BPR2000 numeric pagers, it introduced what it believed to be the next-generation pager, the Sensar. The Sensar was shaped like a pen and was the smallest pager ever produced, weighing less than two ounces. The 1983 Sensar was a tone-only pager followed by a numeric display version in 1985.

Development of the Sensar began a decade before it was finally introduced. It was championed by none other than Weisz and Mitchell, who overrode resistance to the project and insisted that this was precisely the kind of product that COMM ought to be developing— well ahead of any competitor in the marketplace and a tangible symbol of leadership. Unfortunately, the Sensar did not sell as well as had been hoped, at least not initially. (In fact, it now sells better in Japan than anywhere else in the world.) But to general management at Motorola, it is a significant product and a symbol of COMM's commitment to leadership. Fisher explains:

> I still think it is one of the better products we've ever come out with, but it may be ahead of its time in many respects. . . . Relative to some of our expectations, maybe Sensar was what we might call a failure, but it gave us so much technology, it's hard to call it that. We drove for reach-out technology, and we use that technology—the five-spot crystal technology—in a lot of our product lines, including cellular.

Continuing enhancements and renewal. This continuing process of enhancements and product variants following generational changes went on through the 1980s. Just as the tone-only, numeric, and alphanumeric display lines were upgraded and then replaced by new generations, a new tone and voice pager, PageBoy III, was introduced in 1985 and followed by an entirely new line of tone and voice pagers called Keynote in 1989. The Dimension line of high-frequency pagers from the mid-1970s was improved in 1980 by 800Mhz tone and tone and voice models. In 1982, 900Mhz tone and tone and voice versions were introduced, followed by a 900Mhz display version in 1983 and a microprocessor-controlled, 900Mhz tone-only pager in 1985. In 1986, the entire line was subsumed under the Bravo line of pagers (see Figure 3.3).

Many of these product introductions represented relatively incremental extensions of technology. But in 1990, seven years after the introduction of the first Sensar and nine years after the introduction of the Optrix, COMM introduced the first wristwatch pager, a 2.1-ounce tone and numeric display device that stored up to six messages and could be used as both a wristwatch and a pager. Like the Sensar, the wristwatch pager was ten years in development (in this case, undertaken jointly with Timex). Once again, the first version of this new class of pagers represented only the initial step in what was expected to be a continually expanding and improving product line. Of greatest potential significance in this case was that the new technology created the possibility of an entirely new market for paging devices. Jerry Leonard, general manager of the paging business at the time of product introduction, explained:

> Currently, approximately nine million paging units are in use in the United States. . . . Nearly all pagers are held by business users. . . . However, 90 percent of all Americans own at least one watch, and nearly 150 million watches are sold annually in the United States. Since the wristwatch pager sells for under $300 and weighs approximately two ounces, it might expand the paging market to users who had not previously considered buying a pager. . . . The wristwatch pager may have the potential to shift paging to a consumer demand market.[32]

Improving Quality and Shortening Cycle Time

The meaning of leadership within COMM, and in Motorola more generally, began to take on an added dimension in the late 1970s and early 1980s. As the scope of the competitive threat posed by the

Japanese came more clearly into focus, so too did the recognition that the ability to pioneer new businesses and to maintain leadership in established businesses could not be sustained in the long run without much higher levels of quality—not only in manufacturing but in all processes and operations.

COMM had long placed an emphasis on quality and believed that it was the best in the industry. In the 1960s, for example, when Weisz was general manager, his memo on the "philosophies of leadership" (see above) emphasized that the goal of being two years ahead of the competition was compatible with the goal of being a high-quality manufacturer. "I submit to you . . . that it is possible to be a leader, to be years ahead, to have a product that works and is reliable, is built with quality, and to make money in the process."[33] In 1971, in an effort to "achieve the quality and performance that our sophisticated customers demand," COMM introduced an approach to the assembly of PageBoy II that was unprecedented in the electronics industry. Each pager was completely assembled, tested, and packaged by one person who enclosed a signed note in every box.

But while COMM was the best in the industry in the late 1970s, its growing exposure to Japanese competition, punctuated by the NTT experience, led it to the conclusion that its quality could still improve, and more to the point, that the quality of its future competitors already was a lot better. The event that appears to have triggered the heightened concern for quality was a corporate officers meeting in 1979, during which Art Sundry, then vice president and head of COMM's distribution, "ventured the opinion that Motorola was in danger of being buried by the Japanese on quality." His speech, Bob Galvin recalls, "lifted everyone intellectually up off their chairs."[34] Shortly thereafter, a senior executive program was established for which, as Jack Germain describes, Motorola "brought in all the experts, brought in all the managers, and literally stuffed their brains with new knowledge about how the competition was global not domestic." At precisely the same time, COMM was in the midst of its efforts to produce 150 defect-free prototype pagers for NTT.

The Pursuit of "Zero Defects"

In January 1981, a few months after the prototypes had been shipped to NTT, CEO Bob Galvin launched a companywide quality campaign. Germain, who in addition to spearheading the NTT effort had established a Quality Council within COMM, was named corporate vice president for quality and put in charge of the campaign. Germain's experience in the NTT affair, particularly the "eye-opening" success in producing 200 defect-free pagers in a prototype production run, was fundamental to how he approached the new position.

> We learned that perfection is a practical something. It may not be perfect in the theoretical sense, but it will be in the practical sense. All the units will go through, they all work, and when they go out in front of the customer, you don't have any trouble with them. That's perfect. In a statistical sense, you may find that some parts don't quite meet the requirement for that particular component, but the design is tolerant of that, so it never shows up as a customer problem.

Quality, in other words, had to be defined from the point of view of customer satisfaction. A high-quality product in the eyes of the customer, among other things, did not need to be repaired. And experience suggested that the way to deliver such a product was to eliminate defects—to pursue "zero defects"—in the manufacturing process. As John Welty, then senior vice president and chief corporate staff officer, explained, defects "must be eliminated at the source. Prevention is the key."[35]

If quality was to be defined in terms of customer satisfaction, however, pursuit of zero defects could not be limited to manufacturing alone. Customer satisfaction was also in part a function of design and development, marketing, advertising, sales, service, distribution—indeed, virtually every element in the organization. Therefore, the entire company had to "aim at one long-term goal—zero defects." Germain explains:

> Too often, people talk about quality control instead of Quality with a big 'Q.' They talk about end of [production] line analysis, and whether it is good or bad. That kind of thinking is extremely narrow. Quality is about the entire corporation. It has got to start with the chairman. It's a general management issue.

Benchmarking. If zero defects was to be the long-term objective for every part of the corporation, there remained a very practical, near-term question: How far were the various functions from their objective? What levels of quality had they achieved, and more important, how good was their quality relative to the competition's?

Like most companies, COMM had traditionally measured its performance against direct competitors. Product leadership in paging, for example, meant reaching the market with better products in advance of other pager manufacturers. But once quality was defined as pertaining to every function in the corporation, it became apparent that being better than the direct competition in those functions might not be good enough at all.

> Competitor analysis is pretty common, but if you are really going to be number one, you have to ask who is the best in each particular function. If it's a billing issue, it doesn't follow that you will learn anything about billing from your communications business competitor. Maybe you should look at a credit card business, because they do a lot of billing, and compare yourself to them. Or if it's a parts or warehouse operation, maybe you go to a Montgomery Ward or a Sears or a catalogue house, because they are good at filling orders in response to customer requests. You've got to find the leader for every process, and take all your processes and make them better than anyone else's in the world, and then your comfort zone improves. That's being number one. But if you say, we make the best pagers in the world, but our billing is poor, our shipping is not so good, our design cycle time is slow, you really can't say you are number one.

As a result, Germain launched an effort to identify the "benchmarks" to which Motorola's quality should be compared. The level of quality achieved by every function in the organization was assessed and then compared not to levels achieved by direct competitors, but to those achieved by firms that were especially good at that particular function.

The first objective—tenfold improvement in five years. The benchmarking exercise confirmed that Motorola was not a leader in quality in this broader sense. Moreover, the problem was not simply that Motorola's levels of quality were lower than the benchmark levels, but that over time, the benchmarks would rise. Motorola would be chasing a moving target. "We had to figure where the benchmarks were and where we thought they would be five years from then." Next, a judgment had to be reached about where Motorola should be relative to those benchmarks in five years. According to Germain,

> There is a parallel here to technology. You don't wait for technology to happen. You decide you need it, you drive it, invest accordingly, and make it happen. Same thing with quality. If you don't drive it, everything proceeds by extrapolation. You assume your quality is O.K., so why not make it 10 percent better next year. That's the wrong approach. The right approach is to figure out where the benchmarks

will be five years from now and decide where you think you
need to be [relative to those benchmarks].

Germain and his associates concluded that in order to approach
these levels of quality in five years, Motorola would have to improve
not by 10 percent, but by 1,000 percent! In 1981, the Corporate Operating and Policy Committee (comprised of the top 14 executives in
the company) formally established a tenfold improvement in quality
in five years as a companywide objective. Each of the individual
functions in each of the company's businesses had its own set of
benchmarks that it would attempt to improve tenfold. COMM, for
example, identified 30 separate "indices" with which to measure its
progress in quality. Some functions in some businesses would need
more than the tenfold improvement to reach their benchmark, others
would need less. But the idea was to have one target that would
apply across the entire corporation without exception. "There was a
lot of questioning about the tenfold improvement. A lot of people
said, maybe we can make 35 percent or maybe 70 percent, but
tenfold?"

To implement the new program, management quality councils
were formed. Germain describes them:

> We did something that got a little criticism. We didn't have
> any quality professionals on the councils. It was all manage-
> ment. Quality gurus will say that quality problems are 80
> percent management and 20 percent workers. But it's 100
> percent management. Management creates the environ-
> ment, hires the people, they educate—they do everything.
> To be good at this, you have to be a generalist, because we
> are talking about all issues when we talk about quality.

As the companywide effort to achieve a tenfold improvement in quality in five years proceeded, a number of developments unfolded. To
begin with, despite the initial resistance to—even incredulity
about—the objective, many businesses and functions made rapid
progress. In "a lot of areas where we didn't think we had a prayer,"
the objective was reached in only three years. And in the process, it
became clear that improving quality in this way led to significant
cost reductions. By eliminating defects in production, for example, a
business could greatly reduce the costs and investment associated
with inspection, testing, analysis, and repair and, of course, warrant-
ies. In a production line of 1,000 people, a tenfold reduction in defects
would lead to a reduction of the 200 or so people working on inspection and repair to just one or two people. "The heavy focus on cus-

tomer satisfaction," Germain states, "leads to heavy payoffs in financial results. And because it takes virtually no investment, the return on net assets is enormous."

At the same time these encouraging results were being achieved, the benchmarking effort was becoming more sophisticated. Germain's group developed a simple but generic measure. If the number of steps in a process could be counted, and if the overall number of defects—called the yield—in that process could be counted, then with the use of a classic statistical measure of the variation in populations, it was possible to estimate the defect rate of the process. A process that had achieved "three sigma" levels of quality ("sigma," as used in statistics, refers to the amount of variation away from the mean in a normally distributed population) was one in which there would be 66,810 defects per million opportunities for a defect to occur. A four-sigma process was one in which there would be roughly 6,200 defects per million opportunities, and a six-sigma process was virtually defect-free—producing only 3.45 defects per million opportunities.

At the time this metric was formulated, it was clearly understood that it would only lead to a rough approximation of the quality of a process, but given the magnitude of the differences in defect rates between the various sigma levels, imprecision in the estimates was of little consequence. And once this common metric was established, "we really started to learn things." Sending groups literally around the world, and consulting with experts in fields as far from portable communications as medicine and airline safety, Germain's group began to estimate the defect rate of processes ranging from electronic watch and calculator manufacturing to physicians' ability to write prescriptions accurately. In so doing, they discovered that despite the progress Motorola had made toward the tenfold improvement, they were not moving as fast as they needed to in order to catch up with the benchmarks.

A new objective—Six Sigma. And so in January 1987, Motorola took the next step in its pursuit of zero defects. Bob Galvin announced that the "fundamental objective" of the corporation was now *"total* customer satisfaction." The key to this objective was still leadership, but leadership in the broadest sense possible. Motorola would strive to be foremost in every aspect of the organization— "people, marketing, technology, product, manufacturing, and service." And it was to excel in each of these aspects, not just by being better than its direct competitors, but by being "best in class"—better than the world's best.

With the announcement of this objective came a new quality

campaign with new quality targets described in a memo from Galvin to all Motorola employees:

> Improve product and services quality ten times by 1989, and at least one hundredfold by 1991. Achieve Six Sigma capability by 1992. With a deep sense of urgency, spread dedication to quality to every facet of the corporation, and achieve a culture of continual improvement to assure total customer satisfaction. There is only one ultimate goal: zero defects—in everything we do.[36]

An education program was launched to explain to literally every person in the company the meaning and purpose of Six Sigma, how to calculate defect levels, and how to improve quality. In all, the company spent a reported $25 million on employee education in 1987, $50 million (2.9 percent of its annual payroll) in 1988, and $60 million in 1989. A large part of this education was devoted to quality.[37] Throughout the corporation, every organizational component— publication departments, order processing operations, patent attorneys, manufacturing—examined and redesigned their basic operations. The first step involved "breaking down operations into steps and tasks and identifying detailed inputs and outputs for each. We build flowcharts, spot tasks that are prone to error, and measure defect rate . . ." The next step was to redesign these operations in order to make them "mistake proof." This entailed simplifying tasks, increasing training, and changing basic methods. This way, Germain says, "We may completely redefine the way a company is organized, and we begin to think that maybe this really is a revolution rather than just continuous improvement."[38]

At the same time, a corporate-level review process for assessing progress made by each organization toward the Six Sigma objective was established, incentive compensation programs were tied to progress, and a campaign to improve the quality of the company's suppliers was launched. In the opinion of George Fisher, who was named CEO in 1986, even with this companywide effort, the heart of the Six Sigma program was the establishment of clear objectives and the ability, through benchmarking, to assess progress toward them.

> The question of expectation level is so fundamental, and the only way you get the right expectation levels is through a benchmarking process, and then an understanding that everybody is improving over time. Your benchmark is a snapshot, you have to put those snapshots on an experience curve that's moving—that's getting better and better—and

then you've got to time your projects so that you're better, better than the best.

By late in the decade, the results were becoming apparent. In November 1988, Motorola was named winner of the first Malcolm Baldrige National Quality Award. At the end of 1989, the level of defects on a companywide level had been reduced to fewer than 200 per million, down from roughly 3,000 per million in 1983.[39] A number of organizations throughout the company had even surpassed this average. At a pager manufacturing plant in Boynton Beach, Florida (see below), for example, the defect rate by 1989 was well under 100 parts per million.

The financial impact of these changes was striking. By late 1989, Motorola was reported to have saved $250 million (or 40 percent of 1988 pretax income) each year between 1987 and 1989.[40] In 1990, according to Richard Buetow, Jack Germain's successor as corporate director of quality, "We realized a savings of $500 million in manufacturing costs." The target for 1992 was to save $1 billion.[41]

Cycle Time

At the same time that Six Sigma quality was established as a formal corporate objective, a second closely related objective was also set forth: in addition to pursuing zero defects, Motorola would pursue "total cycle time reduction." This objective applied to two distinct "cycles"—new-product development and customer response. The first refers to the time elapsed between inception of a new product idea, through its development, to its first shipment. The second, which applies to products that have already been developed, refers to the time elapsed from when a customer places an order for a product to when the product is delivered.

Cycle time reduction is not a new concept. As George Fisher put it, "Anybody who has grown up in product development has always thought in terms of trying to shorten cycle time . . . although we used to call it speed to market." What changed was the urgency with which speed to market was sought. As Motorola learned more and more about its potential competitors throughout the 1980s, it became very clear that a reduction in defects alone would not be sufficient to ensure continuing market leadership. To be a leader in its businesses, Motorola would also have to strive to be best in class—faster than the world's fastest—in new product development and customer response. "Anybody who is in this business and doesn't realize very early that cycle time is critical," argues Fisher, "is running a race without realizing that the object is to cross the finish line first."

While there are many reasons for the cycle-time reduction campaign, two specific developments during the 1980s had an especially important influence on the importance of cycle time within Motorola. The first was a 1983 effort to develop a new mobile radio for the European market, the second a 1986–1987 effort to reduce customer response time in the paging business.

European land mobile. In the early 1980s, COMM's European mobile radio business was in trouble. Part of the problem was COMM's method of distribution, which was more appropriate to the U.S. market than to Europe. But the more fundamental issue was that COMM was attempting to sell through this inappropriate system of distribution an outmoded product. The product line then being offered had been introduced in 1966. Had COMM followed its normal practice of renewal, it should have introduced new generations in the mid-1970s and again in the early 1980s. But it didn't, and the result was that by the early 1980s, sales had "died." John Mitchell recalls:

> I was sitting as president of the company, interfering with the two-way radio business in Europe. Guys I grew up with were saying, "John, we're going to die." Well, I couldn't wait to get back and design another two-way radio.

Within a year, a new line had been developed, and eventually, the combination of new products and a more appropriate distribution system enabled COMM to regain its leadership position in the market. But the relevance of this episode here is that just as the NTT experience demonstrated that much higher quality was achievable, the European mobile radio experience demonstrated that much shorter development cycles were attainable. Typically, Mitchell explains, product development programs . . .

> took two or three or four years, because everyone would get their fingers in there and want to change it—I have a new transistor, or a new microprocessor, or this new market wants a new feature. We would start with an underspecified product, and then it would take years because we couldn't agree on what we wanted and we would finally bring the product out when we really needed to. There were unbelievable starts and restarts.

Closely related to the problem of shifting product specs was what in hindsight appeared to be a failure to allocate the resources required to meet desired schedules.

Since COMM could not afford any delays in the European mobile radio case, a deliberate effort was made from the outset to overcome the problems of both shifting specs and insufficient resources. All the relevant parties—design, manufacturing, marketing—were brought together at the outset of the project. Not only did they reach agreement on product specs, but they literally signed a contract stipulating that they would stick to the agreement. Terms of the contract could be changed, but only if all parties agreed to the change, and as Mitchell recalls, "Boy, we all knew what a change entailed."

In addition, all the resources needed to complete the project were allocated at the outset. According to Fisher:

> This goes back to a McKinsey [the consulting firm] study which said that if you blow out a development budget by 50 percent, your pretax profit declines by 4 percent. But if you miss the market window by six months, profits decline by 33 percent. Whether those numbers are right is irrelevant. That story, qualitatively, is true.

Operation Bandit. Three years later, COMM's paging business launched a very different kind of cycle-time reduction effort. Here, the challenge was not to develop a new product quickly, but to take an existing product—the Bravo pager—and develop a system for manufacturing it that would lead to major improvements in quality and to a much faster customer-response cycle. The goal was to demonstrate, in Fisher's words,

> a high-quality, lights-out [i.e., fully automated] facility, with minimal cycle time in serving the customer from the time he orders to the time he gets the product, capable of producing lot sizes of one. This was an experiment on all these things, and also on all the peripheral support systems like accounting. . . . How do we make this pager in a clean sheet of paper factory, with clean sheet of paper accounting and order processing practices? How do we minimize cycle time, improve quality, and also have accounting practices that don't penalize the heck out of the thing for using all new equipment?

The project came to be known as "Operation Bandit," a name meant to signify the project's aversion to the not-invented-here syndrome. The project team assigned to design the new manufacturing operation was to behave like "bandits" and take good ideas (legally) from wherever on the globe they might find them.

The idea for Operation Bandit originated with an advanced manufacturing technology group that had been established in the paging business in the mid-1970s. In 1978, this group developed a plan for a lights-out factory for the Sensar (fountain pen) pager then under development. The plan had been put aside because automation technology was not sufficiently advanced, but in 1986, the plan was revived. The motivation for doing so came in large measure from the group's benchmarking activities. (Benchmarking, by this time, was well entrenched throughout the corporation.) Fisher recalls:

> A lot of us felt this was important, but it was pushed by Mauro Walker's [now, corporate vice president and Motorola director of manufacturing] and Bob Hall's [now senior vice president and general manager of COMM's Manufacturing Technologies Group] feeling that we had to get on a steeper manufacturing cost/delivery learning curve, and this was the way to do it. After looking at some of the best-in-class competitors, mostly in Japan, at where they were and more important, where they were heading, it was thought that unless we got to this state at a minimum, we'd be left behind. . . . We all thought we had to be as good as or better than the best Japanese.

As a result, the effort to produce a short-customer-response paging factory was begun in mid-1986. The leaders were Scott Shamlin, then manager of manufacturing operations for the paging business and Chris Galvin, general manager of the business at the time. Eighteen months later, the paging facility was in operation with impressive results. It used to take a total of two weeks to respond to a new customer order for a pager. Now, "seventeen minutes after an order is placed from anywhere in the country, a bar code will be placed on a blank circuit board." Within two hours after the order is placed, the finished product is shipped. Moreover, the plant is capable of producing lot sizes of one. "That bar code contains all the information the factory needs to make the pager. As the board goes down the line, each robot reads the bar code and executes the instructions. The next pager on the line might be for a different customer with very different specifications."[42]

By the time Operation Bandit was completed, cycle time reduction was being aggressively pursued in other parts of the corporation as well. By the end of 1989, for example, the 30-day customer order cycle in one line of two-way radios had been reduced to 3 days. And in the cellular phone business, the new-product development cycle had been reduced from 3 years in 1985 to 15 months. The goal is to reduce this time of development even further, to 6 months.

Despite the progress, however, cycle time reduction was, in Fisher's view, just beginning in January 1991. "We learned one hell of a lot from Bandit; it is a good demonstration, but it certainly is not optimal. . . . We haven't quite gotten our arms around cycle time [the way we have with quality]." There is no simple, generic metric comparable to defects per million, and it may be that a formalization of the process comparable to the Six Sigma effort is not even possible. There are, Fisher believes, certain generic practices that need to be followed, and certain generic obstacles to cycle time reduction. But in the end, it may well be that for both the quality improvement and cycle time reduction, the formal steps taken are not "as important as the realization of how good good really is."

> I can turn this organization loose on any challenge. This organization loves challenges. We all love challenges. We love to beat goals. The problem is management does not often set reach-out enough goals. . . . Don't underestimate the role of benchmarking and expectation levels. Expectation levels are everything because we have tons of good people, all of whom want to be the best, and you've got to let them know how good the best really is, so that they can be better.

Discussion

Business Strategy and Technology

At its core, a business strategy must answer two questions: What markets does the business compete in, and how should it compete in those markets? What is most striking about COMM's business strategy is the consistency with which it answered these two questions over the course of its 45-year history: COMM would compete in the mobile and portable communications markets and it would do so primarily on the basis of product leadership.

The "mobile and portable religion." COMM began as a mobile radio business. Portable communications, on the other hand, did not emerge as an explicit component of its strategic focus until the middle to late 1960s. Before then, as Cooper describes it, COMM had "groped around" in a variety of communications-related businesses, launching or at least investigating new business possibilities in fields ranging from hypersonic burglar alarms to closed-circuit television and remote-controlled traffic light systems. Throughout the 1950s and into the 1960s, Weisz, Mitchell, Cooper, and their associates championed their vision of portable communications, but they represented only one of a number of emerging businesses. It was only as the portable radio and paging businesses began to take off and the small group that had nurtured those businesses rose to leadership positions in COMM that the "groping around" came to an end. When John Mitchell became general manager in 1969, he made mobile and portable communications the explicit focus and began to "infuse this mobile/portable religion much more seriously throughout the organization." Cooper recalls the way the religion was articulated:

> There are many [communications-related] businesses you can get into where there are a lot of ways of getting the job done, and your way is just a little bit better. You can reach the guy sitting in his office in a number of ways—phone, fax, and so on. But the only way you can reach the guy in the car, or the guy walking down the street in the rain, is with a mobile or portable telephone or radio. That was the essence of our thing, and the way Mitchell defined our thing. We were to focus on businesses where there were no alternatives to our product—no other way to reach the guy in the car. And in those businesses, we were to be as close to the customer as we could be, technology leaders, and better always than the competition. So we were not in communications; we were in something much more precise than that. It wasn't communications—it was mobile and portable communications, and that's what defined what we did and had done well, and what we would and wouldn't go after.

In hindsight, it is tempting to see the early successes in portable radios and pagers as a product of the strategy. But the way it actually evolved is closer to the reverse. The portable products business unit built its leadership position during the "groping around" stage of COMM's history, and it did so on the basis of clearly superior product technology, coupled with a better and more cost-effective system for distribution. Once success was established on this basis, the strategic focus followed. In essence, that focus was nothing more than an articulation of "what we did and had done well."

Once this focus was clearly articulated, however, strategy did begin to drive success. Virtually all new technology development was channeled within the mobile/portable focus, as is clearly evident in the pattern of "horizontal" creation of new business opportunities. The first and still the most dramatic example was the push into cellular telephones. What made Motorola's approach unique was not that it was cellular, but that it was portable cellular. Cellular telephones were quickly followed by the effort to develop a business in mobile/portable data communications, which in turn was followed by Iridium and personal communications networks. But it is the persistence with which each of these new business opportunities was (and is

being) pursued that offers perhaps the most compelling evidence of
the influence of this strategic focus. COMM invested $150 million
over 15 years in cellular before it saw its first sale, it has been developing mobile/portable data for well over a decade, and both investments are small compared to the time and resources required to bring
Iridium to fruition.

As COMM and Motorola entered the 1990s, the possibilities for
new business opportunities within the mobile/portable focus were
far from exhausted. The 1989 Annual Report states:

> The 1980s may be remembered as the decade of personal
> computing, but the 1990s may well be remembered as the
> decade of personal communicating. . . . As we move to
> an all-digital world, which allows transmission of data and
> images along with voice, it's not hard to imagine turning a
> personal telephone into a computer terminal and video de-
> vice. Motorola . . . has the platforms to achieve such a break-
> through.

Indeed, by the end of the 1980s, the mobile/portable "religion" had
not only become the driving force of COMM but an integral part of
Motorola's overall strategic focus. The 1989 Annual Report offered
what it described as "a key mission statement that will drive much
of our future growth":

> We will build on our semiconductor technology and market
> position to be the world's premier provider of products, sys-
> tems and services for communication, computing and con-
> trol *for people and machines on the move.*

Leadership. If mobile/portable communications defined the businesses COMM should compete in, the leadership philosophy defined
how it should compete in those markets. This emphasis on leadership
dates back to the earliest days of COMM, but over the years its meaning has become progressively more challenging and ambitious. It has
always meant that COMM should strive to be first to market with
the best-performing products. But as the NTT and dumping episodes
suggest, by the early 1980s, leadership meant striving to be not just
the overall market leader in portable and mobile communications,
but to be (1) the leader in each individual region of the world, and
(2) the leader in each individual price-performance tier, from the lowest end of the market to the highest. And as the quality and cycle-
time reduction campaigns suggest, by the late 1980s, leadership had
come to mean not just best in every segment of the industry but best
in class—better than the best in the world in every individual func-

tion of the organization. The objective was still to be first to market with the best-performing products, but now it was clear that continued realization of this goal required leadership in quality of manufacturing, design, marketing, service, and virtually every other function in the organization, coupled with leadership in speed of new product development and customer response.

Thus, by 1990, pursuit of leadership translated into a cluster of related and continual efforts to accomplish the following:

- pioneer new businesses such as portable radios, pagers, cellular telephones, portable data, and Iridium;
- pioneer new generations of products in established businesses such as PageBoy II, Sensar, and the wristwatch pager;
- incrementally improve existing product lines such as the series of enhancements made to the alphanumeric and numeric display pagers;
- broaden existing product lines into previously unserved market segments such as the expansion of each paging line to include a full range of frequencies;
- serve every market segment—from the highest end to the lowest, and from the United States and Europe to Japan;
- strive for zero defects in every process and function in the organization; and
- reduce the time required to develop new products—both pioneering products and more incremental departures—and reduce the time required to respond to customer requests for these products once they have been developed.

By the late 1980s, advocates of the kind of quality that Motorola was emphasizing had begun to speak in terms of "total quality," in contrast to the narrower, more traditional notion of quality control (i.e., inspection and repair) in manufacturing. The same shift can be seen in Motorola's concept of leadership. The objective by 1990 was not product leadership, but "total leadership"—total in the sense that it applied to every facet of operation, each one compared to the best in the world.

Pursuit of total leadership would be quixotic were it not coupled with strategic focus. The obsession with leadership goes hand in hand with the mobile/portable religion. Bill Weisz, referring to the sale of Motorola's TV business in 1974, argues that "We never regretted the decision . . . the important point is that it was driven by the need to focus resources. You can't do everything. But whatever you are going to go after, devote the resources to do it right, to be the leader." The key is the combination of "selectivity" and leadership. As Weisz stated in a speech in 1983,

> There will continue to be an overabundance of emerging technologies and new product areas in the electronics field. Selectivity will be crucial. We don't want to be in businesses where we can't have a distinctive competence vis-à-vis our competitors. We don't want to be in business where we can't be one of the top one or two companies in the field . . .[43]

Continuity of management. Paralleling, if not driving, this consistent business strategy is a striking continuity of management. The careers of Weisz, Mitchell, Cooper, and Germain illustrate this point well. Weisz began his career at Motorola working for Dan Noble in 1948 as a design engineer. He was responsible for designing parts of the first portable radio line and then in the early 1950s, the first pager. In the late 1950s, he was in charge of the portable products organization, and by the mid-1960s, general manager of COMM. By 1970, he was president of Motorola and he remained a member of the chief executive office through the following two decades, eventually becoming CEO. John Mitchell followed an almost identical track. He began at Motorola in 1953, designing mobile radios. He then worked on the second-generation portable radio and the first VHF pager. He went on to become manager of portable products, general manager of COMM, president of Motorola, and eventually, COO. Cooper and Germain began in technical functions in the 1950s, and also eventually rose through the ranks. Cooper's last position in Motorola, before he left the company in the early 1980s, was corporate vice president for research; Germain, after serving as assistant general manager in COMM, became corporate vice president for quality.

The careers of these four individuals, while out of the ordinary in the degree of success they achieved, illustrate a common pattern of career development in COMM in particular, and Motorola more generally. Mitchell explains it this way. In each product line, each new generation of products was produced by a new generation of managers:

> A guy would start designing a radio, then he would lead a team to design the next product, then he would be promoted to some kind of technical management position, and then to some sort of general management position. In a ten-year

period, you could go through a couple generations of products and be a boss. The success pattern was pretty obvious.
We documented it in the 1980s, but it was already obvious
in the 1950s.

The ranks of management were thus filled with people who had
grown up in the business, typically in either a design engineering or
market development function. Occasionally, key people came from
outside the company, but they were more the exception than the
rule, and once they joined COMM, they followed the usual pattern.
George Fisher, who began his career at Bell Labs, is the most prominent example. He was named assistant director of mobile product
operations in 1977, became vice president of paging by 1981, senior
vice president and assistant general manager of COMM by 1984,
senior executive vice president and deputy to the chief executive
office in 1986, and CEO in 1988.

In light of this continuity of management, the consistency with
which COMM could pursue its strategy—leadership in mobile/porta-
ble communications—is more easily understood. As Marty Cooper
remembers, "One way or another, there was always a Weisz or a
Mitchell there . . . [pushing] to be the product leader and beat the
competition and do it right." Continuity also had another fundamental impact. Cooper explains:

> The managers really understand the business. For a while,
> it looked like managers had to be engineers, but the real
> issue was that this was a technology business and you were
> not likely to understand it adequately without being an engi-
> neer. But it didn't have anything to do with being an engi-
> neer. To be a product leader, to stay ahead of the competi-
> tion, you had to understand the market and you had to
> understand the technology—and not just one technology,
> but a whole bunch of them.

Technology Strategy

It is also illuminating to look at this 45-year history from a technology
strategy perspective. The most striking feature of COMM's evolution
from this perspective is that COMM's technology strategy was virtually indistinguishable from its overall business strategy. From its earliest days, COMM chose to compete in its markets on the basis of
product leadership—and product leadership meant "employing
state-of-the-art techniques in products that we are actually selling

when our competitors are only thinking about them."[44] In other words, product leadership meant technology leadership.

Product-driven technology. Several aspects of this leadership-oriented technology strategy deserve emphasis, but none more so than the way the tight link between business and technology strategy came to be maintained. Initially, it was established more or less intuitively, but by the mid-1970s, it was being formalized in what eventually became the technology roadmap process. The significance of the roadmaps is that they explicitly linked the future product plans of each business to the technology required to achieve them. That is, the products that the business hoped to offer five to ten years in the future were directly tied to current technology development.

This suggests that technology development was product driven. COMM, and Motorola more generally, were (and still are) R&D intensive, but the R&D was very much what Mitchell and Cooper would call "applied" in nature. Even the most radical technology developments, like portable cellular telephones and the Sensar and wristwatch pagers, were product driven. That is, first came the idea of a product target, and then this target drove the required technology development. Mitchell recalls having a "great debate about management of technology" during the mid-1970s when the roadmap process was being shaped:

> Bob Galvin would get really angry because Marty [Cooper] and I would talk about products and applying the technology. He'd say, "Halt, let's just talk about developing technology." But we would say, "You can't develop technology in the abstract; we have got to have something that drives it."

That "something" was future products. The history of COMM is filled with examples of new technology being developed in order to realize plans for future products. The critical relationship between COMM and Motorola's semiconductor business, for example, was very much product driven, with COMM utilizing MICARL to develop the integrated circuits needed to satisfy its particular product requirements. Similarly, R&D in COMM on such core technologies as batteries, antennas, and crystals was driven by specific product needs. Advancement of portable products required new battery technology. Pagers required substantial advances in antenna technology because in Weisz's words, "We couldn't afford the luxury of a stick of wire in the air." In the process of developing portable cellular telephones, Cooper launched an R&D effort in switching technology. Development of the Sensar pager drove R&D in crystal technology. In order to handle the uncertain signalling requirements of NTT, a CMOS-based microprocessor had to be designed and developed, which until that time was unprecedented in the paging industry. The examples of this kind of application-driven research and of the significant advances in technology that resulted are countless. Moreover, as such product-driven research continued over the years, COMM developed substantial expertise—distinctive competencies—in these areas of technology that in turn enabled the establishment of still more ambitious product plans.

The many forms of technology leadership. In Chapter 2 (GEMS), reference was made to past studies of technology strategy that suggest that firms that are first to market with new technology are often not the firms that prove to be the long-term leaders in their markets. Especially in the early stages of an industry before a "dominant design" has been established, and in industries like electronics where patents provide relatively weak protection, it is argued there are substantial benefits to be gained from fast following.[45] Similarly, it is often argued that American firms have often failed to follow up their radical innovations with the continuing stream of incremental innovations needed to sustain leadership,[46] and have also failed to place nearly as much emphasis on process or manufacturing technology as they have on new product technology.[47] A closely connected argument is that American firms have not competed effectively at the low end of their markets and have been all too willing, once foreign competitors attacked those low ends, to retreat toward the shelter of the high end. Thus, contemporary thought about technology strategy points to a cluster of related tensions that have proven difficult for American firms to master—being first to market versus being the long-term leader, pursuing radical innovation versus continual incremental innovation, emphasizing product technology versus process, and competing at the high-performance end of markets versus competing at the low end.

One of the most prominent features of COMM's technology strategy is that it has successfully mastered all of these tensions throughout the course of its history.

> It has repeatedly pioneered new markets with new classes of product technology, such as portable radios, pagers, and portable cellular telephones, *and* has been able to sustain its leadership in those markets for decades.

> It has repeatedly introduced into already established markets new generations of technology such as the PageBoy I

and II, the alphanumeric pager, Sensar, and the wristwatch pager, *and* has been able to sustain the advantage created by these radical innovations with a stream of more incremental product enhancements and variants. PageBoy II, for example, was introduced in tone, and tone and voice variants, and was quickly followed by PageCom (low end) and MetroPage (high capacity). Optrix, the alphanumeric pager, was enhanced several times after its initial introduction and then replaced by the higher-performing PMR2000, which in turn was improved several times.

It has been almost obsessive in its pursuit of product leadership, as this continuing stream of radical and incremental innovations attests, *and* it has been unrelenting for the past 15 years in its pursuit of process improvements, as the zero defect and cycle-time-reduction campaigns attest.

And, it has typically offered the broadest product lines in its markets, competing at the highest end with such products as the Sensar, the wristwatch, and the alphanumeric pager, *and* also at the lowest, as its response to the dumping incident indicates.

The strategic focus on mobile and portable communications is closely related to the ability to achieve this multifaceted technology leadership. Not only did the strategic focus lead to a concentration of technology resources, but over time, the concentration of technology resources led to the development of distinctive competencies in the areas of focus. A self-reinforcing cycle is created: focus leads to concentration of resources, which leads to distinctive competencies, which lead to leadership, which reinforces the focus.

Decision Making and Technology

Another source of insight into the role that Motorola's general managers played in building competitive advantage on the basis of technology is their decision-making style. It is helpful, however, to distinguish between decision making with respect to the periodic efforts to pioneer new businesses or develop radically new products (e.g., the alphanumeric pager) and endeavors toward continual expansion and renewal of existing businesses.

New businesses and radical departures. As we have seen, the history of COMM is marked by the creation of a succession of new mobile/portable communication businesses. Each of these new businesses went through a similar pattern early in its evolution: (1) a preliminary if not primitive version of the technology is introduced into a (2) market that does not exist and for which (3) an infrastructure still needs to be developed. The most striking feature of this pre-emergent stage in each business was high uncertainty. Each new business faced a dizzying array of unknowns about the market, the infrastructure needed to serve that market, regulatory approvals, and the technology. What, for example, were the burning issues facing the paging business in the mid-1960s, ten years after the first pager had been introduced? To Marty Cooper it was very simple: "Would people buy a lot of pagers if we succeeded in making them smaller and lighter?" Was it evident that a large potential market existed even after ten years of development? "No, we believed it would be big, but it was also evident that the world had not caught on to this yet." Similarly, in the early days of the cellular effort, there was substantial skepticism not only outside the company but within. Cellular would require a relationship with the customer different from what COMM was accustomed to; the portable approach was fundamentally different from anything that AT&T or existing mobile telephone markets were accustomed to; and "as we kept spending big dollars year after year in cellular, there were any number of times that . . . [some of the management within COMM] would have killed it." And if there were large uncertainties associated with paging and cellular, those facing Iridium were literally global in scope.

How did decision making proceed in the face of such pervasive uncertainty? The answer, in part, is a process of learning by doing. If the market did not yet exist, and the product that would trigger the market demand was not yet developed, the only way to find out if in fact such a demand would arise in response to the right kind of product was to try to develop it. This chicken-egg problem existed in each of the new businesses, and it was resolved in each instance by advancing the development of the product through successive generations, with each generation based on the lessons learned from the previous one. In paging, for example, the initial approach was based on low-frequency technology and oriented toward private markets. Over the course of the next decade, Weisz, Mitchell, and company learned through experience that the limitations to the low-frequency approach were prohibitive, that a VHF-based system would overcome many of those limitations, that even a VHF system had to be substantially reduced in size and performance before a significant market would emerge, and that that market would be subscriber-based rather than private. "Whether you know it or not," Mitchell argues, "you go down a learning curve." Or as Weisz states, to develop such new businesses, "you have to practice early on; you have got to get the experience, make the mistakes early on, and be the clear leader."

The point is that the direction that paging or any of the other businesses would take was unknown in advance, and given the uncertainties, it could not have been known. There was no market to analyze, because the market did not exist and would not exist until the right kind of product had been developed. At the same time, there was more to this process than just learning by doing. Whether it was portable radios, pagers, cellular telephones, or Iridium, the pursuit of new businesses was shaped by the "mobile/portable religion" and driven forward by a belief that the market would eventually respond. Each new success, each additional level of experience, only served to strengthen that belief. And so decision making in the face of uncertainty was characterized by a combination of a strategic focus or vision coupled to a process of learning by doing. Bill Weisz recalls the early days of the paging business:

> There was no fancy marketing at this stage. When you are pioneering in something the world doesn't even know it wants, you have to have a belief that the world is going to want what you have, that it will start falling over its feet to get it. And so given this view, we gradually progressed and one thing led to another. The kludgie, imperfect LF pagers reinforced our view that portable would take over the world. The first VHF was too big, too heavy, but it was another step in the right direction. All the versions up to the Page-Boys were steps along the way. Each sold a bit more, each did a bit better, each taught us more about the marketplace.

Precisely the same pattern occurred in cellular telephones and, to varying degrees, in the other major new developments, and it still continues today. George Fisher describes the process this way:

> You need a strategic intent—but within that context, you have to be totally opportunistic and aware. . . . Bob Galvin would always say, "You can't know what's around the next corner, so construct an organization that is able to adapt. But you have to have a framework, or you get too distracted and diversified. You keep your eye on the road."

If we can characterize the evolution of each new business as a process of learning by doing shaped by a strategic vision or focus, there still remains the question of how decision makers decided whether or not to embark on this process for any given opportunity.

Marty Cooper believes, "It's much harder to figure out what not to do than what to do. What kills an organization is doing a lot of half-baked jobs." How then were potential opportunities screened? The question becomes all the more important as the magnitude of the resources required to pursue new opportunities grows. In the case of portable radios and paging, the necessary resources were limited and quite manageable, given the rapid growth of COMM at the time. But in the case of cellular, $150 million had to be invested before the first sale, and the requirements for Iridium are much larger than that. How then is the decision reached to proceed or not to proceed with a given opportunity?

Part of the answer is that it is *not* reached through projections of financial returns and discounted cash flow style analysis. The uncertainties about the future shape of the market and the technology are simply too great to allow this kind of analysis to govern decision making. "We hardly ever use discounted cash flow analysis," Fisher explains. "We assume the numbers are the effect, not the cause." This is not to say that "the numbers" are unimportant. "Mind you, we pay a good deal of attention to them," says Fisher, but as measures of results and as constraints on the pace of investment and not determinants of whether to proceed with an opportunity. In cellular, for example, "our investment had nothing to do with the projections." But, Mitchell says, "You have to do these things at an affordable pace. What did it take to do the next mobile, the next portable, the next switch. Could we afford to do it at this pace or half this pace?"

Since the decision to proceed with a given opportunity is not based on model-driven financial analysis, what is it based on? The process is more qualitative in nature and is described by Fisher as being more "Babylonian" than "Euclidean."

> We have tried over the past few years to channel the corporation into "people and machines on the move—communications, computing, and control." So we have a strategic framework within which we make a lot of these decisions. . . . We don't totally focus within the framework, but if it fits in there, it gets a better chance of being funded than if it doesn't. So we have a strategic framework, but at the same time, there is a lot of Babylonian thinking, as opposed to Euclidean thinking, that goes into the process. . . . You get a collective judgment from a lot of people who have been around a lot of years and who have made pretty good judgments and understand the technology and the markets. . . . It's a collegial process, but a collegial process

among people who *know* the technology, *know* the customers, and *know* what you can and can't do.

One way to characterize the decision process that takes place in this
Babylonian, collegial process is that each opportunity is tested against
a sequence of screens or decision hurdles. First, does the opportunity
fit within the strategic focus of the business? Second, does the business have a distinctive competence with respect to the opportunity?
Third, is the opportunity substantial—substantial enough to merit
the risks and resources that need to be devoted to it? And finally, if
the answer to each of these questions is affirmative, how can the
business go about pursuing the opportunity in a way that it can
afford?

If there is a failure in this process, in Fisher's view, it is that
Motorola's success rate is too high.

> Our batting average is way too high; 95 percent are winners.
> In radio communications products, whether two-way or
> paging, we're probably not stepping out far enough, not
> risking enough. We rarely miss. It's indicative of a problem.
> We're not developing the market fast enough. Somebody
> said Sony introduced 1,500 products last year. If we intro-
> duced 1,500, we'd have a few losers, but we'd be moving
> the market a lot faster than we are.

Decision making within existing product lines. In contrast to this
Babylonian decision-making process associated with the establishment of new businesses and major departures from existing product
lines, decision making associated with the more incremental technology advances that were pursued on a regular basis within each product line was a good deal more formalized. Bill Weisz pointed to this
distinction in comparing general management's treatment of nascent
and established businesses. "You need to divide businesses into two
kinds. With the pioneering businesses, you give them money and
support, and leave them alone. But once they grow to a large, more
bureaucratic organization, you need to formalize a lot of these things.
There's a discipline involved." The discipline centered around the
technology roadmap process, coupled to the annual budgetary
process.

COMM and Motorola in general are organized in a highly decentralized fashion. Profit-and-loss responsibility is driven down to the
level of the individual product line. So the responsibility to balance
the need to enhance and renew each product line with the need to
meet financial targets falls to the manager of the individual product
line. The role of general management in this process, as described

by Weisz and Mitchell, is to ensure that this tension between the imperatives to innovate and to live within financial constraints is maintained.

The imperative to innovate is sustained through the technology roadmap process. The individual lines of business are required to take a five- to ten-year product- and technology-planning horizon. At least once a year, each business meets with the chief executive officers, reviews their roadmaps, and agrees with the CEO on technology and product development objectives for the following year. Progress toward the objectives is reviewed the following year. The product and technology development objectives are in turn balanced by budgetary constraints. "Normalized" standards of financial performance (e.g., standard rates of growth and return on investment) are set and then adjusted on a business-by-business basis. Operating management can make the case to adjust the performance standards, but once agreement is reached, "no one is allowed to weasel out of agreed-to [product development] objectives on the claim that they didn't have the resources." This process is summarized by Bill Weisz:

> The way Bob Galvin put it is, "We should do everything we want to do and should do, period. Every good idea should be supported." Obviously, you have to live within your financial environment, so you can't meet this objective every time, but you always strive for it. Finances are a constraint, not a driver. The driver is product leadership.

Notes

1. This study would not have been possible without the permission generously granted by George Fisher, chairman and CEO of Motorola, and without the patient assistance provided by William Weisz, former CEO and vice chairman; John Mitchell, former president and vice chairman; Marty Cooper, former vice president of Corporate R&D; and Jack Germain, former vice president and director of Corporate Quality.
2. Lois Therrien et al., "Motorola: How Much Will It Cost to Stay Number One," *Business Week*, October 29, 1990, p. 96.
3. Through most of its history, Motorola's communications businesses were organized within its Communications Sector. By the mid-1980s, however, several important communications businesses were located outside this sector. In the following, "COMM" refers to this larger family of communications businesses, rather than to the Communications Sector alone.
4. Another third of Motorola's revenue comes from its semiconductor business, and the balance is divided among government electronics, automotive and industrial electronics, and computers and computer networks.
5. Keith Bradsher, "Science Fiction Nears Reality: Pocket Phone for Global Calls," *New York Times*, June 26, 1990, p. 1.

6. William Weisz, "Quality of Performance," internal memo, September 30, 1966.
7. Radio Common Carriers (RCCs) were established in 1948 by the Federal Communications Commission to promote competition in mobile communications. They were granted the same number of channels as the local telephone companies of "wireline common carriers." In effect, an RCC was a utility company offering mobile communications services.
8. T. Kain, "Paging for RCCs," *Communicator*, 1964, pp. 10, 20.
9. John H. Davis, "Cellular Mobile Telephone Services," in Bruce R. Guile and J.Brian Quinn, eds., *Managing Innovation: Cases from the Services Industries* (Washington, DC: National Academy Press, 1988), p. 145.
10. Until this time, the frequencies available for such use were 30–60Mhz, 80–100Mhz (FM band), 140–174Mhz (VHF), and 400–612Mhz (UHF). The new block had originally been allocated to broadcast TV.
11. Davis, "Cellular Mobile Telephone Services."
12. These estimates are cited in Norman Alster, "A Third-Generation Galvin Moves Up," *Forbes*, April 30, 1990, pp. 57–62.
13. "Motorola's New Strategy: Adding Computers to Its Base in Electronics, *Business Week*, March 29, 1982, p. 128.
14. Motorola, Inc., *Annual Report*, 1970.
15. Motorola, Inc., *Annual Report*, 1976.
16. These are 1990 estimates. See Ellis Booker, "Motorola, IBM Go Live with Mobile Data Net," *Computerworld*, vol. XXIV (February 5, 1990), p. 4.
17. See Ibid.; Barbara Darrow and Patrick Burnson, "IBM, Motorola Launch Wireless Data Network," *Infoworld*, vol. 12 (February 5, 1990), p. 1.
18. Booker, "Motorola, IBM Go Live with Mobile Data Net."
19. The figure is from Edward Staiano, president of Motorola's General Systems Sector (which includes the Information Systems Group), as quoted in Margaret Ryan, "Moto Unveils Wireless LAN," *Electronic Engineering Times*, October 29, 1990, p. 1.
20. Joanie M. Wexler, "Motorola First with Microwave LAN Link," *ComputerWorld*, vol. XXIV (October 29, 1990).
21. Seth Malgieri, "Motorola Launches Plans for Global Cellular Network," *RCR*, vol. 9 (July 9, 1990), p. 1.
22. "Motorola Inc., New Global Satellite Cellular Phone System," report by Merrill Lynch Capital Markets, Global Securities and Economics Group, Fundamental Equity Research Department, June 19, 1990.
23. Richard Doherty and Terry Costlow, "Moto Sets 77-Satellite Cellular Plan," *Electronic Engineering Times*, June 25, 1990, p. 1.
24. See "Motorola Looks to Experiment with Private Personal Communications, *Industrial Communications*, June 8, 1990; Keith Bradsher, "Motorola to Announce New Phone," *New York Times*, June 8, 1990, p. D4.
25. T. Kain, "New Growth Market for RCC's," Presentation to the Annual Convention of the National Association of Radiotelephone Systems, Kansas City, Missouri, September 14, 1966.
26. "Motorola's PageBoy II: Tripling the Market," *Business Week*, October 27, 1973, p. 54; see also, "Motorola Paging Receiver Aimed at Consumer Market," *Electronic News*, August 23, 1971, p. 34.

27. For a detailed description of technology roadmaps, see Charles H. Willyard and Cheryl W. McClees, "Motorola's Technology Roadmap Process," *Research Management*, vol. XXX (September–October 1987), pp. 13–19.

28. Japan's telecommunications industry was deregulated and NTT privatized in 1985. For background on paging in Japan, see Mitsuo Otsuki, "Paging Gets Competitive in Japan," *Telocator* (April 1989), pp. 52–55.

29. Quoted from a 1983 Motorola advertisement, which appeared in *Time, Newsweek, Inc.* magazine, *The Wall Street Journal*, and other publications.

30. Economic and Management Consultants International, "The State of the US Paging Industry—Subscriber Growth, End-User, and Carrier Trends: 1990," May 1990. See also, Alan Reiter, "New Pagers Put a Mailbox in Your Pocket," *High Technology Business*, vol. 8 (April 1988), pp. 32–36.

31. Reiter, "New Pagers Put a Mail Box in Your Pocket."

32. Motorola, Inc., "Motorola Wrist Watch Pager Could Revolutionize the World Paging Markets," press release, 1990.

33. William Weisz, "Philosophies of Leadership," internal memo, September 27, 1967, p. 3.

34. Ronald Henkoff, "What Motorola Learns from Japan," *Fortune*, April 24, 1989, p. 164.

35. John R. Welty, "Meeting Competition through the '80s," *Design News*, July 4, 1983, p. 25.

36. Jack Germain, "Motorola's Quality Management System," paper presented at the GOAL/OPC Conference, Boston, December 5, 1989.

37. Thomas J. Murray, "Bob Galvin's Grand Vision," *Business Month* (July 1989), p. 37; Lois Therrien, "The Rival Japan Respects," *Business Week*, November 13, 1989, p. 114.

38. Germain, "Motorola's Quality Management System," p. 7.

39. Therrien, "The Rival Japan Respects," p. 114.

40. Ibid.

41. Glenn Rifkin, "Pursuing Zero Defects Under the Six Sigma Banner," *New York Times*, January 13, 1991, Business Section, p. 9.

42. George Fisher, "Cycle Time a Key Factor in Economic Competitiveness," *Financier* (February 1990), p. 39.

43. William Weisz, "Key Issues in Successful Business Growth," MIT Distinguished Speakers Series, October 6, 1983, p. 12.

44. Weisz, "Philosophies of Leadership," p. 2.

45. See David J. Teece, "Profiting from Technological Innovation: Implications for Integration, Collaboration, Licensing and Public Policy," in Michael L. Tushman and William L. Moore, eds., *Readings in the Management of Innovation*, 2d ed. (Cambridge, MA: Ballinger, 1988), pp. 621–647.

46. See, for example, Ralph Gomory, "From the 'Ladder of Science' to the Product Development Cycle," *Harvard Business Review*, vol. 67 (November–December 1989), pp. 99–105.

47. See, for example, Lester Thurow, "A Weakness in Process Technology," *Science*, vol. 238 (December 18, 1987), pp. 1659–1663.

CHAPTER 4

CORNING INCORPORATED

In 1968, *Forbes* magazine called Corning Glass Works, now known as Corning Incorporated, "one of the strongest companies in American industrial history."[1] In the 15 years between 1946 and 1961, the company's sales quadrupled from $56 million to $230 million, and income increased by a factor of ten from $2.8 million to $25 million. In the half-decade between 1961 and 1966, sales doubled to $444 million and income to $59 million. Return on equity had reached 20 percent in 1966, and in 1967, Corning stock was selling at about 40 times earnings. (The average for Dow Jones industrial average stocks was 17.)[2]

Corning, in the late 1960s, was comprised of a diverse set of glass- and glass-ceramic-based businesses, offering products ranging from light bulb envelopes and TV bulbs, to scientific glassware and telescope mirrors, cookware and ophthalmic lenses, and architectural glass and refractories for high-temperature process industries (see Figure 4.1). Corning was also an equity holder in three large joint ventures—Pittsburgh Corning, Dow Corning, and Owens-Corning Fiberglas—which manufactured architectural glass, silicones, and fiberglass, respectively. These equity ventures contributed roughly 20 percent of total income in 1968.

But for all its diversity, the postwar emergence of Corning as one of the country's most exciting and innovative growth companies was driven by the development of a single business—TV bulbs. On the basis of a string of major innovations, Corning established what appeared to be an insurmountable lead in a large and growing market. By 1966, it was producing two hundred variants of TV bulbs and controlled 125 percent of the U.S. market for TV bulbs. (The extra 25 percent was accounted for by sales to replace bulbs that had been broken by TV manufacturers.) The business accounted for half of Corning's revenues and three-quarters of its profits.[3]

Yet even as *Forbes* was celebrating Corning's success in 1968, the company was on the verge of serious difficulties. The year 1966 proved to be its financial high-water mark. Whereas sales had doubled between 1961 and 1966, they grew only 36 percent between 1966 and 1971. Meanwhile, profits fell from the 1966 level of $54 million

125

Figure 4.1
Corning, 1970

	Percentage of Total Sales
Food preparation and serving, appliances, Steuben glass	25%
TV bulbs, light bulb blanks, resistors and capacitors, Signetics, time-sharing computer terminal	50%
Medicine: Pharmaceutical glassware, ophthalmic glass Science: Laboratory glassware, chemical analysis instruments Construction: PYROCERAM architectural facings, pyrex drainlines, ceramic roofing shingles Industrial Systems and Equipment: glass equipment for process industries, refractories for glass and steelmaking industry Transportation: safety windshield, heat exchangers for gas turbine engines, headlight components	25%

to $37 million in 1971. The primary cause of the difficulties was a decline in the TV bulb business. It began in 1967, when Japanese TV manufacturers began to displace Corning's customer base, the U.S. manufacturers of black and white TVs. What appeared in 1967 to be a temporary slowdown in Corning's dominant business was actually the beginning of a long and painful slide that would eventually force Corning out of the black and white TV bulb market.

To make matters worse, except for the consumer cookware and ophthalmic lens businesses—which were poised for new growth fueled by innovations that led to Corelle dishes and photochromatic lenses—the balance of Corning's businesses offered poor prospects for growth. Signetics, the integrated circuits subsidiary that some of Corning's senior management considered the company's best hope for the future, was faring badly. Eight years after it was acquired, it was still losing money and was far from a leadership position in the market. Meanwhile, a venture into the manufacture of computer terminals was proving to be unsuccessful, the resistor and capacitor businesses were commodity-like, the markets for light bulbs, construction and industrial process equipment businesses were maturing and cyclical, and while the scientific and laboratory glassware businesses were established and profitable, they could not be considered major sources of new growth.

In the 15 years that followed the *Forbes* piece, Corning was staggered by a string of crises, including a devastating flood in 1972, an economic downturn that drove income in 1975 down to $31 million (on $939 million in sales) and forced a significant reduction in employment, a second wave of Japanese imports that decimated Corning's customer base for color TV bulbs, and a slump in 1982 and 1983, during which operating income shrank to 2 percent. (See Figure 4.2 for a summary of financial results.) Yet in 1990, Corning was again being hailed as one of the nation's most exciting and innovative companies. This time it was *The Wall Street Journal* that cited Corning as one of a select few firms that it judged to be "poised to lead" in the 1990s.[4]

The Corning of 1990 was vastly different from the Corning of 1970 (see Figure 4.3). Gone were the businesses in mature markets like lighting, construction, and glass components for the process industries. Gone were the commodity business in passive electronic components, and Signetics, the integrated circuits business in which Corning had never been able to establish a leadership position. Still in place were a handful of the old businesses that had been "renewed" in the past 20 years by a succession of innovations. The consumer cookware business still accounted for 25 percent of the company's sales, although its growth had slowed and it was contributing a disproportionately low percentage (17.6 percent) of the company's operating margin; the ophthalmic lens and auto headlamp businesses were relatively small (roughly $100 million and $50 to $75 million, respectively) but quite profitable; and the TV business, which had shrunk to one aging facility by the end of the 1970s, had undergone a dramatic transformation beginning in the early 1980s as a result of major investments in manufacturing and quality. But it was still far from its former position of market leader. In 1988, it was folded into a joint venture aimed at the U.S. market with Asahi Glass, a global leader in TV glass manufacturing. By 1990, the joint venture was well positioned to take advantage of the rapidly growing video display market (which included the growing market for large-screen TVs).

The key to the revival of Corning's fortunes, however, was several entirely new businesses that had been developed and nurtured since 1970. The "crown jewel" of the new Corning is its optical fiber business, the global leader, with a reported $600 million in sales in a market with tens of billions of dollars of growth potential.[5] Corning pioneered the field of optical fiber for communications. Despite the presence of much larger, technology-rich competitors like AT&T, Sumitomo, and NEC, it has built and maintained both cost and prod-

Figure 4.2
Financial Performance, 1964–1990

Stage One

	1964	1965	1966	1967	1968	1969	1970
Net Sales ($M)	328	341	444	455	479	541	609
Income ($M)	37.6	43.1	59.5	51.3	49.3	34.8	43.9
ROE (%)	16.8	17.0	20.4	15.8	14.0	9.0	10.5

Stage Two

	1971	1972	1973	1974	1975	1976	1977	1978	1979	1980	1981	1982
Net Sales ($M)	603	715	946	1,051	939	1,026	1,120	1,313	1,500	1,623	1,714	1,578
Income ($M)	37	53	70	48	31	84	92	108	126	121	104	75
ROE (%)	8.7	11.6	13.8	8.9	5.7	13.9	13.8	14.2	14.7	12.6	10.0	7.3

Stage Three

	1983	1984	1985	1986	1987	1988	1989	1990
Net Sales ($M)	1,589	1,733	1,754	1,944	2,084	2,121	2,439	2,941
Income ($M)	92	100	136	182	208	211	261	292
ROE (%)	9.0	9.6	11.6	13.9	14.2	13.6	15.9	16.3

Source: Annual Reports; income from equity ventures included. Figures shown here may differ slightly from those reported elsewhere because of adjustments for acquisitions and divestitures.

Figure 4.3
The Transformation of Corning

CORNING, 1970		CORNING, 1990	
Business	% sales	Business	% Sales
Consumer	25%	Consumer	25%
TV, lighting,		Optoelectronics	~16%
capacitors, resistors,		Information Display	~10%
Signetics	50%	• glass for LCD	
		• glass for video	
Ophthalmic lenses,		Specialty Materials	~24%
pharmaceutical glassware,		• pollution control	
chemical analysis		• ophthalmic lenses	
instrumentation,		• auto headlights	
construction and process		• scientific glassware	
industry systems and equipment,			
transportation	25%	Laboratory Services	~25%

uct performance leadership through a continuing stream of innovations, a global network of joint ventures, and an emphasis on total quality.

A second global leader established after 1970 produces Celcor ceramic substrates for automobile catalytic converters. (Celcor is a registered trademark of Corning Incorporated. See the Appendix to this chapter for a list of the registered trademarks cited in this case.) This business has also built its market leadership on the basis of technology leadership coupled with an emphasis on quality. It has spawned a cluster of related businesses including one that supplies molten metal filters for metal foundries and a joint venture with Mitsubishi Heavy Industries and Mitsubishi Petrochemical to produce and market what will in effect be catalytic converters for stationary power-generating systems. Celcor and the related businesses contribute an estimated $225 million to $250 million in sales per year and have strong growth prospects in light of the increasing number of countries that are putting pollution control laws into effect.[6] Also developed during this period of transformation were the world's leading supplier of high-performance glass for flat panel displays—an exploding market with vast potential that is comprised almost entirely of Japanese customers such as Sharp, one of the leading suppliers of liquid crystal displays;[7] a supplier of a new class of substrates for computer memory disks made of a proprietary glass-ceramic material; and a cluster of laboratory services businesses, which account for one-quarter of the company's revenue and operating income and grew 80 percent in revenue and 160 percent in operating income between 1987 and 1990 through a combination of internal growth and acquisitions.

Corning's transformation is thus the result of new business development. And since each of these new businesses was built on the basis of technological innovation—even the nontechnology-based laboratory services businesses is an outgrowth of a ten-year drive to establish a leadership position in medical diagnostics—it is also the result of the strategic use of technology. What follows traces the evolution of the most significant new businesses developed in the course of this transformation. That evolution is described in three chronological stages. Stage One begins in the 1960s, a time of great optimism for Corning, when the company was embarked on what can best be described as an unfettered pursuit of the technological "big hit." Stage Two, which stretches from the early 1970s through the early 1980s, was starkly different—a time of recurring crisis and financial difficulties, when the unrestrained pursuit of the big hit came to an abrupt end, but several new business candidates uncovered in that pursuit were nurtured. Stage Three, the early 1980s to the present, has been a time of renewed growth and profitability as the businesses nurtured during the 1970s developed into their current state.

Stage One. The 1960s: In Search of the Big Hit

The 1960s were Corning's halcyon days. Tom MacAvoy served as president of Corning from 1971 to 1983 and then as vice chairman of technology until 1986. In the 1960s, he was first an R&D manager and then a division vice president. "Everything was growing like mad," he recalls, "and we thought we were causing it."[8] The TV business in particular "was just raining money out of the sky." Above all, this was a time of great confidence in the benefits of R&D—not just at Corning, but nationwide. Corning had been rapidly growing its technical capabilities, increasing its R&D spending from roughly 3.5 percent of sales during the 1950s to nearly 5 percent by the mid-1960s. It built a new corporate R&D lab in 1957 and opened an even larger one in 1965. Throughout this period, the main problem for R&D management was, as MacAvoy recalls, "hiring and finding good people. I spent one-third of my time recruiting and learning what was worth recruiting."

Corning's faith in R&D arose from its history of major technological innovations. The invention of Pyrex in the early 1900s led to the cookware and scientific labware businesses. The development in the

1920s of the so-called ribbon machine for the mass production of light bulb envelopes—a technology still being used around the world—led to Corning's major business during the 1930s and 1940s. In the 1950s, the development of PYROCERAM, a new class of glass-ceramics materials with high strength and heat resistance, gave birth to a new family of cookware, the familiar Corning Ware. It also led to a variety of other new products, including nose cones for missiles. The TV business was also built upon the big hit. During World War II, Corning developed the capability to mass-produce radar bulbs. Immediately after the war, it applied this capability to the manufacture of small, seven-inch TV bulbs. Mass production of larger screens was problematic until the late 1940s when Corning developed a radically new spinning or centrifugal casting technology. This innovation enabled Corning to establish a dominant market position, which it reinforced in the mid-1950s with the introduction of color TV bulbs and in 1960 with the introduction of a TV bulb that eliminated the plate of glass between the viewer and the picture tube.

Thus by the mid-1960s, there was a well-grounded belief within Corning that its well-being, both past and future, flowed from the technological big hit. "We were very conscious," Tom MacAvoy remembers,

> of the idea that the real driving financial power of the corporation derived from a relatively short list of what I would call "home runs." It started with working with Edison back in 1879; by 1900, 75 percent of the corporation's money was being made on the lighting business. When we invented the ribbon machine in the early 1920s, it became the method (and still is) for mass-producing light bulbs. So all during the depression, even though the rest of the business really stunk, that was carrying us. We started fiberglass and silicones in the late '20s and '30s. It took a long time to get them off the ground, but once they did [in the form of joint ventures with Owens Illinois and Dow Chemical], they turned out to be real money makers. Lighting, Pyrex, silicones, fiberglass, Corning Ware, television—these were the technological milestones that created the free cash flow of the company.

New Business Development—the Unfettered Search

Against this backdrop of rapid growth and a history of big hits, the 1960s were marked by a continuing search for the next major line of business. The search does not appear to have been guided by a particular strategic focus. Dr. William Armistead, vice president for R&D at the time and vice chairman of technology during the 1970s, explains that "We were opportunistic; if a good idea came along, we'd go after it." This sense of opportunism was reinforced, if not shaped, by Amory Houghton, Jr., great-great-grandson of Corning's founder. As executive vice president in the late 1950s, Houghton had been responsible for the rapid growth in R&D. He was named president in the early 1960s and CEO in 1966. "Amo had a million ideas," remembers MacAvoy. "If anyone came in with a good one, bang, he'd want to start working on it." He saw the construction industry, for example, as a massive market in which Corning was not participating, so in the words of Jack Hutchins, vice president for R&D from 1973 to 1985, "Amo pushed us into it. He knew we were not in the auto industry, so he pushed us to develop windshields." The net effect was a diversity of efforts to develop new businesses ranging from glass-based lasers, to ceramic roofing shingles and other glass and ceramic components for the construction industry, to high-speed methods for making bottles, high-temperature materials for process industry applications, optical waveguides for telecommunications, ceramic heat exchangers for turbine engines, glass razor blades, and integrated circuits.

Many of these efforts failed, some were modest successes, and several laid the foundation for the new businesses that would drive Corning's resurgence 20 years later. Unfortunately, future successes could not be distinguished in advance from failures. Bill Armistead retired in 1980 but is still considered one of the key figures in Corning's rejuvenation. His view was that

> if you keep track of your projects over a period of years, you
> will find that one-third of them are technical failures where
> you couldn't accomplish what it is you wanted to accom-
> plish. The other two-thirds split 50-50. Half of them are big
> commercial successes and the other half are big commercial
> failures. Although they are technically successful, for what-
> ever reason, the customer won't buy. Now, how can you
> stand half failures? Well, you have to have them. If you
> want any successes at all, you've got to have the failures
> too. I could never figure out which was which in advance.

Safety windshields. One of the largest and most ambitious of these projects involved the development of safety windshields for the auto industry. The project grew out of two separate streams of research, both originating in the early 1960s at the urging of Corning's senior management. One began when Amory Houghton's father, Amory

Houghton, Sr., urged Armistead to develop a process for drawing flat or sheet glass that would eliminate the costly and capital-intensive steps of grinding and polishing. Originally, the goal was to develop a replacement technology for the process used in making commodity sheet glass, but it evolved into a process for making specialty, high-performance glass. At roughly the same time, William Decker, the president of Corning, was urging Armistead to investigate the possibility of making glass that "that would not break." He did not have any specific applications in mind, but Armistead's reaction was that if the lab could indeed figure out a way to stop glass from breaking, "we should have all sorts of applications."

The lab launched two intensive efforts, each following parallel approaches to their respective objectives, and by the second half of the decade, both had achieved results: fusion, a process for drawing thin, high-quality glass without grinding or polishing; and ion exchange, a process of chemically treating glass to make it break-resistant.

These developments spurred a search for potential applications. The most promising appeared to be a new class of windshields that would be stronger and therefore safer than conventional windshields. "What we found in the late 1960s," says Jack Hutchins, "was that the automobile industry needed a safe windshield. And with ion exchange, we could make the front windshield strong, and in such a way that if and when it did break, it would break up into little granules that would never hurt anybody." In 1968, Corning received its first auto windshield contract for the American Motors' Javelin model. A plant in Blacksburg, West Virginia, was refitted for production of the new glass in expectation of growing demand. But the market for the new windshields never materialized. A radically new and less expensive way of making flat glass (the Pilkington float process) had by this time been developed. By using this process, and by doubling the plastic interlayer in its windshields, PPG, the auto industry's leading supplier, was able to make an improved product. While it was perhaps a little less safe than Corning's, it was inherently less expensive. This effectively killed Corning's chances.

By 1971, Corning had terminated the windshield project after having invested tens of millions of dollars. But although the windshield project was a costly failure, the company had succeeded in developing a new, proprietary process for drawing thin, high-quality specialty glass. This process formed the basis for what appeared to be an enormous new business opportunity by 1990—flat glass for liquid crystal displays.

Cercor—Cellular ceramic heat exchanger for turbine engines. A second project that also failed to produce the hoped-for results but that none-theless laid the foundation for one of Corning's new businesses was the development of a key component for automotive gas turbine engines. The component was a heat exchanger that could withstand the high outlet temperatures of the turbine engine, yet be produced cost effectively. Given the then-common view that the gas turbine engine would eventually replace the internal combustion engine in cars, this seemed a promising and potentially enormous application for Corning's expertise in high-temperature ceramics. As late as 1971, Corning's employee newspaper reported that

> the advent of mass-produced gas turbine engines for passenger cars—with heat exchangers from Corning—is . . . predicted to be five to eight years away. The turbine seems inevitable as long as a revolutionary type of engine development does not shove it out of the limelight.[9]

In an offshoot of the R&D that led to PYROCERAM glass-ceramic (the material from which Corning Ware is made), Corning developed a disk-shaped heat exchanger made of a glass-ceramic material in the late 1950s. The material was cellular in structure—that is, shaped like a honeycomb—which greatly increased the surface area and therefore the heat-carrying capacity of the material. The first application was a heat exchanger for a gas turbine used in a marine engine by Outboard Marine Corporation in 1962. Since that time, the heat exchanger—called Cercor—was used in numerous prototype gas turbine applications by a variety of car, truck, and engine manufacturers. The problem, of course, was that gas turbines for automobiles were still a remote commercial prospect. Corning was selling the cellular ceramic heat exchangers, but at a loss and in small volumes.

Optical fibers. In 1966, a Corning scientist reported to Bill Armistead that during a visit to the British Post Office, which operated Britain's telephone system, it was suggested that Corning investigate the development of glass fibers that could be used to transmit light signals for telecommunications. The motivation for the suggestion was concern over the increasing congestion in conventional, copper-wire-based telephone systems. Since light travels at very high frequencies, it has a prodigious information-carrying capability. A light-wave-based telecommunications system promised several orders of magnitude more capacity than conventional systems—if a "waveguide" for transmitting the light could be developed.

Optical fibers were already in use at that time. The total market was estimated at $15 million in 1967. Corning, for example, supplied at least one car manufacturer with what were called "light pipes" to illuminate dashboard controls. The fibers were also being developed as possible probes for medical applications.[10] But these early fibers were useless for telecommunications. The light signals they carried became attenuated or weakened so rapidly that they were useful only for applications involving transmission of light fewer than 10 to 25 feet. The attenuation of a light signal is measured in decibels of light intensity per kilometer (db/km). The typical attenuation level for fibers in 1966 was 1,000 db/km. A famous paper by Kao and Hockham of ITT published in 1966 suggested that the light-carrying capability of glass would have to be improved to 20 db/km (98 orders of magnitude over the then-available "high-loss" fibers) in order for fibers to become a practical telecommunications medium.[11] Nonetheless, when Armistead was told about the British Post Office's suggestion, he decided that the corporate lab should pursue the possibility.

> I could see that if you could really solve this thing, it had some merit to it. I didn't dream what it would turn out to be, or how big it might be, but anyway it looked like an intriguing idea, and I said, "Why don't we solve it?"

The optical fibers would have to be comprised of two parts—a glass core to carry the light signals and a reflective glass cladding to prevent the light from escaping from the core. Since the core would carry the light signals, the critical issue was to make it as free of impurities as possible, since impurities absorbed light, causing signal attenuation. The critical issue for the glass cladding was to have a lower refractive index than the glass core, so that it could reflect back into the core any escaping light.

By this time, a number of industrial groups, including ITT, Nippon Sheet Glass, and Bell Labs, were exploring the potential of optical fibers. They were attempting to develop the core by beginning with optical quality glass and then removing the impurities from it. Corning, of course, had extensive experience with optical glass. It also had been investigating glass-based lasers since the late 1950s. From a commercial point of view, in Tom MacAvoy's opinion, "The laser work led to nothing—no business. But the result was that we had about 20 people who understood quantum optics. We really understood it." And given this base of expertise, when a group at Corning's corporate lab began to examine optical fibers, the optical glass approach was quickly rejected. Armistead recalls:

> We decided that optical glasses were out . . . for several reasons. One was that they have a natural light scattering which was bigger than the 20 db/km loss that was necessary

to be practical. . . . Besides that, they had impurities in them that would come from batch materials and from refractories and so forth. And so there was no question that optical glasses were out.

Instead, Robert Maurer, the section leader of the group that had been working on lasers, proposed basing the investigation on fused silica. From his earlier work, he knew that silica had a natural light scattering of 6 db/km. Indeed, fused silica was the purest known form of glass at the time. The process for making it, developed by Corning in the mid-1930s, involved producing an extremely pure silica glass soot and then depositing it layer by layer onto a rotating heated substrate. By the 1950s, Corning had built a manufacturing facility for making fused silica for defense applications. Unfortunately, silica brought with it several disadvantages, as described by L. C. Gunderson, who managed the R&D effort on waveguides in the mid-1970s:

> There was no assurance . . . that silica could be fabricated in fiber form with the same purity and low attenuation [that it possessed in its bulk form]. Furthermore, the refractive index of silica was among the lowest, and therefore unsuitable as a fiber core material. In addition, its very high melting temperature, in excess of 1700°C, made working with silica very difficult.[12]

Nonetheless, this was the approach pursued by a small team at the corporate lab (the key scientists were Maurer, Donald Keck, and Peter Schultz). After four years of limited progress, they finally achieved a breakthrough. In fall 1970, Maurer announced that the Corning team had succeeded in making optical fibers with lower than 20 db/km attenuation—a stunning development.[13] Industry interest had begun to wane by then, with some experts concluding that low-loss optical fibers were still decades away, so the announcement had a dramatic effect. Corning had achieved one of the remarkable technological breakthroughs of the twentieth century. Yet it would soon learn that while it had added another technological success to its string of big hits, it was not even remotely close to realizing a commercial payoff.

Medical instruments and biology. Two other small efforts in the late 1960s—both outgrowths of Corning's long-established labware business—were also planting the seeds for important future business opportunities. In 1964, it introduced a line of pH meters, a small and very natural diversifying step since the electrodes in the meters were made of glass. The pH meters were soon followed by other analytic instruments, as Martin Gibson, architect of Corning's medical business for two decades and current chairman of Corning Lab Services (a wholly owned subsidiary), describes:

> When the labs business began to change to clinical labs, we had a problem because clinical labs don't use much glassware. So we began poking around for an opportunity, and we were already making a small pH meter. It occurred to us that one of the fastest-growing segments of the clinical labs business was blood pH. We just followed the market.[14]

Corning began to market an instrument for analyzing blood pH and gas in 1967, and by 1969, there was a family of such instruments. In an effort to uncover additional avenues of growth, the business formed Cormedics, a joint venture with Ciba Corporation (now Ciba Geigy) to manufacture and market prefilled disposable syringes. Cormedics turned out to be a disappointment, but the blood analysis instruments were successful and represented the first step in what became a 15-year effort to grow a medical diagnostics business.

While the instrumentation business was taking its first tentative steps, the corporate lab was beginning to explore the life sciences. Jack Hutchins describes how the manager of the effort justified hiring Corning's first life scientist, Ralph Messing:

> He said, "We hired Ralph because we believe there is going to be a biological revolution sometime between now [1968] and the end of the century. We do a lot of business [selling glassware] with biology labs. We anticipate that there may be some problem, some interaction between glass and biological substances. And if that's true, we'd better have somebody on board who knows something about the other side of that interface."

Messing made a serendipitous discovery that had important consequences. He had been using a porous glass (that Corning had developed in the 1930s) to separate proteins. The glass, which absorbs moisture from any material that it touches, is comprised almost entirely of silica and contains thousands of microscopic pores. Messing discovered that as the proteins passed through the glass, they bonded to it and remained chemically active. Eventually, this led to the realization that the porous glass could be a carrier or holder for enzymes that are used in a variety of industrial applications, ranging from fermentation to tanning. In such applications, enzymes are typically used once and then are either lost in the materials being processed or become inactive. The discovery of this new use for porous glass suggested the possibility of reusing the often costly enzymes, and thereby gaining significant economies. Like the first blood gas analyzers, this proved to be the first step in what would become a major effort to create a Corning "big hit" in the field of industrial biotechnology.

Electronics—integrated circuits and computer terminals. The most conspicuous and unambiguous failures during this period stemmed from a foray into the field of electronics. Corning acquired Signetics, a spinoff from Fairchild Semiconductor, in 1962. According to Tom MacAvoy, who had advocated the acquisition,

> We were looking for ways to expand the business on a technological basis into electronics, which was rapidly growing at the time, and still is. Signetics was a tiny little company, but we thought integrated circuits was the wave of the future. That turned out to be right, but Signetics turned out to be the wrong vehicle.

By the end of the decade, Signetics was unprofitable and consuming large amounts of capital. In 1969, for example, it began operations in a new plant, expanded its already established manufacturing facility and research lab, added a plant in Seoul, Korea, and was in the process of building at least two other facilities in Scotland and Portugal. Meanwhile, it lost $6 million on $32 million in sales in 1970, and another $8 million in 1971. But perhaps the most significant cost associated with this business was an indirect one. As a result of its trailblazing R&D, Corning was starting to develop a very strong patent position in optical fibers by 1970. In that year, Corning reached an agreement with AT&T, whereby AT&T would license Signetics to use its integrated circuit and other patents in exchange for a license to use a variety of Corning's patents, including its optical fiber patents. Jack Hutchins remembers that this seemed like a good idea.

> We had these optical waveguide patents and people were saying, "That's not going to be worth anything until the year 2000, so let's exchange the license for the optical waveguide patents for the stuff we can use in Signetics today. Corning by definition is going to win that one." Well, we sure won, didn't we?

Signetics was sold in 1975, while AT&T is today one of Corning's primary competitors in optical fibers.

A less costly, but equally unsuccessful, new business development effort in electronics involved the development of a computer terminal in 1969. Corning had been a manufacturer of passive electronic components since the early 1940s, when it developed high-reliability glass capacitors and tin-oxide-coated glass resistors. By the late 1960s, this was no longer a growth business, although it remained moderately profitable. In this period of unfettered search for the next big hit, the manager of this electronics components business established a new development lab in Raleigh, North Carolina. In an attempt to forward integrate into electronic systems, this new lab developed a time-sharing computer terminal. The terminal, the Corning 904, was introduced in April 1970. After an unsuccessful one-year market trial, the product was withdrawn and written off.

Stage Two. 1971–1982: Financial Crises and Nurturing New Businesses

If the early and mid-1960s were a time of rapid growth, burgeoning profitability, and optimism about the future, the early and mid-1970s were the exact opposite. This was a time of recurrent crises, declining profitability, and retrenchment. Corning faced a host of difficulties during this period but none more devastating than the demise of its TV business. The first signs of the problem had already emerged during the late 1960s. Imported black and white TVs, mostly from Japan, represented 16 percent of the U.S. market in 1965. By 1968, they had risen to 29 percent and a year later, to 43 percent. This erosion of the U.S. manufacturing base, and therefore of Corning's customer base, forced Corning to close one of its two black and white TV bulb manufacturing plants in 1969.[15] In the years that followed, the problem only got more serious.

The difficulties with Corning's TV business can be traced back to the mid-1950s. The story is a familiar one. The CEO of Asahi Glass came to Corning with a proposal to form a Corning-Asahi joint venture to manufacture TV bulbs in Japan. Corning, the overwhelming leader in the industry at the time, was uninterested; it agreed to license Asahi its technology "to get them off our backs." Forrest Behm, who served as manager of manufacturing at the time Corning was transferring its bulb-making technology to Asahi, and who later became senior vice president and general manager of the division that included the TV business before ending his career at Corning as its first corporate director of quality, describes what happened next:

> Asahi was much more thorough about controlling the [manufacturing] process than we were. Although we had a few major breakthroughs, after a few years they were far ahead

of us. You could just see it happening because they were constantly improving their process. We would come through with a brand new glass, and they would immediately adopt it, and start to improve it, whereas we would accept the new process as good enough. We would work on the major breakthrough, and then resist any further changes to the process, whereas you could see them using our major breakthrough and adding constant improvements.

Thus, when the Japanese TV manufacturers began to take over the U.S. market for black and white TVs in the late 1960s, their bulb supplier was Asahi Glass. And because of its practice of continuous improvement, Asahi, it appears, had a cost advantage over Corning.[16] Corning's problems were further exacerbated in 1970 when one of its major domestic customers, RCA, began making its own bulbs. Apparently, RCA's willingness to backward integrate stemmed from this same failure by Corning to make the improvements in its manufacturing process necessary to drive down costs and therefore price. Dick Dulude, current vice chairman of Corning and a key figure in almost all of Corning's growth businesses for the past quarter century, recalls:

What happened in the TV business . . . is that we would invent something that was technically unique, and then we would ride it as long as we could, and we would keep raising prices. People like RCA integrated backward, and we never should have let them. But if I were trying to justify a glass plant and I looked at the prices we were charging, which kept going up and up, I could draw a curve and say Corning is going to continue to raise prices, so I am going to get involved in the business, drive my costs down, and the difference between what Corning is going to sell it for and what I can make it for justifies the plan.

Even after RCA's decision, the difficulties were just beginning. In 1970, Corning was still the leading manufacturer of color TV bulbs. It still had three TV bulb plants in operation—one for black and white and two for color—and the TV business was still the company's primary business. During the first half of the 1970s, the black and white bulb business continued to erode. Import penetration rose to 63 percent of the domestic market by 1975, at which point Corning was forced to exit the black and white bulb business. As it was shutting down this business, precisely the same pattern began to happen with color TVs. Imports as a percentage of U.S. consumption rose from 19 percent in 1975 to roughly 40 percent in 1976. By 1975, the business that had represented three-quarters of Corning's earnings in 1966 was losing money. Its customer base for color tubes had shrunk from 28 companies to 5. "It was as if," Houghton remarked, "General Motors had lost Chevrolet."[17]

Corning's difficulties, however, were not limited to its TV business. After losing $14 million in 1970 and 1971, Signetics recovered temporarily in 1972 and 1973, but by 1974, it was again losing money. Meanwhile, other problems were battering the company. In 1971, a recession year, profits declined to $37 million on revenue of $600 million (from $50 million on $530 million in 1969). In 1972, the company suffered a devastating flood, which brought operations to a near standstill and cost the company $20 million.[18] After a short recovery in 1973, when income rebounded to $70 million on $946 million in revenue, another recession hit the company in 1974 and 1975. In combination with the deterioration in the TV business and Signetics, the recession drove profits down again, to $48 million on $1 billion in 1974, and $31 million on $939 million in 1975. A decade after money had been "raining out of the sky," Corning had reached its financial nadir. The devastating results forced a major restructuring of the company in 1975. Signetics was sold, five plants were shut down, thousands of products were eliminated, and 11,000 of its 46,000 employees, including 1,200 managers, lost their jobs.

Under these circumstances, new business development within Corning took on a very different character. The unfettered search for the big hit ended, and in its place emerged a much more selective, focused approach. Tom MacAvoy, who became president in 1971, describes its origins just before he became president,

> We were probably trying to work on too many projects at the same time. We probably had overcapacity relative to the total organization in the creative technical part of the business. This led to a great frustration among the operating managers of the company and the division managers [one of whom was MacAvoy]. We were working on some things that were really, in my view, off the wall. . . . The labs [the corporate R&D lab] were spending money like it was going out of style.

As the decade progressed, and against the backdrop of recurring and deepening crises, Corning began to practice many of the strategic and portfolio-planning techniques developed during the 1970s. "We were focusing," says MacAvoy. "We were using every tool we could find to focus. We used a lot of GE kind of stuff [GE had been a leader in the development and implementation of strategic-planning techniques[19]]; we tried everything from BCG [Boston Consulting Group's portfolio-planning techniques] to zero-based budgeting." At the same time, the new-business development process did retain at least some of the character of the earlier period. This primarily stemmed from the continuing influence of CEO Amory Houghton. On the one hand, he agreed with the need for a more disciplined, less unfettered approach. "If there is a single lesson that comes out of a period like this, it is concentrate good people and money on the most profitable businesses. . . . The established businesses . . . are the ones that carry the load. . . . If you take your eyes off them and dream solely of tomorrow, the whole profit underpinning falls."[20] But on the other hand, he continued to press the company to push on for the big success. Even though the number of new possibilities being pursued was greatly reduced, it was during this period of recurrent crises that three of Corning's most important future businesses were nurtured. They were Celcor, Corning's automotive emissions business spawned by the gas turbine heat exchanger effort; optical fibers; and the industrial biotechnology business, which grew out of the work on immobilizing enzymes with the use of Corning's porous glass.

Celcor

By mid-1970, the safety windshield project was in its death throes. Amory Houghton, Tom MacAvoy recalls, insisted that Corning had done a poor job in selling the idea to the car companies. So as a last-ditch effort, MacAvoy and several associates met with the heads of GM, Ford, and Chrysler.

> I knew we were dead; we were just having the wake as far as I was concerned. But I was out there with my selling suit on, and before we left Ed Cole's office [president of General Motors], I wanted to know what he thought about the heat exchanger for the gas turbine engines, because we were losing money on the samples, and if he thought it was a winner, we were going to continue to lose money, but if he thought it was very marginal or a loser, I was going to raise prices. When he saw it, he started talking about catalytic converters. . . . Two days later, I was in GM laboratories in Flint, and six months later, we had 50 guys working on it in R&D.

This was at the time the Clean Air Act of 1970 was being negotiated in Congress. The act set emission control standards for cars, to be made effective with 1975 models. The favored approach for controlling emissions was to use a catalytic converter, in which engine exhaust passes through a catalyst, triggering chemical reactions that convert the pollutants in the exhaust into more environmentally benign substances.

The relevance of all this for Corning was that the converter required a substrate to hold the catalyst in place in the exhaust system. That substrate would face conditions not unlike those for which the heat exchanger had been designed. Like the heat exchanger, it would have to withstand high temperatures and be durable enough to survive more than 50,000 miles of operation; this called for a ceramic material. In addition, the substrate would have to provide a large surface area in a relatively small volume, which pointed to the cellular or honeycomb structure of the heat exchanger.

But while there were these similarities to the heat exchanger, there were also differences. An entirely new material would have to be developed, since the glass-ceramic composite used in the heat exchanger was inappropriate for the catalytic converter. More of a problem, the complex cellular ceramic material had only been produced in small amounts for use as prototypes; now it would have to be mass-produced in million-unit quantities. A method of mass-producing the structures would have to be devised and scaled up, and this would have to be accomplished with unprecedented speed, since production of the 1975 models would begin in early 1974. As if these difficulties were not enough, it soon became apparent that GM was pursuing its own approach to the substrate. In addition, a subsidiary of 3M was competing directly with Corning, and the auto companies were lobbying Congress to delay if not rescind the auto emission control provisions of the Clean Air Act. Even if Corning overcame these obstacles, there was a good possibility that the business for its substrates would be short lived—the common view was five years—given the expectation that new approaches to emission control would be found.

It is not surprising that the project met stiff resistance inside Corning. Bill Armistead recalls that for every one of the major innovations, "there was skepticism within the company; you would find people saying, 'Why are you spending all this money for so long and not getting anything?' The worst case of it that I ever saw was Celcor. The resistance to that was just enormous." Part of the problem was the technical difficulties. Part of it was a concern that the business

would only have a short lifetime, either because the regulations
would be changed, a new approach to emission control would be
found, or both. Part of it also was a commonly held view that supplying the auto industry would at best lead to a low-margin business.

Despite the internal skepticism and the large uncertainties, the
project did proceed. The resistance came from what MacAvoy calls
"upper-middle management." But the senior management of the
company—Houghton and MacAvoy in particular—supported the
project. Armistead recalls Houghton's reaction to the resistance:

> Tom MacAvoy was getting awful heat from his division
> managers about their not being able to get things out of the
> lab because the lab was busy on this thing, and he went to
> Amo [Houghton] and said he was worried about that. And
> Amo said, "Well, Tom, you just tell them that if they can
> come up with a project that has the potential that this one
> does, we'll do theirs, too."

What was the rationale for proceeding despite the doubts and
uncertainties? In essence, the market was potentially very large, the
technology was one in which Corning was especially strong, and as
Dick Dulude, vice president of the division that included Celcor, put
it, "You could see how to make money on this," if the technical
obstacles could be overcome.

> We could tell how many of these things we were going to
> make. We knew the car market. And I knew that if we were
> going to take this material, basically a raw material that costs
> 50 or 60 cents a pound and sell it for about $4 a pound, that
> there is enough room in there for me to make money.

Actually, the formal projections of expected returns for the Celcor
project were not particularly promising. The appropriation request
for the initial facility to mass-produce the substrates projected a 12
percent return. But, according to Dulude,

> You can make the numbers come out any way you want,
> especially early in the development. . . . The real question
> is, do you really believe the market is going to happen, do
> you really believe in the people you are working with, and
> do you really believe that you can make the technology
> happen?

Development and scale-up. Development of the Celcor substrates
began during the second half of 1970. It quickly became the single
largest project in the R&D lab, consuming at its peak 25 percent of

the corporate lab's manpower. The primary obstacle was the need for a process that could be used in mass-volume production for shaping the ceramic material into the honeycomb structure. "Nobody could see how to do it," Armistead recalls. When the project started up, "five or six different approaches to manufacturing the thing" were identified and pursued.

> This thing was painful beyond belief, these five or six approaches we were following. I knew in my heart that none of them was going to work. I knew that. But we pursued them anyway, and built up a ferment in the lab. Something had to happen, and it did.

What happened was an invention. One of Corning's scientists, Rod Bagley, developed a die that made it possible to extrude the ceramics. The six teams were combined into one, and the project was transformed into an effort to develop a high-volume process for extruding the cellular ceramic. "It took a lot of effort and a lot of people. We didn't know anything about extruding; we'd never extruded anything." Making the die for the extrusion process quickly became the critical issue. "This thing had to stand 3,000 pounds per square inch of pressure, so the die had to be strong beyond belief, and yet it had to be absolutely perfect." That is, it had to be able to form a cellular ceramic structure with 200 cells per square inch. This translated to a wall thickness for each cell of twelve-thousandths of an inch. Armistead insisted that the die be developed internally, despite the group's lack of experience with extrusion.

> The engineers wanted to go outside and get some engineering company to do it, and I said, "No, we've got to do it ourselves. If we go outside and let somebody else develop this thing, they'll sell it to the auto companies, and we won't have a business."

In order to meet the auto industry's requirements for the 1975 models, the substrates had to be in production by January 1974, which meant that construction of the manufacturing facility would have to begin in January 1973. The manufacturing facility itself required the largest capital investment made by the company in 1973 and 1974, but as it began, the manufacturing process was still under development. Final development of the process, "endless testing," construction of the facility, assembly of the organization, negotiations with customers on price, product specifications and quantities, and ramp-up to full volume all had to proceed more or less simultaneously during 1973. It was by all accounts an extraordinarily stressful time—"the longest summer in my life," in Dick Dulude's recollection.

To make matters worse, internal resistance to the project not only persisted but grew as the odds seemed to get longer. Dave Duke, current vice chairman of technology but at the time manager of Celcor, recalls:

> Some of our corporate financial people would go through the numbers and come back and say, "You're never going to make any money." And one of the top manufacturing guys in the company basically said, "I won't sign your appropriation request because you are never going to make any money on this. You just can't make it." But Amo believed in it, MacAvoy believed in it, Dulude believed in it, and I believed in it. And so we did it.

By early 1974, the first substrates were being shipped, and despite initial technical problems, full-scale production was reached by midyear. The project continued to incur what the 1974 annual report called "heavy development expenses during all of 1974," a year in which Corning's income dropped to $48 million on $1 billion in revenue. By year's end, Corning had shipped 2.9 million substrates in 18 different shapes. Its customers were Chrysler, Ford, British Leyland, Volvo, Volkswagen, and Audi.

Subsequent development. Even with its initial success, the competitive environment facing Celcor was a challenging one. In late 1974, Corning was Chrysler's sole supplier of substrates and Ford's major supplier. But Ford continued to purchase substrates from 3M and W. R. Grace, and General Motors was using an entirely different approach for its converters. Most significant from Dulude and Duke's perspective, there remained the threat that the auto companies would backward integrate and begin manufacturing the substrates themselves, as RCA had done with TV bulbs. This competitive pressure led to a strategic approach to the Celcor business that set the mold for Corning's subsequent major new-business developments. Dulude describes this change in thinking:

> Understanding that it is a tough and very competitive field forces you to think in a certain way. In the TV and other businesses that we were associated with during that era, Corning had a certain philosophy [i.e., invent a technically unique product or process, charge premium prices, and raise those prices over time]. Celcor made us change that. I don't think at that point that we were looking at the TV business

saying we screwed up. I think it was just that Dave Duke and myself and other people said this is a different kind of business and we aren't going to make any money in it unless we drive the cost down and have a better product than anyone else.

And so by 1975, during the first full year of volume production, the R&D lab had turned to the "improvement of manufacturing efficiencies." At the same time, an effort to develop the next-generation substrate (one with 300 cells per square inch) was launched.

By 1977 Celcor had expanded its manufacturing facility, sales had grown to 8.4 million substrates made in 50 different configurations, and the business was supplying substrates for virtually all new cars made in the United States, except those made by General Motors, and for many made by European firms and exported to the United States. (Neither Europe nor Japan had comparable pollution control requirements at this stage.) Meanwhile, R&D to reduce costs and improve the product continued. As Roger Ackerman, now Corning's chief operating officer, recalls, "Our written strategy talked in depth about the need to drive down the cost and quality learning curve . . . [and] we had a very large project team assembled to do just that." Out of this effort came a variety of improvements, including a third-generation substrate (400 cells per square inch).

Despite these efforts, the business did run into difficulties in 1980, when NGK, a Japanese competitor, began to offer Ford and GM "very attractive deals" for their substrate business.[21] According to Forrest Behm, the Japanese "were making a superior quality . . . substrate, pressuring our market position and profits."[22] Corning, however, was able to fend off the threat in the short term by restructuring its approach to pricing its product, and over the course of the next few years, by embarking on a major quality-improvement program at the ceramic substrate facility.

Optical Fibers

Market and technology development. The development of optical fibers continued in the early 1970s following the dramatic announcement that Corning had broken through the 20 db/km barrier. In 1972, the team made another major breakthrough—fiber with loss levels of only 4 db/km. At these levels, the fibers could transmit signals for 20 kilometers without a repeater. (A repeater detects the output of one fiber, converts it to an electrical signal that drives a light source, which in turn retransmits the signal into the next fiber. Conventional cable required repeaters every four miles.)[23]

But while the technology was improving, market acceptance was not. If the challenge posed by Celcor in the 1970s was to develop and scale up technology rapidly enough to take advantage of an exploding market, the challenge posed by optical fibers was almost exactly the reverse. Here was a major technological achievement, but with a commercial payoff seemingly years, if not decades, away. The problem was that market acceptance of the new technology depended on a host of factors beyond Corning's control. Many of Corning's potential customers around the world, since they were vertically integrated, were also its potential competitors. AT&T was the primary example. At least as important, the fibers were only a piece of the overall optical communications system that would have to be developed before Corning's breakthrough technology could be successfully commercialized. Not only did the technology and production capacity for sheathing the fibers with cables have to be developed, they would also be needed for light sources, light detectors (for converting the light signals back into electrical signals), and connectors and couplers (for linking fibers together). Corning possessed neither the wherewithal nor the technology to develop and supply the complete system, but even if it had, the market still would have resisted such a radical change. There were concerns about the reliability and durability of a new telecommunications system, particularly given the expense associated with burying new telephone cable. Moreover, many cabling companies, the natural intermediaries between Corning and the telecommunications companies, had been expanding their conventional, copper-cable-manufacturing capacity, thereby providing an additional reason for resisting the new technology.

Charles Lucy was assigned the task of developing the market for the new technology in the early 1970s. Ira Magaziner and Mark Patinkin, in *The Silent War*, describe the resistance Lucy quickly encountered:

> He expected the telecommunications industry to stand in line for it [optical fiber]. Soon he found that no one cared. No one wanted to buy it. After Corning had won the research race against every company in the world, it seemed the victory would be a hollow one: technical success, commercial failure. Lucy learned what the problem was when he paid a call on AT&T—the biggest potential customer of waveguides since it owned 80 percent of the nation's phone lines . . . "You've done it," they told Lucy. Then they shrugged. They said it would be 30 years before the American phone system would be ready for waveguides. And

when it was, they said, AT&T planned to have its own fiber.[24]

After this disappointing reception from AT&T—and an equally cool reaction from U.S. copper-cabling companies—Lucy turned his attention abroad. Here he found a new obstacle. Telephone companies were usually government owned, which made them resistant to foreign suppliers, let alone foreign suppliers with an entirely new technology. Lucy's reaction was to form development agreements with cable suppliers in England (BICC), France (CGE), Italy (Pirelli), West Germany (Siemens), and Japan (Furukawa).[25] The cablers agreed to develop the components and cabling technology needed to make the optical fibers operational and to pay Corning an annual fee. In return, Corning would grant them licenses to produce the actual optical fibers if and when the market for them developed. The advantage of this approach, Lucy hoped, was that it would stimulate development of and demand for fiber optic systems within the various countries. The disadvantage, of course, was that he is was giving away the rights to produce the fiber once the demand did emerge. Magaziner and Patinkin explain the logic:

> Giving patent licenses to its foreign partners, he [Lucy] knew, meant they could eventually start making their own fiber. But he also knew that if his own company kept improving waveguides, the partners would need Corning to help them remain state of the art. As long as Corning remained the technical leader, it would hold on to a piece of the action anywhere it formed a partnership.[26]

To supply the development partners with fiber samples, a telecommunications product department was established in 1973 within the corporate R&D lab. One year later, the department developed a small facility for cabling the fibers it was producing. By June 1974, Corning began to offer its cabled fiber for sale. The fiber had a loss level of 30 db/km (considerably above the levels achieved in the lab in 1972), was available in lengths up to 500 meters, and cost from $25 to $57 per meter, depending upon the size of the order.[27] By mid-1975, it was selling an improved cable called Corguide at $13.50 per meter with maximum loss levels of 20 db/km. At this point, the cable was being sold not for commercial applications but rather to the various development partners and other companies that were experimenting with and evaluating optical fibers.[28]

Despite this rapid improvement in product and reduction in price, the size of the business was still inconsequential in 1975. All that the company had to show for a decade of development was less than $1 million in sales and an impressive and growing array of competitors, including AT&T, RCA, GTE, ITT, Harris, Thompson CSF, Sperry, and several Japanese firms.[29] Yet optical fibers was beginning to consume an increasing level of resources, and this at a time when Corning was suffering a severe financial crisis. Not surprising, resistance to the project began to grow, just as it had with Celcor. But the effort never slowed, and the reason was the vigorous support given to it by Houghton. According to Armistead, who was vice chairman at this time:

> In the 1970s, we were in trouble profit-wise because of the drop off in TV, and so [optical fibers] was a burden because it took so much effort. Amo just grabbed right ahold of it. He became the champion. . . . He grabbed this thing and he insisted that we put enough technical effort into it and whatever we needed in technical equipment, and he insisted that we vigorously defend our patents.

Likewise, MacAvoy remembers that Houghton

> was after us all the time to keep pushing. He wasn't worried about whether it was going to be a big deal. The only question was when. He wanted us to make it faster, but frankly, if it didn't happen until the end of the century for natural market reasons, he would understand that—as long as when it came we'd be the leader.

The leadership philosophy. The year 1976 was pivotal for the optical fiber business. Early that year, the company began offering uncabled fiber for sale. Six different fibers were available, with attenuation levels ranging from 6 db/km to 10 db/km, and prices between $1.00 and $1.50 per meter. Field evaluations of the fiber by AT&T and other telecommunications companies were soon exceeding expectations. Meanwhile, as Corning recovered from its dreadful financial performance in 1975, the development group at the R&D lab was unable to keep up with the demand for fiber samples. The fibers appeared to be cost competitive with conventional cables in some applications, and optimistic projections for the commercial application of the new technology were once again appearing in the literature. Against this background, Houghton and MacAvoy, along with Leroy Wilson, vice president of the division that would house the optical fiber business, concluded that the time had come to establish a complete business unit to grow the optical fiber business. They asked Dave Duke, who had grown Celcor, to do the same for optical fibers.[30]

From the outset of his involvement, Duke applied an explicit leadership philosophy to the nascent business. Corning would have to adhere to the same continuous pursuit of leadership in both cost and performance that he and his colleagues had used with Celcor for precisely the same reason: strong competition. The dimensions of the problem were made strikingly clear to him when he visited Japan soon after taking over the job. Not only would Corning have to compete with the likes of AT&T, RCA, GTE, and ITT, but Japan's Ministry of International Trade and Industry (MITI) had targeted optical fibers as a priority, and Nippon Telephone and Telegraph was sponsoring development of the technology for Japan's telecommunications markets. Duke attempted to convince NTT to buy Corning's product, but NTT was uninterested in anything but a worldwide license.[31]

To Duke, the scope of the competition magnified the importance of his leadership philosophy. Magaziner and Patinkin describe his viewpoint:

It wouldn't work to merely stay even with the competition. Corning . . . was smaller than its rivals, both here and in Japan. Look at AT&T, he said—it had more people, more money, and itself as a customer. When your competition's bigger, matching it isn't good enough. "I don't want to tie," he said. "If we tie, we lose."[32]

To stay ahead, Duke and his associates explicitly followed a three-part strategy. First, they deliberately pursued a cost-learning curve:

We were doing this in 1976 and 1977. We said we had to have a curve that would get us from two dollars a meter then to ten cents a meter some time in the future. And then we would start talking about how we were going to do that. "Well, we're going to have to go to bigger blanks and faster speeds; we were going to need new equipment," and there were various kinds of things we had to do consciously in terms of draw speeds, blank sizes, and selections to get there.

Second, they deliberately pursued continuous improvement in performance.

Just as important, maybe even more important, is what I call the other learning curve, which is performance against time. And in our case it was things like attenuation and bandwidth. We said attenuation had to go from 5 db/km to .5 over some period of time. And bandwidth [information-carrying capacity] had to go from 200 megahertz to 400 megahertz, up to several gigahertz. And that led us to say, we're going to need to get into single-mode fibers down the road . . . so in the late 1970s, we started working again on single-mode fibers because we knew that by the mid-1980s, we were going to have to be someplace up here on the learning curve. . . . We laid that out in the 1970s. We didn't know exactly how to get there, but we knew where we had to be 10 or 15 years into the future. And as a result we'd brainstorm, and somebody would come up [with a way to do it]. . . . So now we are on our sixth- or seventh-generation optical fiber-making process, whereas our competitors are back at maybe their second or third or fourth.

The third component of the optical fiber strategy was to expand capacity ahead of demand. Once the market finally did develop, the competitor who had the capacity advantage would quickly gain a volume advantage, which of course would translate to a cost advantage. But even apart from the volume-related economies, failure to have the capacity could have delayed the entire market. Duke explains:

If customers couldn't get fiber, then they might have put in a microwave system or they might have put in some more copper. . . . The competition was not just other fiber makers. It was microwaves, it was satellites. In fact, when we were going through this . . . IBM and Comsat, two heavy hitters, were saying, "We're going to put these satellites up and we're going to take all the [long distance telecommunications] traffic away . . . except for the plain old telephone service to the homes." So the competition was microwaves and satellites and copper cable, not just the other fiber [suppliers] . . . . This was a time when the bigger risk was not to keep moving ahead because we would have lost. I mean the whole industry of fiber optics would have lost, not just Corning.

Implementing the leadership philosophy. The rapid scale-up in capacity began in 1976 with a decision to build a pilot facility for manufacturing the fibers. The pilot plant represented a doubling of Corning's fiber-making capacity. As the plant was nearing completion in early 1977, Duke expected it to be able to supply the "domestic and worldwide prototype and evaluation needs" for low-loss fibers for several years.[33] Yet by year's end, in order to meet the growing demand generated by dozens of field tests of the optical fibers, capacity at the pilot plant had been doubled twice, and plans were under way to convert a plant in Wilmington, North Carolina, to a full-scale fiber optics manufacturing facility that would triple the company's fiber capacity by 1979. At the same time, in December 1977, Corning formed a joint venture with Siemens called Siecor, that would manufacture optical fiber cable (that is, sheathed optical fibers) for the U.S. market.

The rapid scale-up continued into the early 1980s. In 1980, "substantial capacity" was added to the Wilmington plant that had begun operation in mid-1979, and Siecor acquired a $90 million (revenue) per year cabling company. The new expansion was completed the following year, and yet another expansion was planned for the Wilmington facility. As Corning was increasing its capacity, it was also introducing major advances in the process being used to make the fibers. The process installed in the pilot plant built in 1977 represented the second-generation optical-fiber-manufacturing process. It was based on the same approach as the first but offered significant improvements in quality as well as reductions in cost of the fiber, as shown in Figure 4.4. The transition from pilot plant to full-scale manufacturing facility in Wilmington, North Carolina, led to an even more significant advance in process technology. Corning had been using the inside vapor deposition process over the past decade, in which silica vapor is deposited inside a tube of quartz. The coated tube is melted and then the fiber is drawn. At the time the Wilmington plant was being built, Corning had a strong patent position in the inside vapor deposition process and was the clear leader in its use. But an alternative technique, outside vapor deposition, that the R&D group had been exploring for some time offered the potential for making superior fiber—lower attenuation, higher bandwidths, and longer lengths—at lower cost and higher volume. Despite Corning's leadership in inside vapor deposition, Duke decided to develop and implement the new process in the Wilmington facility. In Dulude's words:

Figure 4.4
Optical Fibers—Process and Product Improvements

Date	Process (generation)	Attenuation (db/km)	Bandwidth (Mhz)	Price ($/meter)	Product Variants (#)
1976	R&D Lab (1st)	6–10	20–400	1–10.50	6
1978	Pilot (2d)	3–10	200–1,000	.65–3.10	20
1980	Full Scale (3d)	1–5	200–1,500	.30–2.25	new family

We obsoleted ourselves by going with a new generation of equipment. A lot of companies won't do that. When you have a strong patent position, as we did [on inside vapor deposition], the tendency is to hang on. . . . But we decided that we were going to be the lowest-cost, best quality producer in the business.

To maintain that position, Duke and his associates felt it was necessary to push on to the more advanced process.

Product and process advancements continued after the shift to the outside vapor deposition process. In 1980, Corning introduced a new family of fibers called double window fibers; they could transmit light at wavelengths of both 850 and 1,300 nanometers (nm). The most commonly used light sources at the time operated at 850 nm. Using the double window fiber, customers could install a fiber optic system using 850 nm light sources and then upgrade to higher-wavelength light sources as they became available without having to change the fiber. Two years later, two more families of fiber were introduced: "second window fiber," which allowed signals to be transmitted over greater distances and with lower attenuation than any previous fiber, and "short-distance fiber," for linking computers and other short-distance applications. An even more advanced long-distance, single-mode fiber, which could transmit 140 million light pulses a second over a distance of 30 kilometers without the need for a repeater had also been developed in the lab.

This aggressive leadership strategy was extremely resource intensive. Indeed, the company had invested a reported $100 million in the business by the end of 1982.[34] And even though Corning had recovered from its disastrous slump of 1974 and 1975 (see Figure 4.2) and sales of the optical fibers were beginning to grow in the late 1970s and early 1980s, there were still many reasons for concern. A large commercial order had not been received by mid-1982 (most orders were for relatively few kilometers), total sales were reaching only about $10 million in 1982, the business was losing almost as much money as it was bringing in in revenues, and the competitive challenge appeared as strong as ever. As a result, the fiber optics business continued to meet strong internal resistance. Duke recalls that at one point, a top manufacturing executive in the company

pulled out all of his engineers because he said he hadn't realized that Western Electric/AT&T had a license [to Corning's technology]. He said we were never going to make money, and he had better places to put his engineers, so he pulled them off [optical fibers] and started putting them on other things.

But Duke still had the support of MacAvoy and Houghton, and to succeed with a project like this, Duke argues, "You have to have a believer at the top."

> There were a number of times when I would need to add capacity and get something going, and I'd start an appropriation request. And the Corning system is like many systems—it just slows everybody down. You have to get all these signatures and every analyst has got to go through it. . . . But since I knew that I had top-management support, we just went ahead, and in fact, by the time the appropriation was signed on one of the expansions in Wilmington, we actually were putting the roof on. People ask, "Don't you feel that you were taking a lot of risk?" Well, yes, but again, the bigger risk was not having the capacity.

Industrial Biotechnology

While the optical fiber business was scaling up in the second half of the 1970s, another potentially large business opportunity was coming to the fore. It grew out of the serendipitous discovery that porous glass could be used to immobilize enzymes. In 1973, the lab was exploring ways of scaling up the immobilized enzyme process, and the following year, Corning licensed the technology to CPC International, the world's largest producer of corn products (e.g., corn oil). CPC was interested in using immobilized enzymes to convert corn starch to sweetener, and by 1976, the technology was in use at a CPC plant.

In 1976, as Corning was recovering from the slump of the previous two years, Amory Houghton was already beginning to push the organization to identify the next big hit. Celcor was taking off, and progress was being made in fiber optics, but as Hutchins recalls, "There was top management saying, 'That's all terrific, guys, but what's area x?'" MacAvoy remembers the same pressure.

> Amo kept asking, what's the next big one? It was clear that waveguides were going to be a big deal. We didn't know when, but we had the basic technology in hand and we seemed to be in the lead. So what's the next big one? . . . After the recession of 1975, the drum beat got louder. What is the next area? What is "area x"? We spent a lot of time with planners and the Hutchins group [Corporate Lab] trying to figure that out.

Industrial applications of the immobilized enzyme technology were the leading candidates in 1977. Corning owned 30 patents in the field, had explored a variety of applications for the technology, and was building two pilot plants in Europe. One of the most promising near-term applications involved the conversion of cheese whey (a by-product of most cheese-making processes) into sweetener. Research was also being done on using the technology to convert agricultural raw materials, such as starch and cellulose, into chemical products. The goal was to "develop new low-cost industrial processes using not petroleum feedstocks but agricultural raw materials," and then to design and build the plants that would use those processes.[35]

A critical component of this new opportunity was the new field of biotechnology. In the late 1970s, recombinant DNA technology appeared to offer the potential not only for a new and more efficient way of making enzymes but for a way by which enzymes could be tailored to particular applications. According to Dick Dulude, it was thought, "that if we teamed up with a company to make enzymes through recombinant DNA technology, and if we had the technology to immobilize these, you put the two together and maybe you have some kind of unique process that gives you a competitive advantage." And so, in the late 1970s, during the earliest days of the biotechnology industry, Corning was searching for a partner, "looking at a business plan a week."

The biotech company that impressed Corning was a small 1977 start-up called Genentech. Corning contracted with Genentech in 1979 to develop an enzyme for use in the production of fructose.[36] But Genentech was reluctant to work on a contract basis, and its interests were gravitating toward pharmaceutical rather than industrial applications of biotechnology. Therefore in 1981, Dick Dulude, who at the time was responsible for nurturing both the optical fiber and industrial biotechnology opportunities, proposed a joint venture to develop and produce enzymes for industrial applications (primarily, for the food-processing and chemical industries). Since Genentech was cash poor at the time, Dulude proposed that Genentech raise the $20 million needed for its contribution to the joint venture by selling 6.5 percent of its stock to Corning. Genentech agreed, and Genencor was formed in 1982.

At the same time, Corning continued its own internal development, and by 1981, it held 70 patents in the field. It also formed a second joint venture named Nutrisearch with Kroger and Company, a major U.S. food processor and supermarket chain. The initial purpose of this joint venture was to convert whey from Kroger's cheese-processing operations into bakers yeast, which would be used at Kroger's baking operations. A plant was scheduled for completion in 1983.

Medical Diagnostics

In the late 1960s and early 1970s, while Celcor, optical fibers, and immobilized enzymes were in their early stages of development, Corning was also successfully introducing a line of instruments for clinical laboratories—the blood gas and pH analyzers. By the mid-1970s, Corning had taken several additional steps toward becoming a supplier of diagnostic instruments to the clinical laboratory market. It acquired in 1971 Diagnostics Research Inc., a manufacturer of culture media systems used to identify certain types of bacteria. Corning introduced a new blood gas analyzer the following year, and its sales along with those of the already established instruments were so strong that manufacturing capacity was doubled. In 1973, a separate Medical Products division was established. Capacity was once again doubled, new instruments including one that measured calcium levels in body fluids were added to the product line, and a small business that produced equipment for measuring protein in body fluids as well as a 9 percent interest in a small but growing medical-testing laboratory named MetPath were acquired. In addition, several new products were under development. One, which was consuming "a significant portion of the division's budget," was an instrument for classifying and counting different types of white blood cells, called LARC (leukocyte automatic recognition computer). It had been developed not at the corporate R&D lab, but at a lab in Raleigh, which had been part of the electronic components business and had produced the unsuccessful computer terminal. Another product that grew out of the immobilized enzyme work at the corporate lab was a family of radioimmunoassays (RIAs). Two RIAs were ready for commercial introduction in 1974—one tested for insulin, the other for digoxin, a drug used to regulate the heart.

The Medical Products division was renamed Corning Medical in 1976. Its product lines fell into two basic categories: diagnostic instrumentation, primarily blood gas and electrolyte analyzers, and diagnostic reagents. New instruments and reagents continued to be brought out with considerable success in the marketplace, except for LARC which was a major disappointment. Sales grew 16 percent in 1977, 40 percent in 1978, 21 percent in 1979, and 12 percent in 1980. By the end of 1981, the business had grown to nearly $150 million.[37] Through the 1970s, growth was generated almost entirely from internal new-product development. In 1980, however, Corning acquired Gilford Instruments, a $31 million (in sales) manufacturer of analytic instruments and diagnostic reagents for hospitals and research labs. Next, Corning Medical acquired complete ownership of MetPath, the provider of clinical testing services in which it had held a minority interest since the early 1970s. By late 1981, when it was wholly owned by Corning, MetPath had grown into the largest blood-testing laboratory business in the world, with sales of $110 million.

Thus by early 1980s, Corning was in the medical diagnostics products and services business. In the eyes of senior management, the business had joined optical fibers and industrial biotechnology as another of the company's high-growth businesses. Interestingly, this one was not built on the basis of a technological big hit, but rather through the establishment of several small product lines that grew incrementally over the course of a decade and were then combined with two major acquisitions.

Stage Three. 1983–1990: The New Corning

By the early 1980s, Celcor was the world's leading supplier of ceramic substrates to the catalytic converter market; the optical fiber business was the world's technology leader and seemed poised to take off commercially; and in industrial biotechnology and medical diagnostics, Corning appeared ready, in the words of James Houghton (vice chairman through much of 1970s and vice chairman and chief strategic officer since early 1980), "to take part in the fastest growing industry in the United States—health care—and one of the newest technologies—biotechnology."[38]

But while the efforts at new business development seemed ready to bear fruit, Corning was once again running into financial difficulties (see Figure 4.2). The post-1975 recovery reached its high point in 1979, with $126 million income on $1.5 billion in sales. Earnings dropped in 1981 to $104 million on $1.7 billion in sales, and then plummeted to $74.5 million on $1.6 billion in 1982. Operating margins nosedived from a high of 9.5 percent in the first quarter of 1980 to −1.25 percent in the third quarter of 1982. Against this backdrop of promising growth prospects in the midst of sharply reduced profitability, James Houghton was named to succeed his older brother Amory as chairman and CEO in early 1983. The younger Houghton soon announced his strategic objectives. "We have . . . two prime objectives—profitability and growth. Our short-term goal must be a return to profitability. Our long-term goal is to grow at least 5 percent a year in earnings—that's real earnings not counting inflation."[39] Shortly thereafter, he made the profitability objective more precise: operating margins were to be restored to 10 percent by 1985, and then increased to a minimum of 13 percent per year margin.

> That figure of 10 percent is not plucked out of thin air. It's the margin that brings our cash flow above the break-even

point—just barely. . . . It plugs the leak in the boat. Where we're heading after the 10 percent step is 13 percent or more. Thirteen percent gives us the funding we need for steady, long-term growth.[40]

After substantial gains in profitability were made, a new target was set in 1988: Corning was to consistently rank in the top 25 percent of the *Fortune* 500 companies in return on equity.

The emphasis on profitability might easily have been accompanied by a decreased emphasis on new business development, but Houghton explicitly linked his profitability objectives to the growth of new businesses.

What's so urgent about growth? Let me inject the urgency by translating "growth" as "survival." Survival as the Corning we know. Survival as the Corning we want to become . . . there are more and more companies fighting to grow on the same playing field. They'll muscle us out if we let them, grow in our place, and cheerfully watch us shrink. Those are the alternatives: grow or shrink.[41]

To achieve these twin objectives of growth and profitability, Houghton made a number of significant policy changes. He reorganized the company into three business groups that highlighted the major growth prospects: health and science, which combined industrial biotechnology and medical diagnostic products and services; electronics and telecommunications, which combined passive electronic components businesses with optical fibers; and consumer and industry, which contained Corning's traditional glass- and ceramic-based businesses (including Celcor and what remained of the TV bulb business). He also embarked on a five-year process of divesting the company of its low-margin businesses. And most important, he established a corporatewide, total quality campaign. Houghton named then senior vice president for operations, Forrest Behm, corporate director of quality, set aside a training fund of $4 million, established a quality school that every employee in the organization was required to attend, and began a highly visible campaign in which he personally promoted total quality throughout the company. Behm discussed the connection between quality and the twin objectives of growth and profitability:

We're sitting on a gold mine. I mean the cost of not doing things right the first time. Companies that have made quality a way of life have proven this cost to be somewhere between 20 and 30 percent of sales. Those companies have also proven it's a modest goal to cut the cost in half through

> a total quality effort. . . . Cost of quality is the money spent on such things as preventing defects from going out the door, rejects thrown away, customer returns, rewritten memos. Beyond the cost saving factor is the actual gain in sales that total quality can generate.[42]

The quality campaign was an outgrowth of what Behm calls experiments that had been carried out in various parts of the company during the early 1980s. Several businesses had instituted quality improvement and training programs that by 1983 were showing impressive results. Houghton and his senior managers, according to Behm,

> could see six or seven of these experiments that we were doing, how successful they were. . . . In TV bulbs, we made a major move that was purely working on product quality and focusing everything on error-free work. At that time . . . in my estimation we had the worst quality of any in the world. Worst product quality. And with this different approach and different attitude and putting the money into training and not taking chances on shipping bad product, we went from the worst to being equal to anybody. In all of these experiments, we could measure the results; we could measure it in the number of defects, in market share, in what our customers were telling us. You could see it, they were measurable things. . . . And so we had these examples; they were isolated incidents, but they were powerful.

As the decade progressed, so too did the emphasis on growth and profitability through reorganization, restructuring, and total quality. The company was reorganized in 1985 and again in 1987 and 1990, the principle objectives being, in Houghton's words, "reducing costs, increasing the focus on manufacturing and technology, and allowing greater concentration on new market opportunities in each of our . . . segments."[43] The passive electronic components, refractories, and zircoa ceramics businesses were sold. As for the quality campaign, the program laid out in 1983 proved to be only the initial step in a process that gained momentum throughout the decade. Four objectives were established in 1983: make Corning the world leader in quality, have a total quality plan in place in every organizational unit in the company, eliminate surprise quality failures, and produce measurable results—measurable in the sense that they contribute to the 10 percent operating margin objective—by 1985. In 1987, quantitative objectives were established. For example, every organizational unit had to measure its principal errors and reduce them by 90 percent by 1991. Behm reasoned that

> If you tell anybody to reduce something by 10 percent, they don't get around to working on it; but if you say you have to reduce it by 90 percent . . . it forces people to really make fundamental changes. However, if you give people that goal before they have gone through a few years of quality awareness, it won't mean a thing. But once they understand that they don't have to have errors, and that you are willing to invest in training to prevent errors, people say, "Yeah, give us four years and we can do that."

In 1989, the optical fiber business applied for the Malcolm Baldrige National Quality Award. It was a finalist in the competition, but not a winner. To Houghton, that meant that despite the nearly six-year campaign, Corning still had not achieved "world-class quality. The more I looked at what it takes to be world class, the more concerned I became."[44] In 1990, he established a new quality objective— for "all of Corning Incorporated to achieve world-class quality by 1993." By that year, Houghton explained, he expected every individual business unit in the company to be able to compete for the Baldrige award.

This then was the context for new business development in the 1980s—a continued emphasis on developing new sources of growth, but now coupled with a much greater emphasis on profitability and quality.

Celcor

The market for Celcor substrates had stopped growing in the early 1980s. Since catalytic converters were being used on all cars except diesels sold in the United States, sales of the substrates had become a function of domestic demand for automobiles. During the economic slump of 1981 and 1982, Celcor sales declined. It was during this downturn that the business embarked on a major effort to upgrade product quality and manufacturing, and so when the market rebounded in 1983, Celcor was in an even stronger competitive position and the business once again became one of the company's strongest performers.

The problem facing Celcor at this point was not only how to maintain leadership but also how to continue to grow given its leading market share in the fully penetrated U.S. auto market. There appeared to be two potential sources of new growth: new applications of the cellular ceramic technology and the possibility that emission control requirements would be established in Europe. Corning pursued both these prospects while continuing to reduce costs and improve performance.

In early 1985, Corning announced that it would build a facility to manufacture Celcor substrates in West Germany. Catalytic converters were still not required in Europe, although the West German government was offering tax incentives to purchasers of cars equipped with catalytic converters. Still, the political momentum in Europe in favor of emission control standards was gathering strength, and in keeping with its strategy of building capacity in advance of demand, Corning proceeded with the new facility in West Germany. After some start-up difficulties in 1986, the plant reached full-scale production in 1987. By then, European nations were beginning to phase in emission control regulations, and Celcor sales were beginning to increase substantially. Capacity was once again expanded in 1988, with $40 million invested to convert and reactivate an old glass plant in Blacksburg, Virginia.

While capacity was increasing ahead of demand, technology also advanced ahead of the competition. Roger Ackerman, then group president of Specialty Materials (the group that houses Celcor) and now president and COO of Corning wrote in 1987,

> We can sell everything we can make—and if we could make more, we'd be selling it. While we're pushing to get more pieces out the door, we're also stretching our resources to reduce costs, improve quality, and expand capacity. . . . If we continue to drive our costs down and our quality up, we will continue to be the leaders.[45]

Corning developed a continuous extrusion process in 1989, and the following year, it announced a substrate made of a new ceramic composition that allowed for cellular structures with new configurations and thinner walls. Improvements in quality also continued. When the Blacksburg, Virginia, plant was converted to the manufacture of Celcor devices, the entire substrate manufacturing process was redesigned. "The company analyzed each of the 235 manufacturing steps involved, eliminated 115 operations and cut production time to three days from four weeks."[46]

As a result of these actions, Celcor continued to grow through the decade. The business reported in 1990 that it had sold more than 300 million substrates since its inception. (Substrate prices in 1987 reportedly ranged from $10 to $30.)[47] Annual sales were close to $200 million, and the annual report listed Celcor as one of the company's three "outstanding" contributors to earnings (along with optical fibers and laboratory services).[48]

New applications. As Celcor was solidifying its leadership position, several new applications of the cellular ceramic technology were being investigated. One was a filter for capturing soot from diesel engine exhaust, which after nearly a decade of development and testing, seemed "poised for swift worldwide growth" in 1990.[49] A second was a catalytic combustor (as opposed to converter) for wood stoves, which increased heating efficiency and reduced pollution. The first catalytic combustor was introduced in late 1980, followed by a variety of shapes and sizes in 1982 and an improved family of combustors one year later. A third, and to date the most successful, new application was "MetalFilter"—a cellular ceramic filter used to remove impurities during metal casting. The first important application, introduced in 1980, was filtering molten superalloys used to make jet engine parts. The range of applications for the new filter was extended in 1983, and Corning began to describe the disposal filters as "a new filtration system for . . . iron foundries."[50] One hundred and fifty thousand of the filters were sold in 1983. Sales more than doubled each year after that, and in 1987, the metal filter business was described in the annual report as "one of Corning's fastest-growing businesses."[51] By 1988, Corning produced more than 16 different kinds of metal filters, had penetrated 60 percent of the total potential iron-casting market in the United States and Canada, was exploring new applications (e.g., steel foundries), and had extended its marketing efforts to Europe, Korea, and China. A total of 100 million filters were sold from 1986 to 1989. In common with all of Corning's businesses, quality was an important feature of the metal filter's business success. A new facility for manufacturing the filters went into operation in 1989, and as a result of the quality improvements made in the design of the new operation, defects were reduced from 10,000 parts per million to 3; and between July 1990 and May 1991, not a single customer order was returned.[52]

By the end of the decade, yet another application of the cellular ceramic technology had been found. In this instance, the material served as a substrate for the catalysts used for pollution control in power-generating systems. Corning formed a joint venture company, Cormetech, with Mitsubishi Heavy Industries and Mitsubishi Petrochemical, to manufacture and sell the systems. (See Figure 4.5 for a summary of evolution of the cellular ceramic businesses.)

Optical Fibers

The optical fiber business finally took off in 1983. Sales began to "accelerate dramatically" in 1981 and doubled in 1982 to roughly $10 million. Even when the company suffered through a significant

Figure 4.5
Evolution of Cellular Ceramics Businesses

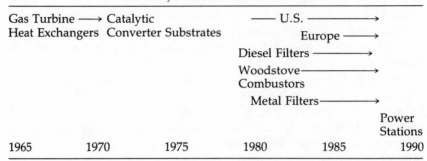

downturn in 1981 and 1982, it continued to invest heavily in the business, doubling capacity at the Wilmington plant in 1981, and tripling it in 1982. But with all Corning's own efforts to develop the market, the triggering event appears to have been the divestiture of AT&T. Shortly afterward, in the fall of 1982, Corning was approached by MCI, which was interested in using optical fibers for the nation-wide long-distance telephone network it was building to compete with AT&T. The MCI request represented the first significant market opportunity for the business, but it posed three interrelated challenges for Duke and his associates. First, MCI wanted single-mode fiber, a new type that Corning was then developing that was capable of transmitting light over a distance of 30 kilometers without a repeater. The fiber had been under development for some time, but at the time of the MCI order, only laboratory prototypes had been produced. Second, not only would the new fiber have to go into production much more quickly than had been anticipated, it would have to be produced in unprecedented volumes. Total capacity at the Wilmington plant in early 1982 was for 100,000 km of fiber per year—MCI wanted 150,000 km. And third, the price that MCI offered was so low that Corning would lose money on the order if it used existing fiber-manufacturing processes. To make a profit, a new generation of processing equipment still under development at the lab would have to be installed. Because of the time constraints, the equipment would have to be scaled up to unprecedented volumes and used to produce a new type of fiber that was still itself under development, without benefit of a pilot plant. The wisdom of such a leap was a matter of considerable debate within the optical fiber group, but Duke insisted on it, as Magaziner and Patinkin describe:

> "I don't want to be in a business where I'm just one of five guys doing the same thing," he said. He again made the

point about how it wouldn't be good enough to tie. As competitive as waveguides were now, he said, the business would be triply so in the future. This was like color TVs in the sixties. If American companies had redesigned their products and factories then, while they were ahead, they'd have kept in front of the Japanese.[53]

By late 1983, plant capacity once again doubled, the new processing equipment had been scaled up, the new single-mode fiber was being produced and shipped to MCI, and the fiber optics business was in the black. Soon after receiving the MCI order, Corning received 100,000-kilometer orders from GTE, Sprint, and U.S. Telecom. In Dulude's words, "The market was suddenly exploding in all directions." Demand in North America alone increased from 200,000 km in 1982, to 600,000 in 1984, and to 1.6 million in 1986.[54] As the market took off, so did Corning's sales, reaching an estimated $100 million in 1984 and $220 million in 1986. (These figures did not include sales from Corning's many joint ventures.) Operating margins appear to have been well over 25 percent in 1985, with the business being "singled out as a major contributor to operating income" by that year's annual report. One analyst reported that the business contributed $75 million in operating income in 1986.[55]

Throughout this period of rapid growth, the business continued to use the strategy that had led to the success it was now enjoying. Whereas in 1981, Corning had a manufacturing capacity of 60,000 km per year, capacity reached 300,000 km per year by the end of 1983, and Duke proposed another expansion that would quadruple Corning's capacity by 1986. This expansion would cost $100 million, the largest one-time technology investment in the company's history. Meanwhile, the pace of new product and process development continued unabated. The new capacity would incorporate a fifth generation of processing technology. A sixth generation was ready to be implemented in 1988, and the development of a seventh was well under way. With continuous process improvement came continuing reductions in price, as shown in Figure 4.6.[56] New products were also developed. In 1985, Corning introduced an improved single-mode fiber and announced research on a fluoride glass that offered the potential for a new class of optical fibers capable of transmitting light over distances one to two orders of magnitude longer than was possible with the silica-glass-based fibers then being used. In 1987, yet another improved single-mode fiber for long-distance applications was introduced.

Market development kept pace with product and process devel-

Figure 4.6
Optical Fiber Prices

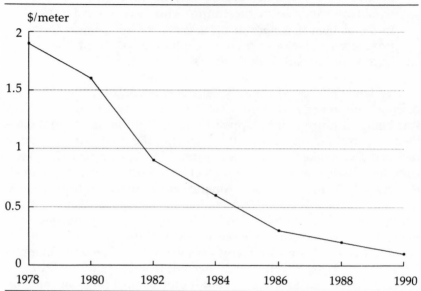

Source: Edward Schollmeyer, "Corning Incorporated: Corning Enters New Dramatic Growth Era," PaineWebber, March 8, 1990, p. 8.

opment as joint ventures or licensing agreements were established in England, France, Italy, West Germany, and Australia, allowing optical fibers using Corning technology to be produced and marketed. These agreements enabled Corning to penetrate these national telecommunications markets. At the same time, Corning was aggressively protecting its patents. This had been an explicit part of the technology leadership strategy from the outset of the business. In fact, the company's first significant battle over optical fiber patents began in 1976, when Corning filed suit against ITT for violating three of its basic patents. A five-year legal battle ensued, culminating in an out-of-court settlement whereby ITT agreed to pay Corning an undisclosed amount of cash and to license the technology from Corning for any subsequent use. At about the same time it was settling with ITT, Corning filed suit against Valtec, a subsidiary of Philips. Corning won that suit in 1984 after a two-year legal fight. Five days later, Philips exited the business and sold Valtec to ITT (which by then had a Corning license).[57] A year earlier, Corning had won a suit against Canada Cable and Wire, which had purchased fiber from Sumitomo that violated Corning's patents. (At this stage, Corning still had not succeeded in having its basic patents recognized in Japan.) Then in 1984, Sumitomo began to export its fiber to the United States. Corning appealed to the International Trade Commission, but while that body was deliberating, Sumitomo built a facility in North Carolina, initially claiming it was an R&D lab and then announcing in 1985 that it was a production facility. Once again, Corning sued. A federal court ruled in favor of Corning three years later, at which point Sumitomo shut down its North Carolina facility and agreed to pay Corning $25 million.

Broadening the business. During the second half of 1986, the explosive growth in the market for optical fibers ended almost as suddenly as it had begun. Although Corning maintained its market share, sales actually declined from about $220 million in 1986 to about $140 million in 1987 (not including sales from joint ventures or licensing fees). This decline resulted from a change in the nature of the optical fiber market, which, though anticipated, had occurred much earlier and more rapidly than expected. By far the largest application for the fibers was in telecommunications. That market was comprised of several distinct segments: the long-distance network; the connections between long-distance lines and the central offices of local telephone companies; the connections or "feeders" between the central offices of the local telephone companies and the "remote terminals" that serve as distribution points in the local network; and the "drops," which connect the remote terminals to individual telephone users. Most of the first wave of optical fiber sales were for the long-distance applications. It was this market that was beginning to be saturated by the second half of 1986. Yet the more local markets—not to mention applications outside telecommunications such as computer networks—were still virtually untapped, and these were expected to be much larger than the long-distance applications. One typical 1989 analysis, for example, projected that the fiber market would grow from $610 million in 1988, to $1.6 billion in 1995, to more than $4 billion in the year 2000. All of this growth was expected to come from shorter-distance applications[58] (see Figure 4.7).

Corning began positioning itself for the shorter-distance market well before the downturn in the long-distance market. In 1984, it introduced a new single-mode fiber for shorter-distance applications and in 1986, a new multimode fiber that could be used for transmitting data, voice, and video in local area networks. A new hermetic coating for fibers introduced in 1987 opened the way for a number of specialty markets such as undersea applications. And then in early 1990, the business introduced a new class of single-mode fiber called "Titan," which was tougher and more durable than conventional fiber and therefore better suited for installation in the local loop.

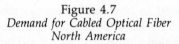

Figure 4.7
*Demand for Cabled Optical Fiber
North America*

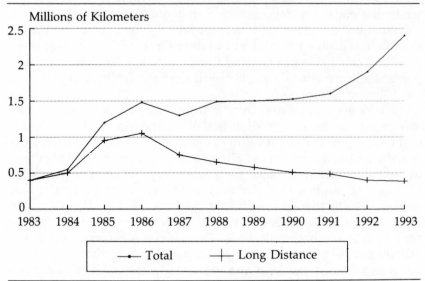

Source: Edward Schollmeyer, "Corning Incorporated: Corning Enters New Dramatic
Growth Era," PaineWebber, March 8, 1990, p. 10.

At the same time it was developing new fibers for the emerging
markets, Corning was developing the components that would be
used with the fibers in these new markets. It established a joint venture with Plessey of England in 1984 to develop optoelectronic devices, but this venture was ultimately a disappointment. In 1987, it
acquired a small firm called Technology Dynamics, which develops
fiber optic sensors for specialty applications such as aircraft, medical
instrumentation, and process control. It entered into a joint R&D
effort with General Instrument in 1988 to develop low-cost optical
fiber systems for cable TV markets. Meanwhile, Corning itself was
developing passive components for local telecommunications applications, such as a fiber optic "coupler" that splits or combines light
signals so that one fiber can be connected to multiple fibers. Corning
introduced fiber optic couplers in 1990 and in early 1991, was building
a facility in France to mass-produce them.

As these developments were under way, the market began to
take off, once again earlier and more quickly than expected, and
Corning resumed its capacity expansions. Capacity was increased 25
percent in 1989, and in 1990, Corning announced it would invest

$100 million in order to increase capacity by an additional 50 percent. By this time, Corning was well established as the world leader in optical fibers, with total revenues (including its share of joint ventures) reaching an estimated $600 million in 1991 and growing at a rate of 15 to 20 percent per year.[59]

Industrial Biotechnology

When he was named CEO in 1983, James Houghton saw industrial biotechnology, along with the optical fiber and medical diagnostics businesses, as the company's best hope for growth.

> I cannot predict the ultimate potential of enzyme technology, but when you consider that enzyme action is important in chemical processing, agriculture, waste conversion, and pharmaceuticals, as well as food processing and medical diagnostics—well, you have the outlines of a vast new marketplace.[60]

As the decade progressed, however, Corning was forced to reevaluate its position. It had become clear by 1985 that in order to establish a leadership position in this business, Corning would have to invest in it at a rate and magnitude comparable to its investment in optical fibers. Even then, given the strength of the competition in biotechnology, Corning would be hard pressed to succeed. Dick Dulude felt that

> It was going to take a half-billion dollars in order to be able to develop a strong position. . . . If you want to be a significant participant in any of these businesses, you are going to have to spend that kind of money. If you are going to end up competing with big guys, you'd better mentally commit enough money up front. . . . [So when] it looked like waveguides was finally going to happen, when the divestiture of AT&T happened and that business started to grow, I didn't see how we were going to find another half-billion dollars to spend on industrial biotechnology. Plus, it was further away from our base technology than waveguides.

And so, after building up its position in industrial biotechnology in the early 1980s, Corning began to sell off its investments in the mid-1980s. It sold portions of its share of Nutrisearch and Genencor in 1985, and then shut down Nutrisearch completely in 1986. In 1987, it sold more of its share of Genencor, and by 1989, Corning had fully divested itself of its industrial biotechnology businesses.

Medical Diagnostics

At the time that Corning was beginning to spin off its industrial biotechnology holdings, its medical business was comprised of Corning Medical, which specialized in instruments (e.g., blood gas analyzers) and diagnostic products (RIAs) for special and emergency blood testing; Gilford Instrument Laboratories, acquired in 1980, which specialized in instruments for routine blood testing; and Met-Path, acquired in 1981, which specialized in blood-testing services. This cluster of businesses had become, as J. Houghton explained in early 1984, "one of the fastest growing . . . in Corning history," even though it competed "in a business area with no direct connection to customary Corning markets or technology."[61] But by the mid-1980s, the company was reaching the same conclusion about this business that it had reached about industrial biotechnology. Developing and maintaining a leadership position would require a level of life sciences capability that the company simply did not possess and a level of investment that it simply could not afford while also pursuing optical fibers. Therefore, in 1985, it spun off Corning Medical and Gilford Instruments into a joint venture with Ciba Geigy, called Ciba Corning Diagnostics. Corning contributed its two diagnostic products businesses (which had combined sales of roughly $160 million in 1984) to the joint venture, while Ciba Geigy paid Corning $20 million and contributed its life sciences research capabilities.

This joint venture marked the end of Corning's attempt to grow a major new business in medical diagnostic products. Ciba Corning actually proved to be quite successful, growing to $300 million by the end of 1988, and for the first time turning a profit that year, despite heavy R&D spending. Nonetheless, Corning sold its share of the company to Ciba Geigy for $75.7 million ($41 million after taxes) the following year because it no longer fit the company's strategic orientation.

Although the nearly 20-year effort to develop a diagnostics products business fell short of the mark, it did lead in a totally unanticipated fashion to a major new Corning business in laboratory services. The laboratory services business can be traced back to the early 1970s, when Corning, a small supplier of diagnostic products to the lab services market, acquired a 9 percent interest in MetPath. When Corning acquired the rest of MetPath in late 1981, it quickly instituted a policy of expansion, building a new laboratory in Chicago to complement the already existing MetPath facility in New Jersey. After a decline in profitability in 1982, because of the expansion plus consolidation in other areas, MetPath began to grow rapidly, reaching $245 million in sales in 1986. In 1987, E. Martin Gibson, then president of Corning's health and medical group, explained his approach to the business:

> Soon after we acquired MetPath in 1982, a variety of changes in analytical and computing technology occurred. As a result, there was strong economic advantage to a decentralized organization where regional labs could provide the same efficiencies as the large central lab. So we made a fundamental change and moved from a highly centralized company to a highly decentralized company. Implementing this change in a relatively short amount of time is the key to MetPath's improved performance. Now . . . we intend to keep on adding new regional labs. Our ultimate goal is to have strong, competitive regional labs in each of the major parts of the country.[62]

To do this, Corning acquired labs in Washington, DC, and Connecticut in 1985, three more labs in 1987, formed a joint venture with UniLabs in 1988 to strengthen its position in the western United States, acquired the eastern operations of Central Diagnostic Labs for $36 million in 1989 (the western operations were part of the UniLabs joint venture), and in 1990, acquired several local labs in addition to Community Clinical Laboratories on Long Island for $21 million. This rapid regional growth was tied to an overall emphasis on quality. In a service business like MetPath, turnaround time is an important source of differentiation. In 1986, MetPath delivered 88 percent of its lab test reports to customers in 24 hours or less; four years later, that rate had been improved to 98.5 percent.[63] By then, MetPath was reported to have grown to more than $400 million in revenues (from $110 million in 1981).[64]

As MetPath grew, the company began to acquire related laboratory services businesses. In 1987, it acquired Hazleton Laboratories, the world leader in chemical testing services for the pharmaceutical and agricultural industry. At the time, Hazleton had nearly three times the market share of its leading competitor. It continued to prosper as a part of Corning, growing 30 percent in 1988 and expanding its range of services to "essentially all phases of the preclinical product development cycle."[65] Two more laboratory service companies were acquired in 1989: G. H. Besselaar Associates, the worldwide leader in providing clinical testing services (complementing Hazleton's preclinical trial services) to the pharmaceutical industry, and Enseco, the leading environmental testing service.

This cluster of laboratory services businesses had grown from

MetPath's $110 million in sales in 1981 to $731 million in sales and $125 million in operating income in 1990, which represented one-quarter of the company's total revenue and income from operations. Late that year, as part of a larger reorganization of the company, Corning spun off the laboratory services group into a wholly owned subsidiary, Corning Laboratory Services. The reason for the change was that Lab Services was so different in character from Corning's other businesses that it would, in James Houghton's words, "be even more successful operating independently of the glass and ceramic portion of our business . . . [and would] have the opportunity to develop a management structure and operating systems best suited to this business."[66] (See Figure 4.8 for a summary of the evolution of Lab Services.)

The Next Wave of New Businesses

Liquid crystal display glass. As Lab Services was being spun off, a new generation of big hit candidates was under development. The most advanced was a business that manufactured glass substrates for liquid crystal displays (LCDs)—the display technology that had become the leading approach for the flat panel displays used in porta-ble computers, video cameras, compact disk players, miniature TVs, pocket calculators, and digital wristwatches. The LCD market was exploding by 1990—already more than $1 billion, and growing at more than 35 percent per year[67]—and was completely dominated by Japanese firms. Nonetheless, Corning was by far the leading supplier of the flat, high-performance glass used in the LCDs, and this new Corning business was being compared to optical fibers. According to John Loose, the executive vice president of the group that contains the business, "Advanced Display Products is following a pattern sim-ilar to that set by Corning in the optical fiber business, and we expect the return to be equally as big."[68]

The LCD glass business can be traced back to the late 1960s and early 1970s. The glass is made using the same proprietary process—fusion—that was used to make the commercially unsuccessful safety windshields. Later, Corning applied the technology to several minor applications such as windows for aircraft and self-cleaning ovens and then sheets of photochromatic glass for eyeglass lenses. In the 1970s, Corning also began to make LCD glass for digital watch makers, but most of this glass was manufactured by a more conventional process.

As LCDs became more sophisticated in the early 1980s, and their applications more demanding, it was apparent that higher-performance glasses would soon be required to satisfy the needs of

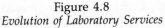

Figure 4.8
Evolution of Laboratory Services

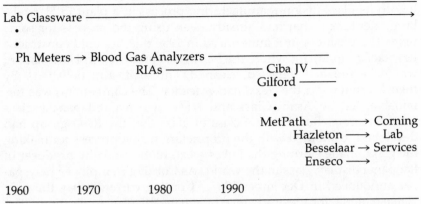

LCD makers. A small group at the corporate lab began to explore new types of glass that could withstand the high-temperature requirements of LCDs and, if made with the fusion process, would satisfy the latest LCD glass performance requirements. William Dumbaugh, who led the group, "saw a tremendous future for Corning in this area if we could develop some glasses that would be able to take the higher processing temperatures." By 1985, the group had succeeded. "We felt we had a natural combination of things working for us—we had the fusion technology and we had these glasses." No other potential supplier of LCD glass could match Corning in either category.

Even though the group at the lab believed it had a performance advantage, it was not at all clear that the business of supplying glass to LCD makers was a worthwhile opportunity. As late as 1985, LCD technology was still not the dominant approach for making flat panel displays, and perhaps more important, the timing and magnitude of the market for flat panels, whatever the underlying technology, were very much in doubt. Cathode ray tubes offered better performance at lower cost. The picture began to change in 1986 and 1987, however. LCDs became the technology of choice for flat panel displays, and rather than displacing the conventional cathode ray tube display technology, flat panels were used for entirely new and potentially large display applications, such as miniature TVs and portable computers. As the market for LCDs grew, so too did orders from Corning's Japanese customers. And as orders increased, Corning turned to its old fusion process and the new LCD glass that the lab had developed.

By the end of 1987, Corning had introduced the new glass, established a new business unit to pursue the LCD market, and was scaling up its glass-fusion-manufacturing process in a plant in Harrodsburg, Kentucky, that had already been using the process for some time. The business unit announced in 1988 that it would construct a new facility in Japan, where the LCD glass produced in Harrodsburg would be finished (beveled, cleaned, annealed, and polished). By then, Corning was the clear market leader. The competition was formidable, led by Asahi Glass and NEG, two major Japanese glass manufacturers. But the new class of glass that the R&D group had developed, combined with the proprietary fusion process for making the glass, made Corning the lowest-cost, highest-quality producer of flat panel display glass in the world. As Corning's employee newspaper announced in December 1987: "Corning currently has the only viable material for these advanced flat panel display applications. The challenge is to maintain the leadership position for this market, which is based largely in Japan."[69]

Corning attempted to meet the challenge with the same strategy it had used in optical fibers and Celcor: pursue continuous improvements in product performance and quality and do so ahead of the competition; maintain cost leadership by continuously pursuing process improvements; and build capacity ahead of demand. According to Dave Duke (now vice chairman), this approach

> is a model that I keep using with a lot of our developing businesses; we set out with the two learning curves [cost and performance] . . . and I come on kind of heavy-handedly with the division managers and the technical people in their divisions saying, "Don't tell me what you want this year, tell me what you want to look like in five years . . . where do we have to be in terms of flatness and warp and the number of pixels they can put on [the LCDs] and costs?" That's the way you drive the manufacturing program and your technology program and your standing against the competition, because by the time they catch up to where you are now, you are way up here someplace.

To reach these goals, Corning had a team of 27 scientists working on improving the fusion process and developing new glasses in 1991, and was expected to invest $100 million in this area by 1995.[70] As for product quality, perhaps the clearest indication of the priority it was being given by the business came from one of its customers. Sharp Corporation, one of the leading makers of LCDs in the world, selected Corning in 1990 as winner of its "Outstanding Supplier Award for Materials and Technological Support."

Other new business. The LCD glass business was the most prominent of Corning's new wave of potential big hits, but it was by no means the only one. Two in particular stood out at the end of the 1980s. One of them involved a new kind of substrate for computer memory disks developed at the R&D lab. Made from a tough glass-ceramic, by early 1991, the substrate was in field tests with customers around the world. It does not warp or dent, and compared to conventional, aluminum-based memory disks, it lasts longer, carries twice as much data, and is one-third the width.[71]

Another potential big hit appeared to offer even greater long-term benefits than the LCD glass or memory disk substrates. This was an entirely new class of material that the R&D group was developing. Named Placor, the new material is a composite of glass and plastic. The company had patented 20 such composites by 1991 and was beginning to explore a potentially vast range of applications for materials that combined the strength and durability of glass with the formability of plastics.

Discussion

Business Strategy

Which markets? Unlike GE Medical and Motorola, which have focused on specific market segments such as diagnostic imaging equipment and mobile and portable communications, Corning has always competed in widely diverse markets: optical fibers and their related components, catalytic converters and automotive headlights, ophthalmic lenses and consumer cookware, magnetic memory disk substrates and video display bulbs, telescope mirrors and plastic cell culture products used in laboratory research and testing, and a cluster of related laboratory services businesses. The reason for this diversity, in MacAvoy's opinion, is that

> You can't sell glass the way you sell something like polystyrene. When you melt glass, you have to form the object while it is still hot. You can't just make it in a reactor, chop it into pellets, and ship it to someone else in bags. To capture the economics, you've got to form something out of it. A light bulb, for example. You've got to go a step forward toward the market. Intrinsically, you are in the components business, not the materials business, so that throws us into a wide variety of component businesses of different sizes. Some of them are little tiny things. And some of them grow up to be big businesses, and some of them die, and some of them are just bait until we can find out what they can lead to.

Even though Corning competes in diverse markets, like GE Medical and Motorola, it has had a consistent strategic focus over its long history—a focus defined not in terms of markets, but in terms of specific technologies. Corning has always defined itself as having a core technology base from which it pursues new market applications. This was how Amory Houghton saw the company in the early 1960s, when he was the newly named president of Corning. "The main problem of Corning," he said then in an interview with *Forbes*, "is to make a product reality out of a research phenomenon. . . . You can't help but get excited about finding applications for glass."[72] When Houghton became CEO in the mid-1960s, he maintained this philosophy: "Corning's long-term growth continues to rest substantially on our abilities to research the new, and pull through to the marketplace products made from ever stronger and more usable glass."[73] He still held this view in 1982, shortly before stepping down as CEO. "The core of this company has been to be masters of technology, wherever our basic technology happens to lead us."[74] This was also how James Houghton described the company shortly after becoming CEO in 1983. "You must begin with the company's mission. We express Corning's in four words: to market technology profitably."[75] The same idea was expressed graphically in 1985 by Corning's senior management committee when it described the company as a hub and wheel (see Figure 4.9), with segments of the wheel representing the company's four broad business sectors and the hub representing Corning's technology. In 1990, when Corning Laboratory Services was spun off as a wholly owned subsidiary, the old vision of a company pursuing a range of market applications for its core technology was reinforced. According to James Houghton, one of the reasons for the reorganization was that it allowed the company "to tie our other three sectors and our core technologies closer together."[76]

Corning did stray from its focus on glass and glass-ceramics in the 1960s when it attempted to establish a position in electronics, and in the 1970s and early 1980s, with its forays into industrial biotechnology and medical diagnostics. In each case, Corning recognized the significance of an impending technological revolution (first, microelectronics, then, biotechnology) and positioned itself to take advantage of it well in advance of other firms. Nonetheless, the company was never able to build the technological capabilities needed to achieve a leadership position in these new fields, and one of the consequences seems to have been a reinforcement of the historical strategic focus.

> I [Dave Duke] think we've concluded that it's going to be very difficult for us to compete in the long term, with sus-

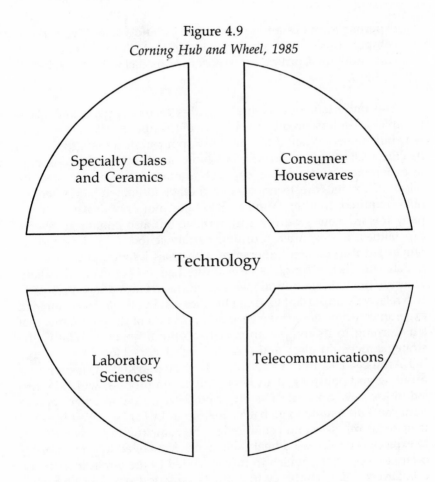

Figure 4.9
Corning Hub and Wheel, 1985

Specialty Glass
and Ceramics

Consumer
Housewares

Technology

Laboratory
Sciences

Telecommunications

tainable competitive advantage, in things that are out of our main area of expertise. When I look at it [i.e., Corning's expertise], I look at materials in general: glass, ceramics, glass-ceramics, and the interfaces between these and polymers, metals, and so forth. But to compete in medical, medical diagnostics, biotechnology—it requires an enormous amount of R&D and technology, and we just couldn't compete. So we said, let's try to refocus. . . . Each time we got too far from our home base, we didn't know enough about the technology or the markets and therefore we had to find partners or sell off the technology. We have been able to get into new areas like optical fiber, where we took our knowledge of glass and leveraged that to get ahead into more of the telecommunications business. So we've now built an expertise in optics and optoelectronics, and we feel we can compete pretty well with anybody in that. But that's again core stuff for Corning as opposed to medicine or biotechnology.

The importance of maintaining this focus on glass and glass-ceramics is underscored by the history of Corning's efforts to develop new businesses. When it has pursued opportunities that grow out of its core technologies, Corning has built on an ever-expanding base of experiences and capabilities. Each attempt to develop a new application for its core technology—whether ultimately successful or not—required another round of R&D that not only drove the company toward new products and markets but also enhanced its core capabilities. For example, Corning's strategic focus on glass and ceramics led it to diverse experience with glass lasers, optical glasses, and fused silica. The glass laser effort had no commercial payoff, whereas the work in optical glasses and fused silica did contribute to two relatively important Corning businesses. But it was the combined experience from these three very different sets of developments that led Corning to its unique approach to optical fibers. Similarly, the strategic focus on glass and ceramics led Amory Houghton to urge Bill Armistead to find a way of making high-quality glass without grinding and polishing. This led to the fusion process, which in turn led to the development of safety windshields, several other applications, and ultimately to global leadership in LCD glass. And the strategic focus on glass and ceramics led the company in the early 1960s to explore ceramic-based heat exchangers, which led to substrates for catalytic converters, which in turn have led to the application of the cellular ceramic technology to markets ranging from filtering metals in iron foundries to catalytic combustors in wood stoves. The underlying cellular-ceramic technology stems from the R&D that led to Corning Ware, which in turn was an offshoot of the development of photosensitive glass.

Rather than independent forays into new markets, each new attempt to grow a glass- or glass-ceramic-based business is thus part of a stream of such efforts, each drawing from and in turn contributing to a growing base of experience. Over time, this base of experience develops into a formidable source of competitive advantage—but only if Corning remains true to its focus. Entering new fields like integrated circuits and biotechnology neither draws on this base of experience nor contributes to it. The many attempts to develop new products and businesses within the strategic area of focus do both.

This iterative process between an ever-expanding body of glass and ceramic technology and diverse efforts to develop new glass- and ceramic-based products and businesses exemplifies what a growing number of scholars refer to as the "core competence" of the corporation.[77] Prahalad and Hamel, and Teece, Pisano, and Shuen, for example, argue that the successful competitors in global markets are best understood by examining not the strategic positioning of their individual lines of business (which is the approach dictated by conventional wisdom), but rather their critical competencies that cut across those lines of businesses. The diversified company, Prahalad and Hamel write, should be conceived of as

> a large tree. The trunk and major limbs are core products, the smaller branches are business units; the leaves, flowers, and fruit are end products. The root system that provides nourishment, sustenance, and stability is the core competence. You can miss the strength of competitors by looking only at their end products, in the same way you miss the strength of a tree if you look only at its leaves.[78]

When viewed in these terms, Corning is rooted in the technologies associated with material composition, processing, and application of glass and ceramics. Its major limbs include optical fibers, which in turn is comprised of several smaller branches and leaves such as specialty fibers, optical fiber components, long-haul fibers, fibers for the local loop, and cable; Celcor, which branches off into catalytic converter substrates, diesel filters, molten metal filters, wood stove combustors, and power plant pollution-control devices; and display glass, which has two major branches, video and flat panel.

How to compete in those markets. In the diverse markets in which it does attempt to compete, Corning's goal has always been to be a market leader. As *Forbes* described in 1962, in the post-war period, Corning often found itself "in the happy position of pretty much leading its field in nearly every product line."[79] The TV bulb business, with its 125 percent market share, was the outstanding example. The new businesses that Corning has built since that era continue to emphasize market leadership, but it is a class of leadership very different from the one practiced earlier. In the TV business, Corning built its position on being first to market with unique, high-performance products for which it charged a premium. For Celcor, fiber optics, and LCD glass, leadership still means first to market with superior product performance, but now it also means cost leadership. Leadership in the new Corning means being first to market with the best-performing, lowest-cost products. In each of its new businesses, from Celcor to memory disk substrates, it has explicitly attempted to drive down a cost-learning curve (e.g., reducing the cost of optical fibers from $12 per meter to $.15), to drive down a performance-learning curve (e.g., reducing the attenuation levels of fibers by several orders of magnitude), and to do so on both counts ahead of its competitors.

The same applies to Corning's Laboratory Services business, where if anything, the drive to combine both cost and performance leadership is even greater given the reduced basis for product differentiation in a business that offers services not unlike those of the competition. The corporatewide emphasis on quality also contributes to this pursuit of leadership. The drive to improve total quality—which in the optical fiber business reduced the number of defects in a new coating process from 800 parts per million in 1986 to 275 parts per million in 1987 to zero in 1988—has a dual effect of reducing costs (by simplifying production processes as well as reducing the need for inspection, rework, and recall) and enhancing product differentiation (through higher quality).

What motivated a form of leadership that is far more ambitious than the more conventional version of the traditional Corning businesses? The answer is competition. Duke's warning—"If we tie, we lose"—highlights the critical issue. When competing against larger firms, with substantially greater resources and better access to markets, product parity is the first step to a failing business. The competition had the capacity to outspend Corning in R&D, outinvest Corning in new plant and equipment, and outsell it with superior market access. If the terms of the competition were ever to shift from technology to access to resources, Corning would inevitably lose. By maintaining performance and cost leadership, Corning was able to prevent this shift.

The threat of Japanese competition in particular proved to be a major stimulus for this approach, Duke remembers:

> It was very clear to us as we looked at the history of what had happened in consumer electronics and automobiles and so on that Japan had been very successful at deciding where it wanted to put its bucks, protecting its internal industry, doing a lot of cooperative work early, getting to the point that all the early R&D was done, and then turning everybody loose and knocking each other's brains out and coming down the learning curve, while still protecting Japanese markets. And then when they were big and strong, they'd just go out after the world and take over an industry. If I were in Japan, I'd probably use the same strategy, but for

an American firm trying to compete with that, it is very tough, and so we used to say that we have to fight the Japanese everywhere. We have to fight them in the United States, we have to fight them in Europe, we have to fight them in Australia, we have to fight them in Japan. And we are going to fight them every way we can. We've got to use all the political influence we have [to open up their markets], and all the legal means [to protect Corning's patents], but in addition, we must beat them the old-fashioned way. We have to fight them with better products and lower costs.

As the history of the optical fiber business makes clear, this leadership strategy is extremely resource-intensive, requiring continuing high levels of investment in R&D and plant and equipment. No company, and certainly not one of Corning's size, can afford many such efforts. This suggests an important relationship between Corning's pursuit of leadership and its strategic focus. If it had any hope at all of achieving a leadership position, it would have to limit its efforts to growing new businesses in domains where it possessed unique strengths—that is, opportunities that built on its unique store of experiences. Corning's strategic focus and leadership strategy thus went hand in hand. The decisions to exit industrial biotechnology and medical diagnostic products, for example, stemmed as much from the recognition that Corning did not have the technical strengths to achieve leadership in these new fields as it did from the recognition that it would have to concentrate its resources in those areas where it was strong.

In those limited areas where it did pursue leadership, Corning also exhibited a cluster of related practices: aggressive protection of patents, building capacity ahead of demand, and when necessary, utilizing joint ventures to gain market access. The battle to protect patents was especially important in the field of optical fibers. Why did Corning protect its patents so vigorously in optical fibers when its leadership strategy dictated that it continuously strive to make its technology obsolete? This question was often raised, especially in light of the expensive legal battles that Corning was forced to wage in order to protect its patents. Some inside Corning argued that it made more sense

> to get on with the next generation of product than fight over the current one. . . . But Duke pointed out the long picture. Few materials companies, he said, put as much into research as Corning: over $100 million a year. Out of all that, he said, the firm might get one major breakthrough a decade. The

only way to continue a high level of research was to get the maximum possible profit from each of those breakthrough products.[80]

This does not imply that Corning limited its pursuit of leadership to areas where it had a unique patent position. In LCD glass, for instance, the patents on Corning's fusion process have expired. If anything, this has only intensified the drive for technology improvements.

A second practice that complemented the leadership strategy was building capacity ahead of demand—not just in optical fibers but in Celcor, when the European market began to take off in the late 1980s, and in the emergent businesses in LCD glass and memory device substrates as well. Again, the driving force was competition—direct and indirect. Having the capacity to meet demand when it finally did emerge in each of these businesses enabled Corning to build volume ahead of the competition, which is critical for cost leadership in businesses like optical fibers, LCD glass, and Celcor, which have strong learning effects and scale economies. At the same time, it enabled Corning to stay ahead of competing technologies. In the early days of optical fibers, for example, Corning was competing not just with other fiber suppliers but with suppliers of satellite, microwave, and conventional telecommunications equipment. If Corning had not been ready to meet the early large orders from MCI and GTE, those companies may well have turned not to competing fiber vendors, but to vendors of competing technologies.

Corning's reliance on joint ventures, in contrast, had less to do with competition than it did with market access. By far the most important joint venture in Corning's history is Dow Corning (the worldwide leading supplier of silicones), which in 1990 had total sales of $1.7 billion (compared to total Corning 1990 revenues of $3 billion), and contributed $82.7 million to Corning's total net income (after taxes and interest) of $292 million. This joint venture was established in the early 1940s, after Corning had developed the underlying technology but decided it needed Dow's manufacturing and marketing expertise in order to exploit it. Unlike Dow Corning, which is unrelated to Corning's primary strategic interests, the joint ventures that Corning formed during its transformation were of direct strategic concern. In effect, they enabled Corning to extend the markets in which it could take advantage of its technology and product leadership. Most of these joint ventures were formed as part of the attempt to develop the optical fiber business. Many provided Corning with access to relatively closed foreign telecommunications markets. Others enabled Corning to integrate forward into related markets.

Siecor, Corning's joint venture with Siemens for manufacturing fiber optic cables (as opposed to unsheathed fiber), is the primary example. It was formed in 1977 and grew to a reported $300 million in sales by 1990.[81]

In the LCD glass business, Corning has not had to rely on this kind of market-extending joint venture, even though most of its customer base is in Japan. Part of the explanation is historical. Corning has been supplying LCD glass to Japanese display makers since the earliest days of the industry. A more important explanation may be the degree of fragmentation of the regional market for LCD glass as opposed to optical fibers. In the latter case, it was not uncommon for the market in each country to be controlled by a national telecommunications organization of one sort or another (e.g., NTT in Japan or the British Post Office). Each organization typically had an interest in ensuring local participation in the development of any telecommunications network, which led Corning to form its many joint ventures. The LCD market, in contrast, is highly competitive in Japan. And in a highly competitive market, it is in the interest of each competitor, whether it be Sharp or Matsushita or Hitachi or NEC, to seek out the best-performing components for its LCDs at the lowest available price.

One other set of joint ventures prominent in Corning's recent history grew not out of a desire to leverage Corning's leadership, but rather out of an inability to establish its leadership. Genencor (the joint venture with Genentech in industrial biotechnology) and Ciba Corning (the joint venture with Ciba Geigy in medical diagnostics) were designed to compensate for Corning's relative weakness in life sciences. The company has since divested its interest in both. Similarly, in 1988, Corning transferred its TV and video display glass business into a joint venture with Asahi Glass—Corning Asahi Video Products. In effect, this joint venture represented an acknowledgment by Corning that despite a major commitment to upgrade both products and manufacturing in the mid-1980s, it could not achieve a leadership position in this business on its own. This joint venture strengthens Corning's relations with Japanese manufacturers of TV and display equipment, and it also provides access to Asahi's technology, particularly glass technology for large-screen TVs where Asahi is especially strong.

Technology Strategy

Corning's technology strategy, like Motorola's, is so thoroughly tied to its business strategy that it is difficult to distinguish one from the other. The pursuit of cost and performance leadership in its markets hinges on technology leadership. Corning's ability to create new lines of business, like optical fibers and LCD glass, has been a result of its successful efforts to pioneer developments in and applications of its core glass and ceramics technology. And its ability to maintain leadership in those new businesses once they were created has been a result of the success with which it continually renews and improves the technology underlying them.

Creating new businesses—in search of the big hits. One of the most distinctive features of Corning's technology strategy is its overt "big hit" mentality. This is not to say that more continuous incremental innovation is unimportant to Corning, but, except for laboratory services, the major new businesses that Corning has grown during the past 20 years, like the major businesses it grew in earlier times, have been built on the basis of technological breakthroughs. Dave Duke agrees that it is also important

> to keep doing the incremental improvements. We have got to maintain the products we have. All of us look very hard at the products we do have. How do we extend them? How do we improve them? How do we make more money this year and next? But one of the things that I think Corning has done really better than many others has been this kind of home run mentality. And if you go back in our history, it seems like about every ten years we get one big one. I mean we get a lot of little ones, we get a lot of singles, but we get these big ones every once in a while.

As is true for Motorola and GE Medical, general management plays a critical if not driving role in Corning's pursuit of the big hit. During the 1960s, Amory Houghton actively encouraged an unfettered pursuit of the "next whale." In the 1970s, a time of financial crises and restructuring, it was Houghton again, along with Mac-Avoy, who protected the nascent Celcor and optical fiber businesses from the many skeptics and insisted that they receive sufficient funding, just as it was Houghton who began to push for the next hit (which turned out to be industrial biotechnology) in the second half of the 1970s. In a telling interview with the Corning employee newspaper shortly after the company had to drastically reduce its workforce in 1975, Houghton had this to say about pursuing the big hit:

> I'd have to cite my father. His warning: "Don't worry about being schizophrenic in running an organization today. Hold costs tighter than a drum, but spend the money and drive home the big opportunity when it comes along." . . . Nine-

tenths of wisdom is being wise in time. So the question I always ask myself is this: Are we moving fast enough on some of the bigger, more far-reaching developments? Time is so critical, because others—maybe not as creative in some areas—catch up and pass us by if we're not equally good at using as well as developing technology.[82]

Why is the active involvement, if not interference, of senior management critical to new business development? The answer seems to involve the magnitude of the required investments and time horizons. Each successful big hit emerged only after large risks had been taken, similar to Motorola's experience with the decade-long, pre-emergent stage in each new line of business that it created. Celcor required a massive R&D effort, with unprecedented capital investment and speed of scale-up, for customers who were lobbying Congress to repeal or limit the legislation that had created the market. Optical fibers consumed 17 years and $100 million of R&D (in addition to investment capital) before Corning finally received the MCI order and began to turn a profit. Comparable levels of R&D and investment are now being spent in the LCD display glass business. This kind of investment and risk simply cannot be made without, as Duke put it, "top-management sponsorship or having a believer at the top who can get rid of all of the nonsense that you have to put up with." Incremental innovation offers more predictable outcomes and more comforting levels of risk. But new business creation—pursuit of the big hit—by its very nature creates legions of skeptics, and it is only general management that can protect new business prospects from those legions. In Tom MacAvoy's experience,

> the organization has this desire to allocate resources in a rational and democratic process. Ultimately though, [to bring a big hit candidate to fruition] something irrational has to be done, and by irrational I mean deciding that something like optical waveguides or the automotive emissions control . . . requires resources that transcend the normal allocation process. You have got to marshal a lot of resources for a major thrust, and it is when top management recognizes two or three steps along in the innovative process that something has the potential for being big that it starts thinking about how [it] can . . . get more resources into this thing.[83]

Existing businesses—pursuing the learning curves. If creating new businesses through the technological big hit is a dominant feature of Corning's technology strategy, maintaining cost and performance leadership once those businesses have been established through continuing improvements in technology is its complement. This pattern was first set in Celcor, then explicitly pursued by the same team of managers in optical fibers, and is now being applied with equal rigor to LCD glass and memory substrates.

Corning's practice of continuing innovation is similar to Motorola's technology roadmap process. Future levels of product performance and cost required to maintain market leadership are projected, and these projections drive today's R&D. Duke describes this process:

> What you have to do is anticipate what the technology is going to look like, what consumers are going to want, what's going to make them satisfied. . . . You've got to be looking out three or five years ahead and say, Where do I want to be? What kind of product do I want to have? How will I do the manufacturing? How do I get that kind of a cost curve? And that says you've got to have some forward vision of where you're going to go, and then you have got to have the courage of your convictions to allocate the resources to make it happen.

Achieving these projected levels of performance and cost require innovations in both product and process technology. In the optical fiber business during the 1970s, for example, Duke and his associates projected that single-mode fiber would be required by the mid-1980s and that costs would have to be reduced from $12 a meter to $.15. They therefore began R&D on both the new product and new processes well in advance of the projected need. As it turned out, the MCI order forced them to move even more quickly on both fronts than they had anticipated, but the fact that they had been applying this discipline enabled them to respond successfully. Similarly, 15 years later in the LCD business, R&D was being targeted both at developing new types of glass and at improving the fusion process for making the glasses that had already been introduced. Most of the emphasis was being placed on process improvements because they led to both improved product quality and lower costs.

The class of innovation required to satisfy this continuous pursuit of product improvements and cost reductions involves much more than incremental extensions of existing technology. In optical fibers, for example, the innovations that have enabled Corning to maintain its competitive standing have been entirely new generations of products and processes. In 15 years, Corning has progressed through seven generations of processing equipment, each one making the preceding generation obsolete. The introduction of each new generation was followed by incremental improvements that enhanced efficiency. As these improvements were being made, the next generation was being readied for implementation, and yet another generation was under development.

Centralized R&D. Underlying Corning's ability to create new businesses with the occasional technological big hit and then to successfully renew those businesses with generational innovations in product and process technology is a strong, centralized corporate R&D lab. The importance that the company attaches to the lab is reflected in its senior management structure. Corning has had a vice chairman of technology, to whom the lab reports, since 1971. The current vice chairman is Dave Duke who was general manager of two of Corning's most important new businesses—Celcor and optical fibers; his predecessor was Tom MacAvoy who was president of the company for over a decade; and MacAvoy's predecessor was Bill Armistead. Although he never ran a business, he worked closely and directly with Amory Houghton during the 1970s.

Corning spends roughly 5.4 percent of operating revenues (excluding the laboratory services businesses) on R&D, the bulk of which is accounted for by the corporate lab. This is roughly comparable to its past R&D spending and is not an especially large amount of R&D for a research-intensive business. But more significant than the rate of growth and relative magnitude of Corning's R&D spending is its centralized nature. Glass and ceramics technology represents Corning's core competence, and the corporate lab is the depository of that competence. It is the lab that transfers much of the knowledge and experience gained from one iteration between core technology and market application to the next.

The lab also serves as a "force in waiting" that can be quickly marshalled and applied to major new opportunities on the occasions when they do arise. In each of its major successes, Corning mounted large, concentrated R&D efforts. For example, at its peak, Celcor consumed one-quarter of the corporate R&D lab's total resources. Dave Duke traces the practice back to Bill Armistead (former vice chairman of technology): "Bill is the role model I [as current vice chairman of technology] use. He had this passion—when he saw a big one, it was 'Katie bar the door and let's go do this thing and really make it happen.'" Duke can only take this approach because Corning, unlike many other U.S. firms, has maintained a strong corporate R&D lab. MacAvoy explains:

> When we come up with an optical waveguides, which we
> do every once in a while because we're working on the outer

fringe of this core area of technology, one of the reasons we can implement it is because we have what I like to call a flexible critical mass of technical people. We can put together people . . . and provide a driving wedge into the future. We've done it over and over again. Every seven to ten years, it seems, we blow the whistle, and everybody forms up. . . . So there is a certain kind of critical mass that we have to have. We don't know exactly how big it has to be, but we know we have to have it.

In recent years, corporate labs have fallen out of favor in many U.S. firms. They are often viewed as too isolated from the operating businesses and their markets. It is therefore interesting to note that most of the corporate R&D that led to Corning's big hits was triggered and driven by customer requests or perceived market needs. To be sure, a good deal of fundamental research was involved, but most of the major R&D had a specific, applied target. Celcor was initiated by interactions with General Motors and was from the outset aimed at developing substrates for the catalytic converter. Optical fibers grew out of interactions with a potential customer—the British Post Office—and was originally aimed at developing glass fibers with attenuation levels below 20 db/km so that they could be used to replace the capacity-limiting, copper-cable-based telephone networks. The current LCD glass business was a result of the realization by a group at the corporate lab, later reinforced by customer requests, that LCD makers would need higher-performance glass. The most notable exception was industrial biotechnology. The outcome of the serendipitous discovery of a new use for Corning's porous glass, it was more reminiscent of the classic pattern of technology push—of a technology "solution" in search of a market "problem."

Decision-Making Style and Technology

The search for new businesses and learning by doing. Turning from general management's business and technology strategy to the decision-making style behind them, there is again a pattern consistent with that seen in our other cases. The most striking feature of the style of decision making employed by Corning's general management is how closely it conforms to the "learning by doing" style found in the histories of both GE Medical and Motorola Communications. Each of Corning's major new businesses evolved in piecemeal fashion, one development or experience leading to the next, few of them anticipated. Two examples are laboratory services and LCD glass. In laboratory services, experience supplying glassware to scientific laboratories led Corning into the pH meter business. This led to the blood gas analysis business, which grew into a diagnostic products business, which in turn led to Corning's entry into diagnostic services with the acquisition of MetPath. The subsequent successes of Met-Path led to an expansion into the scientific (as opposed to medical) lab services businesses. Meanwhile the diagnostic products businesses that had been the driving force behind the diversification into services was eventually spun off into a joint venture and then divested. Twenty-five years of mostly incremental steps forward, each building on the experiences of the previous step, led to an entirely unforeseen cluster of businesses unlike any in Corning's history and which, in the span of a decade, had grown to one-quarter the size of the entire corporation.

LCD glass followed a similar pattern. Development of the fusion process was triggered by the desire to develop a method for making sheet glass without grinding or polishing. It evolved instead into a process for making thin, high-quality specialty glass, which was first applied unsuccessfully to safety windshields and then, among other things, to the production of sheets of photochromic glass for lenses. Meanwhile, during the 1970s, Corning had been supplying the nascent LCD market with glass made from a more conventional process. As the market grew and customers began requesting higher-performing glass, the company turned in the mid-1980s to the fusion process, first using it to make an already established glass and then a glass specifically developed for LCDs. As Corning continued to respond to the ever-increasing market demand for high-performance LCD glass, it found itself in the late 1980s with not only a new business opportunity but also an opportunity with a long-term growth potential comparable to optical fibers.

Celcor evolved more closely along the path that had been expected when Houghton, MacAvoy, and their associates began to support its development in the early 1970s, but even here, the pattern of building on often unexpected experiences is apparent. When MacAvoy went to GM to talk about cellular ceramics, he had in mind the gas turbine heat exchanger that had been under development for a decade. Out of his visit came the totally unforeseen opportunity in catalytic converters, which spawned a series of new business opportunities in molten metal filters, diesel filters, and the like a decade later. As for optical fibers, the road to eventual success is filled with unexpected developments, from the surprising lack of market interest in the early 1970s, to the divestiture of AT&T in the early 1980s, to the earlier and more severe than expected slump in the long-distance market in the mid-1980s, to the more rapid than expected emergence of the local loop market in the late 1980s. None of this is to suggest that the businesses evolved in random or blind trial-and-error fashion. In each instance, they followed the general course that had been hoped for, but the specific form they took, the specific market and technological developments to which they had to respond as they followed that general course, were not, and could not have been, anticipated.

Evaluating new business opportunities. Given the uncertainties and unexpected developments that marked the evolution of each of the major new businesses, it is not surprising to find a good deal of caution, if not skepticism, expressed by senior management about the uses to which traditional financial and market analysis tools should be put, particularly in the early stages of new business development. As MacAvoy explained when he was in the midst of the optical fiber effort in 1978:

> You can't allocate resources to a business like that on the basis of internal rate of return calculations. It's a major strategic decision—either we're in the business or not—and we're in it. The main question we ask is whether they can use more engineers or capital funds than they've requested.[84]

Dick Dulude, looking back on Celcor, optical fibers, and several other new businesses that he had been responsible for, makes a similar argument:

> You can make the numbers come out any way you want, especially early in the development. I can give you a generic business plan that has $50 million dollars worth of sales in five years, 10 percent net profit after tax, the net present value is right—they're all the same. Another thing you know is that the business plan you see is not what you are going to actually get. The numbers all change. I'll sell a generic business plan to anybody that wants to go into business because they all look the same. I know I sound cynical about this, but if you're spending all your time replanning the business plan and putting down the projections to the eighth decimal point, you are worried about the wrong thing, you really are.

This does not mean that Corning is uninterested in achieving returns that exceed its cost of capital. "It's not that any of us are saps, you know. We all want to make money," states MacAvoy. Nor does it mean that Corning did not perform financial analyses. The issue is the extent to which general management was guided by the results of such analysis during these critical early stages in the development of each of the new businesses. Dave Duke explains that in the several new-business development efforts that he managed, discounted cash flow calculations were performed as a matter of course. However,

> I didn't believe most of them. In fact, in a lot of the big ones that I went through, the financial people cranked out the numbers and we were never going to make any money. But those of us who were close enough to it knew that if you changed two or three assumptions, you could get the numbers to come out any way you wanted. We crank the numbers. We go through what the cash flows will be, how much it's going to take, and what the market shares will be. We have the analysts crank out all kinds of numbers to make sure we get a feel for them. . . . But I rely on my experience and intuitive sense of what assumptions to make.

If senior management's decisions about new business development were not based on projections of future financial performance, what were they based on? The answer to this question has changed considerably over the past three decades. During the 1960s' unfettered search for big hits, the determination of whether to pursue a new business opportunity seemed to be most heavily influenced by the company's focus on glass and ceramics. With the notable exception of its foray into electronics, the opportunities pursued during this period—for example, glass razor blades, glass drainpipes, glass lasers, ceramic roofing shingles, safety windshields, optical fibers, ceramic heat exchangers for automotive gas turbines—were the product of what is best characterized as an undisciplined pursuit of glass- and ceramic-based opportunities. During the financially difficult 1970s, the emphasis shifted to screening out from among the many possibilities that had been identified in the 1960s, the opportunities that appeared to be most promising from a market perspective. At the same time, however, the focus on glass and ceramics weakened. The only major new opportunities identified for development in the mid- and late 1970s—medical diagnostics and biotechnology—fell outside the traditional areas of strength.

The strategic decision making exhibited during James Houghton's tenure combines elements of both earlier eras. On the one hand, we see a renewed emphasis on the traditional domains of strength, which is reminiscent of the 1960s. On the other hand, reflecting James Houghton's overriding concern with improving the profitability of the company, the search for new businesses based on these traditional areas of strength is much more disciplined than it was in the 1960s, which is reminiscent of the 1970s. Glass- and ceramic-based opportunities are once again emphasized—but only if they lead Corning into young, fast-growing markets. Corning is still "trolling" for big hits, to use MacAvoy's analogy, but it is doing so much more selectively.

Criteria for screening opportunities. Over the course of this 30-year period, Corning's general management has thus evolved a decision logic for screening and selecting new business opportunities that in many respects is similar to the qualitative, experience-based logic applied by Motorola's general management. Duke, Dulude, and Mac-Avoy each have a different way of describing this decision calculus. In Duke's words:

> We have a whole series of checklists and guidelines, our own internal innovation guide with a series of questions that you need to answer at the research stage or development stage or pilot plant stage. But we also have a lot of experience. I have been doing this for 30 years now. I've been through 4 or 5 of them [major new-business development efforts] for Corning and as a result, we can look at it, and determine what will be our sustainable competitive advantage. Do we know something about the market? Do we see access to customers? Do we have some sort of real advantage—some unique process or unique product that we think gives us that advantage to win over not just the first year, but over the 10 or 20 or 30 years or the lifetime of the product? We look at these questions and we analyze them . . . Is it real? Can you win? Is it worth it?

"Is it real?" is a question about both the market and the technology. "Can you win?" is a question about Corning's strengths relative to the competition, and, of course, "Is it worth it?" has to do with the potential magnitude of the opportunity and the potential return.

Dick Dulude describes a similar logic, though he places special emphasis on what might be considered the profit potential inherent in the business opportunity.

> This sounds really simplistic, but I have a question that I always ask: "How do we make money on this?" If I can't understand in simple terms how you can make money on this, we probably shouldn't be involved. . . . It's very different from asking, "How *much* money are you going to make on this?" *How* are you going to make money on it?" . . .

Technology is interesting, marketing is interesting, but if you can't figure out simply how you are going to make money on something, . . . I don't believe that it is ever going to happen.

Tom MacAvoy, from a third perspective, argues for much the same kind of decision-making logic: "We have this visceral conviction that if it's important and you can be the leader, and the market is going to happen, and it builds on your strengths, do it."

Decision making and the maintenance of leadership. Once the business has been established and the product is approaching or is already out in the marketplace, the general managerial decision-making task in each of these businesses shifts from whether and how to pursue the opportunity to how to maintain leadership in the face of intense competition. At this stage, the greatest uncertainties have been reduced. A better understanding of the market, of competitive standing, and of costs and selling price have been achieved, and financial projections become more meaningful. But even here, they serve more as a constraint than as a driver of the decision-making process. The impetus in each new generation of Corning's businesses remains the imperative to maintain cost and performance leadership.

This is not to say that the financial performance is unimportant; on the contrary, as we have seen, rising profitability was one of James Houghton's continuing points of emphasis through the decade, with return on equity growing steadily from 9 percent at the end of 1983, to 14.2 percent in 1987, to 16.3 percent in 1990. But within Corning's major new-growth businesses, financial performance was seen by general management as the measure of results rather than as determining decisions about the future. The continuing pursuit of leadership shapes the plans for investment and R&D spending—unless and until that pursuit fails to achieve acceptable returns. At that point, the response is not so much to cut back on investment, which will only weaken the business's competitive position and therefore its long-term financial prospects, but to rethink the viability of the business. In Dick Dulude's opinion,

That's what general management is all about—balancing the need to stay ahead and the need to maintain the high, steady rate of investment against the financial resources available to you. . . . The bean counters are necessary and useful, but they don't run the business. The time that they are really important is when you have the business in a deep dive, and their role is to wave the red flag and point out that last year you didn't have the returns, and the previous year you didn't, and that's when they start asking you the tough questions. But the way you decide whether or not to continue to invest to maintain that leadership—you do that by asking those same questions: Is this a big market? Do I believe in my people? Can I make money at this? If the answers are there, you do it.

Notes

1. This study would not have been possible without the permission generously granted by David Duke, vice chairman, and without the patient assistance provided by William Armistead, former vice chairman for Technology; Forrest Behm, former senior vice president, general manager and corporate director of Quality; Richard Dulude, vice chairman and former group president; John Hutchins, former senior vice president of R&D; Thomas MacAvoy, former president and vice chairman; and from the Corporate R&D Lab, William Dumbaugh, research fellow; Theodore Kozlowski, director Technical Products Development; and William Prindle, division vice president and associate director for Technology.

    Unless otherwise specified, the study is based on interviews with these individuals; Corning's annual reports, 1967–1990; and Corning's employee newspaper, *Corning World* (formerly, *The Gaffer*), 1971–1990.
2. "Corning Glass Works: Long-Term Gains Seen," *Forbes*, November 1, 1968, p. 43.
3. "The Trials of Amory Houghton Jr.," *Forbes*, August 1, 1977, p. 34.
4. Lawrence Ingrassia, "A Select Few Poised to Lead into the '90s," *The Wall Street Journal*, June 23, 1989, eastern edition, p. A3.
5. For a typical projection of the future optical fiber market, see Edward Schollmeyer, "Corning Incorporated: Corning Enters New Dramatic Growth Era," PaineWebber, March 8, 1990; the $600 million annual sales estimate is from Keith H. Hammonds, "Corning's Class Act," *Business Week*, May 13, 1991, p. 71.
6. Sales estimate compiled from Schollmeyer, "Corning Incorporated," and Corning Annual Report, 1990, pp. 6, 24.
7. For an analysis of the LCD market, see H. Wakabayashi, "The Expanding Liquid Crystal Display Market," Nomura Securities International, April 1990.
8. "Corning Glass Works: Corporate Strategy and Managerial Philosophy," Video, 9–880–507, Harvard Business School Publishing Division.
9. "Turbine Engine Progress Slow but Sure," *The Gaffer* (November 1971), p. 4.
10. Jack Robertson, "Fiber Optics Market Due to Sprout," *Electronic News*, May 6, 1968, p. 32.
11. K. C. Kao and G. A. Hockham, "Dielectric Fiber Wave Guides for Light Communications," *Proceedings of the Institution of Electrical Engineers*, vol. 113 (July 1966), pp. 1151–1158; L. C. Gunderson, "A Case History of the

Optical Waveguide Project at Corning Glass Works," Corning, Research and Development Laboratory, L-2291, May 13, 1980, p. 2.

12. Ibid., p. 3.
13. John N. Kessler, "Fiber Optics Sharpens Focus on Laser Communication," *Electronics*, July 5, 1971, p. 47.
14. Stephen Kindel, "It Takes a Lot of Patience," *Forbes*, September 13, 1982, p. 83.
15. "CTV Imports Double in '76, ITC Told: Statements of Amory Houghton, Jr., and Allen W. Dawson," *The Gaffer* (February 1977), p. 7.
16. Ironically, in 1988, Corning folded its TV and video display business into a joint venture with Asahi Glass—but this JV was aimed primarily at the U.S. market rather than Japan's.
17. "The Trials of Amory Houghton, Jr.," p. 35.
18. Ibid.
19. GE was facing a similar problem in the 1970s, although its was an order of magnitude larger in scale. See Francis J. Aguilar, *General Managers in Action* (New York: Oxford University Press, 1988), pp. 258–308.
20. Dennis Mog, "What We Did Was Essential . . . Houghton," *The Gaffer* (December 1975), pp. 8, 11.
21. Arthur Daltas and Philip McDonald, "Corning Converts to Strategic Marketing," *Planning Review*, vol. 15 (March–April 1987), pp. 38–39.
22. "1983's Powerful New Words: Total Quality," *The Gaffer* (March 1984).
23. Ira Magaziner and Mark Patinkin, *The Silent War* (New York: Vintage Books, 1989), p. 280; "Glass Guide Loss Is Cut to 4 db/km," *Electronics*, September 11, 1972, p. 30.
24. Magaziner and Patinkin, *The Silent War*, p. 275.
25. Thomas MacAvoy, "Corning Glass Works and Optical Waveguides—A Pioneering Innovation," University of Virginia, Darden Graduate School of Business Administration, 1991.
26. Magaziner and Patinkin, *The Silent War*, p. 279.
27. Michael E. Porter, *Cases in Competitive Strategy* (New York: Free Press, 1983), p. 369.
28. Lucinda Mattera, "Fiber Optic Cable Is Multichannel," *Electronics*, May 15, 1975, p. 121.
29. "Light Wave of the Future," *Business Week*, September 1, 1975, p. 48.
30. Magaziner and Patinkin, *The Silent War*, p. 281.
31. Ibid., p. 282.
32. Ibid.
33. "Production at Pilot Plant for Waveguides Due by Summer," *The Gaffer* (April 1977), p. 2.
34. Hammonds, "Corning's Class Act," p. 71.
35. Corning Glass Works, Annual Report, 1978, p. 9.
36. Gary Taylor, "Genentech Plus Corning Equals Genencor," *Business Month* (July 1989), pp. 40–41.
37. Myron Magnet, "Corning Glass Shapes Up," *Forbes*, December 13, 1982, p. 100.

38. James R. Houghton, "Corning Glass Works Poised for an Exciting Entrance to a New Era," *The Gaffer* (April 1983), p. 7.
39. Ibid.
40. James R. Houghton, "Ahead: Tough Goals and a Hard Climb," *The Gaffer* (March 1984).
41. Ibid.
42. "Top Managers Commit Company to Total Quality Effort," *The Gaffer* (October 1983), p. 3.
43. Corning Glass Works, Annual Report, 1987, p. 3.
44. James Houghton, "Reach Again," *Corning World* (January 1990), p. 4.
45. "Specialty Glass and Ceramics Concentrate on Picking the Winners," *The Gaffer* (July 1987).
46. *The Wall Street Journal*, June 23, 1989, p. A3.
47. Corning Incorporated, Annual Report, 1990, p. 6; Philip Goodman, "Corning Glass Works," Duff and Phelps, July 8, 1988, p. 5.
48. Corning Incorporated, Annual Report, 1990, p. 2; Schollmeyer, "Corning Incorporated," p. 5.
49. Corning Incorporated, Annual Report, 1990, p. 7.
50. Corning Glass Works, Annual Report, 1984, p. 4.
51. Corning Glass Works, Annual Report, 1987, p. 17.
52. Hammonds, "Corning's Class Act," p. 70.
53. Magaziner and Patinkin, *The Silent War*, p. 288.
54. Corning data, as cited in Schollmeyer, "Corning Incorporated," p. 6.
55. 1984 sales estimate is from Robert Barker, "The Future Is Now," *Barrons*, August 12, 1985; 1986 sales estimate is from Mark Hassenberg, "Corning Glass Works (GLW)," Donaldson, Lufkin & Jenrette, 0198–89, February 27, 1989, p. 5; income estimate is from Anthony Baldo, "Why Give Chase to Corning?," *Financial World*, August 22, 1989, p. 8.
56. Corning data, as cited in Schollmeyer, "Corning Incorporated," p. 8.
57. Anne Hyde, "Patent Nonsense: The Fight over Fiber Optics," *Electronic Business*, November 15, 1984, pp. 24–26.
58. Schollmeyer, "Corning Incorporated," p. 4.
59. Hammonds, "Corning's Class Act," p. 71.
60. James R. Houghton, "The Role of Technology in Restructuring a Company," *Research Management*, vol. XXVI (November–December 1983), p. 16.
61. Corning Glass Works, Annual Report, 1983, p. 5.
62. E. Martin Gibson, "Consumer, MetPath, Science: Reduce Costs, Meet Market Needs," *The Gaffer* (March 1987).
63. Hammonds, "Corning's Class Act," p. 70.
64. Author's estimate, based on data in Hassenberg, "Corning Glass Works (GLW)," p. 5, and Corning Incorporated, Annual Report, 1990, p. 26.
65. Corning Incorporated, Annual Report, 1989, p. 26.
66. James R. Houghton, "Corning Reorganizes," *Corning World* (November–December 1990), pp. 1, 4.
67. Wakabayashi, "The Expanding Liquid Crystal Display Market," p. 5.

68. John Loose, "Expecting a Big Return," *Corning World* (January–February 1991), p. 7.
69. "Technical Products Reaches for New Market Share," *The Gaffer* (December 1987).
70. Hammonds, "Corning's Class Act," p. 71.
71. John Holusha, "Corning's Slenderized Hard Disk," *New York Times*, May 5, 1991, Sec. 3, p. 8.
72. "Their Most Important Product," *Forbes*, February 1, 1962, p. 21.
73. Corning Glass Works, Annual Report, 1968, p. 2.
74. Kindel, "It Takes a Lot of Patience," p. 84.
75. Houghton, *Research Management*, p. 9.
76. Houghton, "Corning Reorganizes," p. 1.
77. C. K. Prahalad and Gary Hamel, "The Core Competence of the Corporation," *Harvard Business Review*, vol. 68 (May–June 1990), pp. 79–91; David Teece, Gary Pisano, and Amy Shuen, "Firm Capabilities, Resources and the Concept of Strategy," University of California at Berkeley, Center for Research in Management, Consortium on Competitiveness and Cooperation, Working Paper 90–8, December 1990.
78. Prahalad and Hamel, "The Core Competence of the Corporation," p. 82.
79. "Their Most Important Product," p. 20.
80. Magaziner and Patinkin, *The Silent War*, p. 293.
81. Schollmeyer, "Corning Incorporated," p. 4.
82. Mog, "What We Did Was Essential . . . Houghton," pp. 8, 10.
83. "Corning Glass Works: Tom MacAvoy Talks About Technology," Video, 9-882-555, Harvard Business School Publishing Division.
84. Thomas Clough and Richard Vancil, "Corning Glass Works: Tom MacAvoy," 9-179-074. Boston: Harvard Business School, 1978, p. 4.

Appendix

Registered Trademarks of Corning Incorporated Cited in This Case
Celcor
Cercor
Corning Ware
PYROCERAM
Pyrex

PART II

ANALYSIS

CHAPTER 5

GENERAL MANAGERIAL PRACTICE AND TECHNOLOGY-BASED ADVANTAGE

Underlying the disappointing performance of U.S. firms in dynamic industries such as semiconductors, consumer electronics, and factory automation is a curious and disturbing paradox: technology-rich firms, based in a technology-rich society, are failing to compete effectively in technology-intensive industries. The goal of this book is to understand why. Why are some firms—whether foreign or domestic—more adept than others at competing on the basis of technology? Part of the explanation is macroconditions external to the firm. Another is the relative efficiency with which firms manage their technology functions. But there is a third factor at work, general management, and this has been the focus of our attention. How does general management contribute to (or detract from) the ability to build and sustain competitive advantage through technology, and is it possible to identify patterns in general managerial practice that are especially conducive to that process?

In seeking answers, we have retraced the history of three U.S. businesses competing in high-tech markets. These businesses are anything but typical. They are outliers—successes in precisely the kinds of fast-changing, short-cycle-time, technology-intensive markets in which U.S. firms have been notoriously unsuccessful. In history and culture, they could not be more different from each other. Motorola is a product of the Midwest and the pre-World War II evolution of the U.S. car industry; GE is the epitome of the diversified, multinational, East Coast, *Fortune* 100 giant; and Corning, while also highly diversified, is an order of magnitude smaller than GE, rural, and family dominated. But for all their differences, it is the similarities in how these businesses have gone about building their positions of global leadership that are most compelling. Their general managerial practices are as striking in their departure from conventional wisdom as they are in their similarity to each other. There are differences among them, but the similarities overshadow those differences and suggest the outlines of a model for successful, technology-based general management.

Business Strategy and Technology

Consistency of Strategic Focus

The similarities begin with the way general management defines the domains in which the businesses compete. In each case, a strategic focus is consistently articulated and applied not for years, but for decades. For GE Medical Systems (GEMS), the focus has been on diagnostic imaging since the mid-1970s; it does not view itself as a medical equipment business, as it did during its nearly disastrous effort to diversify in the 1960s and early 1970s; nor does it view itself simply as an X-ray equipment supplier. It is a diagnostic imaging business and strives to compete in every market for every diagnostic imaging modality. Similarly, since the 1960s, Motorola's communications business (COMM) has defined itself as in mobile and portable communications; it is not in communications per se, or in radio-based communications, but in communications with "people and machines on the move." And for Corning, this focus is defined in terms of its core technologies. It pursues virtually any new market to which its glass and ceramics technology can be uniquely applied. Its focus weakened during the 1970s, when it ventured into biotechnology and medical diagnostics in addition to pursuing glass- and ceramic-based opportunities, but by the mid-1980s, it had reaffirmed that its domain is based on glass and glass-ceramics technology.

Strategic focus and technology development. The strategic focus shapes the context for technology development in all these cases. This is especially apparent in the pursuit of major new-product lines or businesses. To most observers in the middle to late 1970s, optical fibers appeared to be a distant, high-risk possibility. But for Corning, while an optical fiber business sometimes seemed far off, it was of direct strategic relevance. It might not be successful for decades, and by then Corning might have grown an entirely new set of businesses in biotechnology, but for CEO Amory Houghton and president Tom MacAvoy, it was imperative that Corning be a major participant in the optical fiber market when it finally did emerge. Similarly, the risks associated with Iridium—the global portable cellular system that Motorola is developing—make COMM's 15-year, $150 million development of cellular telephones look like child's play. But the dimensions of that risk look very different to a firm that has "communication with people and machines on the move" as its strategic focus than they do to other firms. Iridium fits strategically; it is part of a stream of new mobile and portable communications business opportunities—from portable radios to pagers, to cellular telephones, to mobile and portable data equipment, to personal communications networks—that Motorola has been pursuing for more than 30 years.

GEMS has been evolving in a similar fashion. Since it established itself in computerized tomography (CT), it has followed up virtually every potential diagnostic imaging technology it has identified. It has not always succeeded, as attempts to develop ultrasound and digital X-ray systems attest. But it has been consistent in its pursuit of emerging diagnostic imaging technologies. Failures in ultrasound and digital X-ray were followed by the highly successful development of magnetic resonance (MR), which in turn has been followed by more recent explorations of new approaches to diagnostic imaging, including renewed efforts in ultrasound.

The influence of the strategic context on technology development is further illuminated by asking a classic question from the field of technology management: Was technology development in these businesses characterized more by "technology push" or "business strategy [or market] pull"? That is, were the technology development efforts of these innovative firms driven by new technologies and the vision of technologists, or were they shaped by the demands and interests of the businesses served by those technologists? On the one hand, there is considerable evidence of technology push. Innovations such as optical fibers, cellular phones, and high-field MR imaging were the result of opportunities created by technology well in advance of the interests and demands of the established lines of business. On the other hand, all these innovations fit the strategic focus of the firms where they were developed. They may have grown out of technology push, but the technology push was itself shaped by strategy pull. Marty Cooper (COMM's champion for portable cellular telephones) was a maverick, but he was also one of the leading disciples of the "mobile and portable religion." The interest Red Redington and his associates (the scientists at GE's corporate lab) expressed in MR in the late 1970s may have seemed infuriatingly irrelevant to GEMS as it struggled to make CT a success, but it clearly pertained to diagnostic imaging. The quest for optical fibers may have seemed quixotic to a company that had to struggle for profitability in the 1970s, but surely its strategic relevance was never in doubt. Every major technological innovation in these cases extended well beyond the field of view of the established businesses, but they fit well within the strategic focus.

At the more continuous level of innovation, this pattern is even more pronounced. The targets for technology development are shaped by the strategic interests of the current lines of business. The technology roadmaps employed by COMM illustrate this point most directly. Technology under development today is defined by the products projected to be needed for the business to maintain its leadership three to five to ten years in the future. Technology development in all three firms is product driven. In the lexicon used by the federal government, it is "applied" rather than "basic" research. Path-breaking science and engineering are still required at times, as are long time horizons; but in these three firms, technology development occurs within a clearly defined strategic context.

Strategic focus and persistence. In addition to defining the relevance of new technology-based opportunities, strategic focus also fuels the persistence required to bring opportunities to fruition once they are recognized as relevant. These cases are studded with examples of general management doggedly supporting the development of a major new line of business, despite daunting market and technology uncertainties and growing internal resistance. It is tempting to attribute this persistence to the vision of extraordinary individuals, or to the blind faith of the lucky. But a more accurate interpretation is that general management persisted because these opportunities made strategic sense. They fit the strategic focus. What to the outsider appears to be an act of extraordinary risk taking or uncommon vision appears to those operating within the strategic focus as good strategic sense. This is in large measure what Walt Robb meant by "We really didn't have any choice" but to persist with CT despite the long string of setbacks. If the controversial fan beam approach to CT had not been successful in the end, "we would have shifted to the fourth generation," the contending approach being pursued with some success by the competition. "You just never give in. You just *have* to make it one way or another."

Strategic consistency and managerial continuity. We would expect to find continuity of management in businesses that exhibit strategic consistency, and in these cases we do. Bill Weisz and John Mitchell, who served in Motorola's chief executive office in the 1970s and 1980s, were design engineers in COMM's mobile radio business in the 1950s. Tom MacAvoy, president of Corning in the 1970s and early 1980s, began his career in the corporate lab. For a quarter-century, Dave Duke managed Corning businesses that had grown out of the corporate lab, before becoming Corning's vice chairman for technology. And while Walt Robb came to GEMS from GE Silicones, he did serve as vice president of GEMS for 13 years. He began his career at GE's corporate R&D lab, and when he left GEMS in 1986, he was named senior vice president in charge of the lab.

This kind of continuity is more the exception than the rule in many American firms, where it is not uncommon to find a high rate of managerial turnover. At the same time that GEMS was developing MR under Walt Robb, for example, GE's robotics and vision business had three general managers in 5 years. A similar pattern—eight general managers in 13 years—was found in a recent study of a business in a major U.S. chemical company.[1] And Rosenbloom and Abernathy describe a pattern in U.S. consumer electronics firms of "high-level American executives seem[ing] to come and go and switch around as if playing a game of musical chairs at an Alice in Wonderland tea party."[2] Sometimes general managers are replaced because of their ineffectiveness, but often the turnover is the result of promotion and a reward system that places a premium on rising rapidly through the managerial ranks. What these cases of success show is that a high degree of turnover—even when associated with success—is fundamentally incompatible with building advantage on the basis of technology. The effort to develop the new generations of technology required to renew established businesses, let alone the far more difficult and time-consuming process of creating entirely new businesses, takes years of investment without significant return, inevitably accompanied by a string of crises, surprises, and disappointments. It is far less likely to be pushed to fruition if along the way the original general manager is replaced. The new manager, particularly if he or she comes from outside the organization, is likely to bring a different strategic point of view. The project that seemed imperative might seem like a luxury to the newcomer. And, if it is no longer imperative, then as the inevitable crises and conflicting demands for resources arise, the project is increasingly likely to be compromised. Moreover, in the absence of managerial continuity, new projects are less likely to build on prior experiences. Instead of a decades-long process, building on lessons from prior successes, partial successes, and even failures, one finds a more staccato pattern of individual projects, each given high priority for short periods of time before being eclipsed by a new high-priority effort directed at a new target.

   The chicken-egg question. How does the strategic focus originate? Does it predate the establishment of competitive advantage through technology, or does it follow from it? As Motorola's John Mitchell asks, "Which came first—the strategy or the success?" The answer is a combination of both. The strategic focus follows initial successes and, once established, promotes further success by channeling resources so as to sustain and expand the early successes. The egg leads to the chicken, which leads to more eggs.

   This pattern is perhaps most evident in the history of Motorola.

In the 1950s and early 1960s, COMM was "groping around" in new business areas ranging from hypersonic burglar alarms to precision test and measurement equipment and aircraft navigation and communication equipment. It was only in the 1960s, once the portable radio business was firmly established and the pager business was finally taking off, that the focus on mobile and portable communications was explicitly formulated.

During the late 1960s and early 1970s, GEMS was also groping. First it unsuccessfully attempted to diversify into a variety of medical equipment markets, and then during the early days of Robb's tenure, it retrenched and concentrated on the domestic market for X-ray equipment. The strategic focus on diagnostic imaging only emerged in the second half of the 1970s with the success in CT. Corning's history is somewhat different, but the same lesson applies. Its strategic focus on glass and ceramics technology was already well established when, in the 1960s and 1970s, it too went through a seemingly unfettered search for new businesses. Many of the opportunities it pursued—safety windshields, ceramic components for gas turbines, glass lasers—were within its traditional focus. But it was also during this period that Corning's focus weakened. It launched major drives to establish itself first in integrated circuits, then in medical equipment and industrial biotechnology. The eventual failure in these areas, particularly when juxtaposed against the successes in the new generation of glass- and ceramic-based businesses, had the same effect as did the initial successes in COMM and GEMS. They highlighted the company's unique strengths and led to a reinvigorated strategic focus on glass and ceramics.

In each instance, the strategic focus resulted from general management's recognition and identification of the unique capabilities of the business. General management must articulate what may be obvious in hindsight but is nonetheless critical for future success in a world of strong competitors and many more opportunities than can possibly be pursued. By affirming or reaffirming the business focus, the general manager is saying to the organization, "This is what we are good at. This is the kind of business that we succeed in, and therefore, this is the kind of business we should concentrate on." On the other hand, a strategic focus, no matter how eloquently it is described, cannot substitute for unique capabilities. A well-articulated strategic focus is essential for exploiting such capabilities, but it does little good in their absence. This is the lesson Corning learned from its forays into biotechnology and medical diagnostic products. As it pursued these opportunities, it began to describe its strategic focus as "technology" rather than the more focused "glass-ceramics technology." But while it rationalized these new-business-development efforts by broadening the definition of its focus, experience demonstrated that it had extended itself well beyond its capabilities. Even though Corning's laboratory services businesses proved to be enormously successful, the primary lesson learned from these expeditions outside its traditional areas of strength was the importance of building on core capabilities. Dave Duke explains:

> We've concluded that it's going to be very difficult for us to compete in the long term, with sustainable competitive advantage, in things that are out of our main area of expertise. . . . Each time we got too far from our home base, we didn't know enough about the technology or the markets.

Leadership within the Area of Focus

Within their areas of focus, these businesses are the world leaders. This leadership is a matter of explicit managerial philosophy. At COMM, it was first espoused by Dan Noble in the 1940s and carried forward by subsequent generations of management. As Bill Weisz wrote in his mid-1960s memos, the objective of the business was to be the "worldwide leader" in its field by providing products that were "orders of magnitude better" than the competition's. During the long and uncertain development of Corning's optical fiber business, CEO Amory Houghton insisted that the company make the investments required to achieve leadership. Houghton's philosophy was mirrored by Dave Duke and Dick Dulude who set the mold for Corning's new generation of businesses. It was Duke who concisely articulated the essence of Corning's leadership philosophy in his admonition, "If we tie, we lose."

Walt Robb established the tradition of leadership at GEMS. During the early stages of CT, when the corporate lab and GEMS' engineers proposed a me-too CT system, he insisted on a leapfrog approach. "If you can be number one," Robb argues, "no matter whether that market turns out to be $200 million or $1 billion, you have reason for confidence. If you have to spend $50 million to be number one in a $200 million market, that's much better than skimping . . . and being a loser in a $1 billion market."

The changing nature of leadership. While the influence of general management on leadership is apparent from the outset in these cases, the form that leadership takes evolved dramatically during the 1970s and 1980s. Corning's TV bulb business epitomizes the form of market leadership many U.S. firms strove for in the post-World War II era, prior to the emergence of Japan as a formidable competitor. According to Dick Dulude, ". . . we would invent something that was technically unique and ride it as long as we could, and we would keep raising prices." But once there was significant competition from Japan, this form of leadership became obsolete. By the mid-1970s, Corning was practicing a new form of leadership. The pattern was first established with Celcor, and then repeated with optical fibers, LCD glass and ceramic memory disks. Like the TV bulb business, these businesses were based on pioneering unique products and processes. But here the similarity between the two generations of businesses ends. Once introduced, these unique products and processes were continuously improved. And of greatest significance, not only performance, but cost was continuously improved. By the time Duke was running the optical fiber business in the late 1970s, Corning was explicitly using two distinct learning curves—one for performance and one for costs. The objective in all the new businesses was and is to be a leader on both dimensions. Whereas in the 1960s, the pioneering development of a unique process for making glass bulbs represented the culmination of the pursuit of leadership, by the 1980s, this would be only the starting point. Corning's total quality campaign during the 1980s reinforced this dual pursuit of cost and performance leadership. By improving quality, each business improved its performance while reducing cost.

COMM's leadership philosophy also became progressively more ambitious over time. In the 1950s and early 1960s, market leadership meant being first to market with unique products. By the 1960s and early 1970s, leadership meant also being first to market with product improvements. And by the early 1980s, an even more ambitious form of leadership, reminiscent of Corning's simultaneous pursuit of leadership in cost and performance, was taking shape. The campaigns to eliminate defects, to produce better products that were cost-competitive at the low end, and then to reduce both development- and customer-response-cycle times, culminated in the goal of "best in class." By the late 1980s, COMM was striving not only to be first to market with the best-performing products and first with such products in every market segment, from high end to low and from Europe to Japan, but to be better than the best performers in the world in every organizational function.

The meaning of leadership also became progressively more ambitious at GEMS, though less markedly so than at Corning and COMM. During the late 1970s, leadership for GEMS meant achieving the largest share of the U.S. diagnostic imaging market by introducing clearly superior products, and then maintaining that leadership with continuous improvements in advance of the competition. Leadership

Figure 5.1
Changing Meaning of Leadership

1960	1970	1980	1990

Unique Products

Superior Performance plus
Continuous Improvement

Superior Performance, Continuous
Improvement, Low Costs

"Best in Class"

in the early 1980s meant the largest overall share of the worldwide diagnostic imaging market. And by the late 1980s, with John Trani as senior vice president, it meant achieving the number one or number two market share position worldwide in every diagnostic imaging modality in both sales and profitability. One of the most important consequences of this evolution toward a more ambitious form of leadership was that by the mid-1980s, GEMS was confronting, rather than retreating from, the low ends of its markets. Unlike Corning and COMM, however, GEMS never succeeded in competing directly in these cost-sensitive market segments. It was much slower to embrace the total quality management and process simplifications that Corning and COMM had begun to adopt in the early 1980s. But, through YMS, its joint venture with Yokogawa Electric Works, it did manage to develop a vehicle for competing in cost-sensitive markets.

Toward "Best in Class." These three businesses have evolved along this path of increasingly more ambitious forms of leadership at different paces, and through very different sets of experiences. Motorola is somewhat farther along the path than Corning, and Corning is somewhat farther along than GEMS. But all are headed in the same direction. All have moved inexorably toward becoming best in class (see Figure 5.1). Best in class creates a horizon that always recedes and, therefore, that always propels the firm forward. It is a form of leadership that forces the firm to set ever more ambitious objectives and that is totally intolerant of complacency. This is what George Fisher (the current CEO of Motorola) means when he says that the most enduring significance of the quality and cycle time campaigns at Motorola are the expectation levels they create.

The problem is management does not often set reach-out
enough goals. . . . Don't underestimate the role of bench-

marking and expectation levels. Expectation levels are everything because we have tons of good people, all of whom
want to be the best, and you've got to let them know how
good the best really is, so that they can be better.

The idea of aspiring to be best in class undercuts a widely accepted precept about business strategy. The conventional wisdom is
that there are two generic approaches to competing in any particular
market—differentiate or be the low-cost performer.[3] The two are usually considered incompatible. In any given market, companies that
follow a cost-leadership strategy (e.g., clone makers in the personal
computer markets) usually pursue a very different course with very
different sets of resources from those that follow differentiation strategies (e.g., Apple, IBM). Best in class, however, implies pursuit of
both courses simultaneously. On the one hand, the firm that strives
to be better than the best in all organizational functions is striving
for maximum differentiation. Relative to the competition, it aims for
a wider range of products and services that offer better performance
and quality, and that are developed and continuously modified in
shorter amounts of time. On the other hand, the firm that strives to
be best in class is also, in effect, seeking the low-cost position in any
given price tier of its market. Whether in the high end or the low,
best in class means fewest defects and shortest cycle times, but these
can only be achieved by drastically streamlining and simplifying organizational processes, which in turn lead directly toward the low-cost
position! One of the most surprising outcomes of Motorola's early
attempts to improve quality was the discovery that this led to dramatic cost reductions with minimal investments. Similarly, one of the
most important components of Corning's drive for substantially better returns on equity has been its total quality-management campaign.
     Best in class is more ambitious than the apparent goal of many
U.S. firms that undertook vigorous restructuring programs in the late
1980s and early 1990s. Streamlining the organization and significantly
reducing the cost structure are useful and important steps. But they
are a far cry from achieving maximum differentiation at the same
time. Best in class is also more ambitious than total quality management, another popular objective of the late 1980s and early 1990s.
Best in class means not only striving to eliminate defects and to become more responsive to customers but also striving to be first to
market with superior products. Total quality, important as it is, is
not a substitute for the latter. It cannot compensate for the absence
of the long, sometimes painful, and always expensive process of de-

veloping superior products and bringing them to market in advance of the competition. Total quality strengthens the firm that does these things; but it cannot transform a firm that lags in new product development into a leader. Total quality is necessary for total leadership, but far from sufficient.

Leadership and competition. The march toward increasingly ambitious forms of leadership in these businesses is closely tied to the realization that they were facing ever-stronger competition. This is especially apparent in the histories of Corning and COMM. Corning first began to practice a more complete form of leadership in Celcor (the cellular ceramic substrates for automotive catalytic converters), where competition from 3M, W. R. Grace, and the car companies themselves made Dulude and his associates realize that "We aren't going to make any money . . . unless we drive the cost down and have a better product than anyone else." In optical fibers, the threat from such resource-rich competitors as AT&T, and NTT and its suppliers, motivated the pursuit of cost and performance leadership. And, Corning's LCD glass business is the leading supplier for an industry totally dominated by Japanese manufacturers. If Asahi Glass or any of Corning's other Japanese competitors catch up technologically, Corning will lose.

The mutually reinforcing relationship between leadership and competition is equally apparent in COMM's history. It was general management's insistence on market leadership that drove COMM to break into the Japanese paging market, for general management believed that if the business was not able to compete in Japan, it was not a complete market leader. Similarly, Weisz and his associates realized that if Motorola could not compete at the low end of the pager market, when it was threatened by low-priced competition, it "might as well get out of the whole damn business." The insistence on leadership in all segments of its market forced COMM to confront rather than retreat from competition. And when it did, COMM learned that in important respects it was not the leader it had always believed itself to be. This was the genesis of the total quality campaign, which ultimately led to the goal of best in class. The pursuit of leadership drove COMM to confront competition, which in turn drove it to the more ambitious forms of leadership. Total leadership and exposure to world-class competition go hand in hand.

Focus and Leadership

In the end, the most important attribute of the business strategies of COMM, Corning, and GEMS is not the consistent strategic focus and not the ever more ambitious pursuit of leadership, but the mutually

reinforcing combination of the two. Strategic focus channels resources into a market-technology domain where the business has
been successful. These resources reinforce the business's strengths
in the area of success and, over time, lead to the development and
continuing enhancement of a unique set of capabilities. These capabilities reinforce the business's leadership in its area of focus. The
continued success, in turn, reinforces the commitment to the area of
focus, which leads to a continued channeling of resources, which
further fortifies the business's capabilities and leadership in the area
of focus.

But if focus and leadership are mutually reinforcing, how do we
distinguish between businesses that are building leadership in their
area of focus from businesses that are so focused on their existing
domains that they become hidebound and closed to new opportunities? The old adage about sticking to one's knitting is as much a
prescription for success as it is a description of firms that failed to
adapt to a changing world. History is filled with examples of firms
that stubbornly stuck to their knitting as the world passed them by.
The combination of a consistent focus and the single-minded pursuit
of leadership within that area of focus can also plant the seeds of the
firm's demise.

GEMS, COMM, and Corning avoided this by repeatedly attempting to grow new businesses that represented major departures
from their existing lines of business but that nonetheless fit their
areas of focus. All of COMM's new businesses—paging, cellular telephones, portable data communications, Irridium, and personal communication networks—fit this pattern. So too do most of Corning's
new businesses: the cellular-ceramic-based ventures, optical fibers,
LCD glass, and most recently, memory disks and glass-plastic composites. (The notable exception is Corning's cluster of laboratory services businesses, which does not fit within the glass and ceramics
envelope.) And even though GEMS was less of a pioneer, its history
is also marked by attempts to leapfrog into entirely new lines of
business within its strategic domain. The result is that over time,
COMM, Corning, and GEMS expanded their areas of focus. When
combined with the will to grow new businesses, a consistent strategic
focus becomes more of a road than a wall, more of a framework
than a constraint. Its boundaries become malleable, changing and
stretching in new directions with each effort to grow an entirely new
line of business. Although Motorola has had mobile and portable
communications as its explicit focus for more than a quarter-
century—and Corning glass and ceramic technologies for considerably longer—their opportunities for growth seem to be multiplying
rather than drying up. And ever since its success in CT, GEMS has

been exploring one potentially important new diagnostic imaging modality after another.

It could be argued that the reason these firms have been able to grow within their area of focus is that they are operating in domains that are especially rich with opportunity, domains in which technology is changing rapidly and creating many possibilities for growth. In other fields, those with inherently longer life cycles and more engineering-intensive product development, for example, the pattern might look much less dynamic. There may be some merit to this argument. It is certainly true that these cases were selected precisely because they represented success in high-tech dynamic markets. But on the other hand, in any field, the argument that the opportunities for growth are depleted tends to be self-fulfilling. It is difficult to find any industrial environment that is not being reshaped by changes in technology. How dynamic or static a firm's strategic focus is may depend more on how management defines and operates within that focus than on the inherent richness of the field. If management defines the strategic focus in terms of current lines of business (e.g., catalytic converter substrates), it is more likely to eventually find the field exhausted of opportunities than if it defines the focus in terms of the capabilities that have developed with those lines of business (e.g., expertise in glass and ceramics technology). Once the focus is defined in terms of unique capabilities, each effort to grow a new business on the basis of those capabilities—whether successful or not—enriches them, which increases the likelihood of discovering and developing yet more new business opportunities. The primary obstacle to continuing growth becomes not a lack of opportunities, but a lack of general managerial will to strike out at new opportunities that build on existing strengths.

Technology Strategy

Did general management in these cases exhibit a technology strategy? The answer is unequivocally yes. For each business, market leadership in the area of strategic focus was to be established through technology leadership. The technology strategies of Corning, COMM, and GEMS exhibit a number of important features. Although there are important differences among them, it is once again the similarities that are most striking.

Pioneering Versus Fast Following

Corning and COMM are unabashed technology pioneers. Their objective is to be first to market with superior technology. Throughout their history, they forged new markets and then created successive generations of new technology within those markets. The strategy of fast following was pursued only when the business failed to be first to market, as when COMM was beaten to the punch by NEC in numeric pagers.

GEMS, in contrast, was not among the pioneers of either CT or MR, but it did not pursue a fast-follower strategy either. Rather, in both cases, it was slow to react to newly emerging markets. Once it did, it had one objective: be the leader, leapfrog the competition with new technology, and then stay ahead with still more technology. So although GEMS was never a pioneer in developing new markets, once it saw the importance of these markets, it behaved like a pioneer.

The argument against pioneering and in favor of fast following is that pioneering entails high risk. There can be advantages to allowing other firms to confront the uncertainties associated with exploring new markets with new technologies, and then moving quickly to take over the market once the pioneers have effectively reduced the uncertainties and defined the important dimensions of the market.[4] The problem with this approach is that it does not fully take into account the nature of the competition. If the firm that pioneers a market is capable of continuing to pioneer new generations of technology, it is almost impossible to catch. It develops a learning-curve advantage, which is constantly reinforced as long as the pioneer continues to press ahead with ever-newer technology. This has occurred repeatedly in the history of COMM and Corning. The followers in optical fibers, presumably striving to be fast, are always two or three manufacturing process generations behind Corning. And nearly a decade after COMM pioneered portable cellular telephones, the competition is still struggling to keep up. In 1989, COMM introduced a new generation of portable cellular telephones called Micro TAC that weighed only 10.7 ounces, 40 percent as heavy as the preceding generation. It was a year and a half before Japanese competitors were able to introduce a comparable product. In mid-1991, a few months after the competition caught up, Motorola brought out Micro TAC Lite, which weighed only 7.7 ounces.[5]

If, on the other hand, the pioneering competitor has relatively limited resources, as EMI did in CT, then it may indeed be possible to do what GEMS did—enter the market late and leapfrog the competition. Unfortunately, in the important high-tech markets, there are few EMIs left in the 1990s. The competitors are companies like NEC, Toshiba, and Canon—and Corning, COMM, and GEMS. They are focused on their domains of strength and determined to lead in their areas of focus. Against this kind of competition, fast following is a recipe for at best, constantly threatened profitability. This becomes all the more true as cycle times shrink—and the shrinkage is most apparent in high-tech markets like the ones described here. The shorter the time between generations of products, the smaller the window for profitability, and therefore, the more important it becomes to be first to market.

Radical Plus Generational Plus Incremental Innovations

As should be apparent from the preceding discussion, the pioneering practiced by COMM, Corning, and GEMS takes three distinct but mutually reinforcing forms. Corning and COMM were first to market with radical innovations; all three were first to market with generational innovations; and all three also have been first to market with incremental innovations.

Creating entirely new businesses through radical innovations is a hallmark of Corning's history. Optical fibers is the most dramatic recent example, but Corning's other new businesses fit the mold as well. The LCD glass business is based on a unique method of forming glass, the family of pollution-control-related businesses grew out of a unique method of making cellular ceramic structures, and Corning's latest new business prospect—glass-plastic composites—represents an entirely new class of materials. These radical innovations were followed by generational innovations and, within each generation, by incremental improvements. In optical fibers, Corning repeatedly made its own manufacturing capability obsolete by developing and introducing seven distinct generations of processing technology over the course of 15 years. As one generation was being implemented, a second was nearing completion, and development of a third was under way, a pattern that is striking in its similarity to the process of generational change in the semiconductor industry. Each generational innovation was followed by incremental improvements, which led not only to increased efficiency but also to a growing variety of products. In the cellular ceramic family of businesses, the early ceramic structures were replaced by new generations of progressively denser structures. At the same time, within each generation, the business produced a growing variety of shapes, while pursuing continuous reductions in cost and, since the early 1980s, improvements in quality. Meanwhile, new classes of cellular-ceramic-based products were being developed, and all were produced in a variety of shapes, with continuously improving performance and quality and continuously declining costs.

COMM exhibits a comparable balance among the three forms of

innovation. Every new mobile and portable communications business was a pioneering effort. As each grew out of its pre-emergent state, COMM followed up with generational innovations. It was first to market with a genuinely useful VHF pager, PageBoy I, which was 25 percent cheaper and lighter and offered 80 percent greater range, than the first VHF pagers. PageBoy II, which was one-third the size of PageBoy I, was again well ahead of the competition. PageBoy II was followed by MetroPage, a high-capacity pager capable of serving 100,000 subscribers at a time when the highest-capacity pagers on the market could serve only a few thousand. COMM subsequently led the competition in introducing high-frequency pagers, alphanumeric pagers, pen-shaped pagers, and most recently, the wristwatch pager. These generational innovations were followed by an expanding number of product variants and extensions in advance of, and with the explicit purpose of bracketing, the competition. To take just one of many possible examples from the history of paging, following COMM's introduction of the first alphanumeric pager in 1981, it introduced a model with twice the message capacity, as well as a low-frequency model in 1983, a vibrate-only model in 1984, a battery charger and printer accessory in 1985, and in 1986, an entirely new generation of alphanumeric pager capable of receiving four times as many messages with ten times the information. By 1988, the competition still had not caught up with the product COMM introduced in 1986.

GEMS established its leadership through generational innovations that leapfrogged each market's radical innovators, and then it sustained its advantage through subsequent generational and incremental innovations. The first enhancements to the CT 8800 were introduced at about the same time the first 8800s were being shipped. Development of the 9800, the next generation CT system, began less than a year after the 8800 was introduced. Similarly, within five years of the introduction of its first MR system, Signa, GEMS introduced five major upgrades, several additional enhancements, and an entirely new generation of product, the Signa Advantage.

The three sides of pioneering versus the conventional wisdom. A common charge in the late 1980s and early 1990s is that U.S. firms are failing in high-tech markets because they place insufficient emphasis on incremental innovations. In *The Breakthrough Illusion,* for example, Richard Florida and Martin Kenney write that "the United States makes the breakthroughs, while other countries, especially Japan, provide the follow-through" on which competitive advantage is built.[6] Apparently in reaction to this alleged failure to continuously improve technology, many U.S. firms have been reorienting their

R&D operations away from longer-term, higher-risk R&D and toward more incremental improvements and extensions of existing product lines. The order of the day in many firms is to make R&D operations "more responsive" to their businesses, which is a euphemism for focusing attention more completely on existing products and processes.

The histories of Corning, COMM, and GEMS offer absolutely no evidence to support this change in industrial R&D. To be sure, the demise of Corning's TV bulb business is consistent with the charge that U.S. industry has neglected the incremental improvements that sustain leadership. But Corning and the others have long since learned this lesson. All three businesses vigorously pursued incremental improvements to their product lines. The important point is that they did so *in combination* with an equally vigorous pursuit of more radical and generational innovations. What sets these three businesses apart from so many other U.S. firms is that for their general management, continuous improvements in existing product lines and discontinuous innovations leading to entirely new product lines are different sides of the same coin. If these firms had focused in the past on the kind of incremental R&D being advocated today, the COMM of 1990 would be primarily a mobile and portable radio business; GEMS, an X-ray or at best a CT business; and Corning, a dying specialty glass maker. These businesses built and renewed, and continue to build and renew, their competitive advantage through radical and generational innovations. They sustained that advantage over time through more incremental product line improvements and extensions, but it is on the basis of the riskier, failure-laden, expensive, and time-consuming efforts to pioneer new businesses and new generations of technology that their competitive advantage was and still is established.

New business creation and general management. It is difficult to overstate the importance of this ability to develop new businesses while continuously improving existing ones. In the fastest-growing high-tech markets of the late 1980s and early 1990s, the most conspicuous failing of U.S. firms is not a lack of incremental improvement, but the failure to successfully establish any business presence at all. For all its explosive growth and fundamental importance, the liquid crystal display market is devoid of any strong U.S. participants, even though it was U.S. firms that developed the technology. In the emerging markets associated with electronic imagery, U.S. players seem to have lagged in growing new businesses. The largest U.S. supplier of facsimile machines, Pitney Bowes, sells equipment made by Japanese firms. Even in laptop and notebook computers, the fastest-growing segments of the computer industry, Toshiba is more of a pioneer than the traditional U.S. manufacturers. Moreover, the recent history of some of the most widely respected and historically innovative U.S. firms is replete with examples of incremental improvements to existing product lines but almost devoid of examples of successful new-business creation. IBM has been a master of continuous incremental improvement in its mainframe computers. But since the introduction of its enormously successful personal computers in the early 1980s, it has failed to establish leadership in any new business despite overwhelming technological strengths and marketing advantages. Xerox failed to take advantage of an extraordinary opportunity in the late 1970s to grow a new business in personal computing. RCA, for all the depth and breadth of its technological capabilities, somehow failed to capitalize on the wave of new business opportunities in consumer electronics. And apart from GEMS, GE failed in every one of its attempts during the 1980s to grow new high-tech businesses—from factory automation to computer-aided design to ceramic components.

This dismaying failure of U.S. industry to grow new businesses underscores the uniqueness of the achievements of Corning, COMM, and GEMS. Their profitability in the early 1990s is a direct result of their new-business development efforts in the late 1970s and early 1980s. Yet even in these firms, we have seen that the process of nuturing new businesses is long and painful. GEMS failed in its initial efforts to develop digital X-ray and ultrasound, and it did not break even on MR until 1988, seven years and $300 million after it decided it had misread the market and had to respond. The time to break even was not nearly as long in CT, but GEMS did have to persist through four years of repeated failures and setbacks before it began turning an operating profit in 1978. Similarly, the long new-business incubation period has become so familiar to COMM that it even has a name for it—the pre-emergent stage. Cellular telephones took close to 15 years of development and $150 million of investment before the first sales were recorded, and then the business lost $50 million in its first year. We see precisely the same pattern throughout Corning's history—an enormous investment over a long period in a business opportunity with uncertain prospects. The investment in optical fibers exceeded $100 million at a time of serious financial difficulty.

When the investment and time required to grow new businesses is balanced against their always uncertain prospects, the reasons that new business development is resisted quickly become apparent. As the years pass with no immediate prospect for a return on a growing investment, internal skepticism, resistance, and outright opposition intensify. While established lines of business scrape to stay ahead in a struggle against increasingly strong competition, new-business development efforts drain badly needed resources and scarce managerial talent in a seemingly endless pursuit of opportunities with receding time horizons. Indeed, there appears to be an inherent conflict between the managerial attributes required to manage the continuous improvement of established product lines—discipline, an almost obsessive focus, careful attention and responsiveness to customers—and those required to manage the discontinuous leaps into new businesses and markets. Yet if there is an underlying conflict between these two sets of innovation, it is equally clear in hindsight that it is precisely the ability to pursue both that distinguishes COMM, Corning, and GEMS from so many of their counterparts.

In each instance, it was general management that nurtured the new business development. Marty Cooper recalls that as time passed without any prospect of a return on the efforts to develop the cellular telephone business, "There were any number of times that it would have been killed had it not been protected by [John] Mitchell." At roughly the same time, Amory Houghton and his associates were pushing ahead with optical fibers, despite "getting awful heat from . . . division managers," and Robb and his associates were persevering in trying to differentiate GEMS from the competition amid growing doubts from both within their organization and above. Yet the same general management that protected new business development also insisted on the continuous improvement of the established product lines. Bill Weisz believes general management needs to be somewhat schizophrenic about supporting both the discontinuous and the more continuous kinds of innovation. "You need to divide businesses into two kinds. With the pioneering businesses, you give them money and support, and leave them alone. But once they grow to a large, more bureaucratic organization, you need to formalize a lot of these things. There's a discipline involved."

Another general manager from an entirely different GE business describes the role of general management in growing new businesses in a strikingly similar fashion. Charles Reed was in charge of GE's engineering plastics business during the 1960s and early 1970s when it too was going through this process of both continuous and discontinuous change. (In 1974, as a member of an internal advisory board to Jack Welch, Reed was among those urging GEMS to respond to the developing CT market.) GE Plastics, now the world leader in engineering plastics, was founded on a family of entirely new materials. While these materials were being developed, the established product lines were themselves scrambling for resources. Just as in these three cases, management of the established lines saw the new business development as a distraction and drain of resources from the more pressing needs of growing and strengthening the existing businesses. It fell to general management to achieve the proper balance—to insist on the continuous form of improvement while encouraging the discontinuous. "The key," Reed says, is the involvement of "management one step removed" from product line management. "That's what you need—someone who is at a bit of a distance, who won't worry too much if it fails. They are the ones who have to push to move into new areas."[7]

Technology Leadership and Marketing

Marketing and distribution play an important role in the success of these three firms. One of the keys to COMM's early success was its dedicated sales force, which enabled COMM, in Bill Weisz's words, "to know the customers better than they know themselves." Similarly, GEMS enjoys the strongest marketing and distribution in its industry. "We have a good understanding of what the potential applications are of this [MR]," states GEMS' Morry Blumenfeld, "better than the MDs do. We understand them better than they understand themselves." But although marketing and distribution were strengths for COMM and GEMS, their primary impact was to reinforce the competitive advantage first achieved by technology leadership. COMM's dedicated sales force promoted the development of a proliferation of product variants tailored to the particular needs of particular customers. This unquestionably entrenched COMM in its position of market leadership, but in all its major new businesses, market leadership was first established through superior technology. COMM was first to introduce portable radios, transistors in radios, fully transistorized mobile and portable radios, a truly useful pager, high-capacity pagers, high-frequency pagers, portable cellular telephones, and so on. It was also through technology leadership that GEMS won market leadership in diagnostic imaging. In 1976, GEMS had 20 percent of the CT market. Its share was as high as it was in large measure because of superior marketing and distribution, but that strength could not compensate for a mediocre product. Its market position began to weaken as the limitations of the early CT product became known. Less than two years later, with the market collapsing and the industry suffering from overcapacity, GEMS catapulted to a 60-percent market share. The reason was the introduction of a clearly superior (faster and with substantially better resolution) product— the CT 8800. The combination of a superior product and unsurpassed marketing and distribution was formidable. The latter reinforced the former, as understanding of the radiology and cardiology markets led to the identification of new applications and the development of new product variants to serve those applications in advance of the competition. But when GEMS did not enjoy product superiority—in CT before it introduced its 8800, in ultrasound for much of the 1980s—its marketing strengths were insufficient to establish a position of competitive advantage.

Corning never enjoyed the luxury of superior "complementary assets." Because of its tendency to follow glass and ceramics technology into markets as diverse as computer peripherals and pollution-control devices, it seems to have relied even more exclusively on technology leadership for its competitive advantage than its two counterparts. This does not mean Corning neglects marketing and distribution, but rather that they are not a source of competitive advantage. The result is that it has come to rely much more heavily than COMM and GEMS on the use of strategic alliances, through which it has often been able to gain access to the marketing and distribution required to fully exploit the advantages built on technology leadership. In this respect, Corning illustrates the point most forcefully. In all these businesses, competitive advantage is established through technology leadership; that advantage is reinforced with complementary assets such as strong marketing and distribution, but the technology leadership is the necessary condition.

Decision-Making Style and Technology

The decision-making style of the general managers in these cases is best described as driven by strategic imperatives. Decisions regarding investment, R&D spending, and new business development are shaped by the imperative that the business remain a leader in its field. The analytic, financially driven style of decision making that is so much a part of American management culture is absent here. Financial considerations are constraints on general managerial decision making rather than its determinants. In every case, once a course of action is deemed strategically necessary or desirable, financial considerations determine the pace and approach, and they are the ultimate measures of performance. But the decisions about whether to set out on or to continue the course of action are shaped by strategic considerations. For any major potential investment, the driving question is: "Given that we are committed to this area of business, what steps must we take to stay ahead?" rather than, "Given that we must achieve a certain rate of return from our investments, is this a wise investment?"

Decision making by strategic imperative, and its divergence from the more analytic style, is most apparent in the repeated efforts at COMM, Corning, and GEM to develop new businesses, which, as we have seen, is a critical and distinguishing feature of these cases.

New Business Development and the Knot of Uncertainties

New business development typically occurs under conditions of extraordinary uncertainty. The technologies are still under development; the markets exist barely, if at all; and often the infrastructure required to deliver the technology to market is not yet established. The picture is further muddied by questions of timing—time required to develop the technology, timing of market emergence, speed with which competitors and competing technologies are moving—and invariably, by exogenous factors such as government regulations over which the firm has little or no control. But what makes these uncertainties so difficult to deal with is that they also interact with each other. The form the still-developing technology should take largely depends on how the still-developing market responds to early versions of the technology; yet paradoxically, how the market responds depends on the form the technology takes. COMM's earliest pagers, for example, were fragile, kludgie, low-frequency systems that did not require FCC approval, were limited to use within buildings, required extensive wiring in those buildings, and were sold directly to private organizations. After a decade of iterations among technology, market, and infrastructure, PageBoy I was introduced. It operated on VHF frequencies over a citywide area, was significantly smaller and more durable, required FCC approval, and was sold through intermediaries called radio common carriers, several of which COMM itself helped to develop. During its 15-year struggle to develop the optical fiber business, Corning faced not only a challenging new technology but a thoroughly entrenched competing technology (copper cable), fast-developing alternative technologies (e.g., satellite communications), closed markets both at home and abroad, strong competitors that otherwise would have been Corning's largest and earliest customers, and significant doubts about when the market would finally emerge. In the end, it was an exogenous and largely unpredictable event—the divestiture of AT&T— that broke the logjam.

One would expect the knot of intertwined uncertainties to be less complicated for GEMS, since it was relatively late to market with both CT and MR. But one of the most striking features of GEMS' history is the string of surprises and unexpected developments it encountered. GEMS initially underestimated the importance of CT; later, it attacked the wrong target (breast scanning) and then went on to attack the right target with the wrong product (a whole-body scanner that could not perform acceptable head scans). Throughout this period, it continued to underestimate the increasing demand for CT. Next, it was surprised by the sudden collapse of the market, which was triggered by one of those seemingly inevitable exogenous changes.

These uncertainties were exacerbated by the pursuit of total leadership. A conventional response to the high uncertainties associated with new business development is to fast follow—to leap into the fray after the unknowns have been reduced and future prospects clarified. But fast following is incompatible with total leadership. Total leadership in an area of focus means among other things, striving to be first to market, which drives these businesses into the thick of the uncertainties.

New Business Development and Learning by Doing

The general managers in all three businesses are well aware of the uncertain nature of new business development and, as a result, are skeptical about the utility of analytic, model-based approaches to decision making. In Walt Robb's opinion, "You can't make financial models that can be relied on. You can make the numbers come out any way you want." Dick Dulude agrees: "You can make the numbers come out any way you want, especially early in the development." At Motorola, George Fisher explains, "We hardly ever use discounted cash flow analysis. We assume the numbers are the effect not the cause."

Rather than grounding their new-business development decisions on analytic projections, general management in these cases engage in what is best described as "learning by doing." They develop new businesses through a serial, iterative process, with each subsequent step building on the experiences—both positive and negative—gained from the previous step. Uncertainty reduction becomes an active process; insight into the technology and market is gained, not by waiting for the market to reveal itself or by perfecting the technology in the lab, but by bringing an early version of the product into the still-undeveloped and ill-defined market. Experience from this initial foray provides the basis for judgment about whether and how to proceed. Sometimes, experience leads to the conclusion that the opportunity is not worth continued pursuit, as GEMS decided once it began to develop digital X-ray, and Corning concluded about medical diagnostic products and industrial biotechnology after a decade of development. In other instances, however, experience reinforces the conviction that the opportunity deserves attention, as when COMM learned that despite all the shortcomings of its low-frequency pagers, "if you went to Mount Sinai Hospital and tried to take back the first pagers . . . they wouldn't give them to you." Experience can also point to possibilities that were entirely unanticipated when the initial project was launched. For example, Corning's efforts to develop glass-ceramic heat exchangers for automotive gas turbines led to ceramic substrates for catalytic converters. Each step offers an opportunity to learn, reassess, and if necessary, adjust. New business development becomes a process of continuous assessment and adaptation. As George Fisher explains, "Bob Galvin [the former CEO of Motorola] would always say, 'You can't know what's around the next corner, so construct an organization that is able to adapt.'" Bobby Bowen of GEMS makes the same point. "A lot of people think of product development as involving a lot of planning, but . . . the key is learning, and an organization's ability to learn."

Corning's 25-year search for new businesses is filled with examples of learning by doing. The laboratory glassware business led to the blood gas analysis business, which grew into a diagnostic products business and prompted a series of acquisitions, including the diagnostic services business called MetPath. During the 1980s, MetPath was expanded step by step into a highly successful cluster of laboratory services businesses, while the diagnostic products business that had initially spawned the services was spun off into a joint venture and eventually divested. Similarly, the LCD glass business grew out of an ultimately unsuccessful effort to develop a superior method of making commodity glass. This led to a unique process for making specialty glass, which was unsuccessfully applied to safety windshields and then successfully used in several minor applications before blossoming into a major new-business opportunity. The decade-long effort to develop an industrial biotechnology business began as a serendipitously discovered method of immobilizing enzymes, grew into a major R&D effort, led to several joint ventures aimed at producing enzymes that could be used in industrial process applications, and finally was spun off and divested in the 1980s.

Learning by doing at COMM is most apparent in the pre-emergent phase of its new-business development activities. In all of COMM's new businesses, progressively smaller and more useful versions of products are introduced to progressively better-developed markets through progressively more sophisticated infrastructures. COMM's early pagers were hardly market successes, but according to Bill Weisz, "Each sold a bit more, each did a bit better, each taught us more about the marketplace." "Whether you know it or not," says John Mitchell, "you go down a learning curve."

Learning by doing is even more prominent in the history of GEMS. When GEMS finally realized that the CT market was becoming much more significant than expected, it established a crash project in mammography. In reaction to the unexpectedly rapid growth in the market, GEMS launched a parallel project in whole-body scanning and licensed a head scanner. After the mammography and head-scanning systems proved disappointing and the body scanner flawed, GEMS shifted its emphasis to improving the body scanner. When the body scanner finally reached the market and was found to be of doubtful competitive value, GEMS began a concentrated push to develop substantially better detectors. Once achieved, these led to the development and introduction of the very successful CT 8800. Like virtually all the examples of new business development in these cases, development progressed step by step, in often unanticipated directions and in reaction to often unanticipated developments.

The Strategic Context for Learning by Doing

Learning by doing dictates that the way to determine if a new business opportunity is worth pursuing is to pursue it. Unfortunately, this is an extraordinarily time- and resource-consuming way to reduce uncertainty. No firm can afford to research even a fraction of available opportunities in this fashion. General management must distinguish between opportunities that are worth learning about and those that are not. But how does it do so? The caldron of uncertainties surrounding new business development makes analytic projections of future returns suspect, which is why learning by doing is relied upon in the first place. So how does general management screen opportunities for new business development and select from among the many possibilities those that are worth an initial foray?

Selectivity. From the many instances of successful new business development in these cases, it is possible to derive a decision logic that general management used to identify worthwhile new business opportunities. It is more qualitative than quantitative, and dominated by strategic considerations. First, there are two closely related sets of questions that have to do with whether the opportunity makes strategic sense:

1. Does the opportunity fit the focus of the business? Does it represent a step in the right direction?
2. Does it build on the unique capabilities of the business?

Is it in an area where the business has an unfair advantage and where it can establish and sustain leadership?

For firms that exhibit both a strategic focus and a drive for total
leadership within the area of focus, a positive answer to the first set
of questions will often imply a positive answer to the second. In fact,
if it does not, that in itself ought to be a source of concern, for it
indicates that in some aspects of the domain of focus, the business
is unable to lead.

Next, there is a set of questions that have to do with whether
the opportunity is worth pursuing, whether it is worth the time,
investment, and inevitable setbacks required to bring it to fruition.

3. Is it "real"? Is it big? Can we make money on this? Is it
   worth it?

Answering yes to these questions is not by itself sufficient for proceeding. Strategic fit (yes to the first two sets of questions) is usually
a necessary condition; the combination of good fit and a substantial
potential opportunity (yes to the third) is sufficient.

The evolution of strategic thinking at Corning helps illuminate
this decision logic. During the unfettered search for new businesses
in the 1960s, the company pursued many opportunities—for example, ceramic roofing shingles, glass razor blades, new bottling
methods—that violated the third criterion. In contrast, the efforts of
the late 1970s and early 1980s to develop the industrial biotechnology
and medical diagnostic businesses satisfied the third criterion, but
not the first two. It was only in the 1980s, because of the combination
of James Houghton's (Corning's current CEO) emphasis on profitability and the reaffirmation of the traditional focus on glass- and
glass-ceramic-based businesses that all three criteria came to be consistently applied. The new opportunities pursued by Corning in the
late 1980s and early 1990s—LCD glass, new cellular-ceramic-based
pollution control devices, glass-ceramic substrates for computer
memory disks, and the new family of glass-plastic composites—all
fit Corning's strategic focus, build on its unique strengths, and are
potentially significant in magnitude.

If in the judgment of general management an opportunity satisfies these three criteria, there remains an additional question:

4. How do we pursue this opportunity in a way that is affordable?

This is not the same as "Can we afford to pursue the opportunity?"
This question is conditional on the preceding answers: Given that it

makes sense to pursue it, how should we do so? At what rate should investment proceed; what is the proper balance between investment targeted at renewing existing product lines and investment targeted at growing new businesses? Thus, for GEMS, the question was not whether the pursuit of MR made financial sense, but rather how to pursue MR in a way that made financial sense. In Walt Robb's judgment, the answer was to cut back on CT in order to support the burgeoning MR. Similarly, one of the most important challenges facing Motorola in its high-risk effort to develop Irridium is to manage its financial exposure—which it is doing by limiting its share of the ownership of the overall network. John Mitchell explains that "You have to do these things at an affordable pace. What did it take to do the next mobile, the next portable, the next switch? Could we afford to do it at this pace or half this pace?" Achieving this balance is, in the end, a test of managerial judgment. It is, in Dick Dulude's words, "what general management is all about—balancing the need to stay ahead and to maintain the high, steady rate of investment against the financial resources available to you."

Failure and persistence. Failure is inherent in learning by doing. Success is achieved over time, through a sequence of missteps and partial successes. Every successful new business in the three cases is marked by initial disappointments and setbacks. CT is perhaps the most striking example, but MR also met with unwelcome surprises, as did optical fibers, LCD glass, pagers, cellular telephones, and mobile and portable data equipment. In each instance, the reaction was not to give up, but to modify the effort according to the lessons learned, and then try again. On the other hand, these cases also reveal examples of learning by doing ending with failure. In digital X-ray and ultrasound at GEMS, and diagnostic products and industrial biotechnology at Corning, disappointment eventually led to disengagement. Sometimes general management persisted through failure; other times it did not. This leads to another obvious but critical question about the decision-making process that underlies learning by doing: Once general management has selected an opportunity for development and launched the sequential, iterative development process, how does it distinguish between opportunities that merit persistence and those that do not? Persistence, after all, means a growing level of investment with little or no return. It is seen as a virtue when it leads to success but folly when it ends in failure. So when does it make sense to persist?

The answer involves the same criteria management uses to screen opportunities initially. As more and more experience is gained with the opportunity,

1. Does it continue to appear to fit strategically?
2. Does it still seem to be in a domain in which the firm can dominate?
3. Does the potential payoff still seem substantial?

For Walt Robb, digital X-ray satisfied the first two criteria, but once GEMS began to develop the technology, he learned that it did not satisfy the third. Digital X-ray was never as useful diagnostically as had been hoped. At Corning, experience began to suggest that diagnostic products and industrial biotechnology were not satisfying the second criterion. Both were still promising from the perspective of the third, and in fact Corning earned a substantial return on its investment in biotechnology when it finally divested itself of its cluster of holdings. But it had become apparent by the mid-1980s that Corning was unlikely ever to become a leader in either field. Corning's strategic focus was also narrowing by this time, so these opportunities were also beginning to appear questionable from the perspective of the first criterion.

None of COMM's efforts to develop new mobile and portable communications businesses ended in disengagement, but its consumer electronics business did in 1974. The logic of that decision to divest was similar to Corning's in biotechnology and diagnostic products. It was, in Bill Weisz's words, "driven by the need to focus resources. You can't do everything. . . . We don't want to be in businesses where we can't have a distinctive competence vis-à-vis our competitors. We don't want to be in business where we can't be one of the top one or two companies in the field. . . ." The decision about when to persist and when to get out, then, is shaped by the same logic that drives the selection of opportunities in the first place. This is described by Dick Dulude: "The way you decide whether or not to continue to invest to maintain that leadership—you do that by asking those same questions. . . . If the answers are there, you do it." Persistence, like selection, is driven by strategic imperatives and paced by financial constraints. The primary difference between the two is that over time, as experience is gained, general management is able to make increasingly more informed judgments about whether a particular opportunity satisfies the strategic imperatives.

Failure and strategic context. If failure is inherent in learning by doing, and learning by doing in these cases is shaped by the strategic context, it follows that how failure is interpreted is also a function of the strategic context. Imagine two different businesses pursuing the identical opportunity. For one business, the opportunity fits the strategic focus, whereas for the other, it represents a chance to diversify into an entirely new domain. These cases suggest that the two businesses will interpret the inevitable missteps and setbacks along the path of new business development very differently. The business for which the opportunity is not strategically central will be much less likely to persist through the initial hardships, precisely because the opportunity is of less central importance. For a pharmaceutical company seeking to diversify into medical equipment in the mid-1970s, for example, the mammography failure would probably have been seen as just that—a failure. Moreover, since the business is operating outside its area of focus, there is little if any information of value to be gained from such a setback. Disappointment in a diagnostic imaging venture teaches a pharmaceutical company little about its core technologies and markets. The lessons of the failure apply to a market-technology domain that is foreign to the primary focus of the business. They are therefore unlikely to be useful in subsequent forays, in the way that Corning's unsuccessful effort in glass lasers helped to lay the foundation for its eventual success in optical fibers. In contrast, the business operating in its domain of strategic focus is more likely to persist through the initial setbacks and more likely to learn lessons of value. Not only did GEMS' general management feel it had no choice but to continue in its pursuit of CT, it also learned important lessons from the mammography failure about both its technology (it was feasible) and the market (GEMS was aiming at the wrong target).

This suggests that the likelihood of ultimate success in pursuit of new business opportunities will be greater for the firm that stays within its strategic envelope than for the firm venturing outside it. It has more reason to persist through the early setbacks, and it is better able to bring to bear the experiences gained from prior failures (and success). This may help explain why for many companies, internal venture operations aimed at spawning entirely new businesses are so often disappointing. By design, the new ventures tend to fall outside the strategic focus of the parent company. Learning by doing within the strategic envelope in no way guarantees success, as GEMS learned in digital X-ray and ultrasound; and learning by doing outside the envelope in no way guarantees failure, as Corning learned in laboratory services. But the likelihood of ultimate failure is surely greater outside the envelope than within, and the likelihood of success is surely greater inside the envelope than outside.

Managerial judgment and the strategic context. In both the selection and continuing reassessment of opportunities, managerial judgment clearly plays an important role. When GE's corporate lab first urged

GEMS to launch a program to develop an MR system, for example, MR was still in its infancy. GEMS would have been a pioneer in this market had it proceeded, but Robb chose not to. Although MR was of obvious strategic relevance, it did not, in Robb's judgment, appear to be a substantial enough opportunity (criterion 3). Once it became apparent that it would be substantial, Robb moved quickly. But the point is that managerial judgment is required to screen opportunities and assess progress. This suggests yet another way in which the strategic context shapes the process of learning by doing. Judgment builds on experience; continuity of strategic focus breeds experience. Dave Duke explains:

> We have the analysts crank out all kinds of numbers to make sure we get a feel for them. . . . But I rely on my experience and intuitive sense of what assumptions to make. . . . I have been doing this for 30 years now. I've been through four or five of them [major new-business development efforts] for Corning, and as a result, we can look at it and determine what will be our sustainable competitive advantage. Do we know something about the market? Do we see access to customers? Do we have some sort of real advantage . . . ?

George Fisher makes a similar point: "You get a collective judgment from a lot of people who have been around a lot of years and who have made pretty good judgments and understand the technology and the markets." If the new business opportunity fits within the domain of strategic focus, it builds on what was learned in past efforts. Fisher stresses the importance of such experience in the decision-making process: "It's a collegial process, but a collegial process among people who *know* the technology, *know* the customers, and *know* what you can and can't do."

It is illuminating to speculate about how management would reach these judgments in the absence of experience. For a general manager who is new to a business, who does not know the technology, customers, and "what you can and can't do," the most likely course of action is to fall back on the conventional, model-driven projections of future returns, which, as we have seen, are inherently unreliable under conditions of high uncertainty. In the absence of strategic continuity and the experience it breeds, analytic projections will tend to drive, rather than support, managerial decision making.

Decision-Making Style and Growing Existing Businesses

By the time a business grows out of its pre-emergent stage, the technological and market uncertainties are greatly reduced. Even so, we still find in these cases a style of general managerial decision making that is shaped more by strategic imperative than by financial dictates. The critical question becomes What does it take to stay ahead? Maintaining and enhancing leadership are the dominant concern.

COMM, Corning, and GEMS have all developed a discipline for guiding decision making in the established businesses. This discipline finds its most explicit expression in COMM's technology roadmaps. Product performance and cost trends are projected three, five, and even ten years into the future, and then used to determine the R&D and investments required to maintain leadership. Corning's new generation of businesses engage in a similar process, described by Dave Duke: "You've got to be looking out three or five years ahead and say, Where do I want to be? What kind of product do I want to have? How will I do the manufacturing? How do I get that kind of a cost curve? And . . . then you have got to have the courage of your convictions to allocate the resources to make it happen." Similarly, Morry Blumenfeld describes that at GEMS, "We are very explicitly driven to stay ahead. . . . We know exactly now [summer 1990] where we would like the product to be in 1992, 1993, and 1994."

As with new business development, financial resources are the constraint, not the driver. Financial performance is the measure of results, not the determinant. Decision making in these firms, about both when and if to grow new businesses and about how to maintain them once established, is driven by the strategic imperative to stay ahead in the area of focus.

Profitability

By most standards, these businesses have been financial successes. They have thrived in highly competitive, investment- and R&D-intensive markets at a time when virtually all their domestic counterparts were being driven out of the business. In the ten years between 1981 and 1990, COMM's operating income quadrupled, with operating margins hovering near 10 percent. Corning's profitability nearly tripled during this same period, with return on sales growing from 6 to 10 percent and return on equity growing from 10 to more than 16 percent. While comparable figures are not publicly available for GEMS, operating income appears to have grown by an order of magnitude in the past decade, and the business is now one of GE's most important profit contributors. So if decision making is driven by strategic imperatives rather than by projected financial performance, this in no way implies a lack of interest in profitability. These businesses have achieved financial success by pursuing total leadership within their respective areas of focus. To the extent that total leadership is realized, financial performance follows.

This conclusion, however, leads to another important question. What if the investments required to maintain total leadership lead to a decline in near-term profitability? Should the investments be made nonetheless? The answer suggested by these cases is yes. There is no doubt that Corning's pursuit of optical fibers damaged its profitability, just as COMM's profitability was hurt by the drive to establish leadership in cellular telephones. In 1984, the business lost $50 million. In 1990, again because of increased new product and business development, COMM's operating income declined from roughly $650 million to $585 million (see Figure 3.1). The alternative was to forgo or delay these investments, but this would have weakened COMM's ability to maintain leadership and would in the end have been even more damaging to the bottom line. The logic of general managerial decision making in these cases is that to maximize profitability in highly competitive high-tech industries, strive obsessively to build and maintain leadership within the strategic envelope. Good financial performance, over the long haul, will follow.

Conclusion: Building Advantage Through Technology— A Model of General Managerial Practice

This book began with a series of questions about the role general management plays in translating technology into competitive advantage. As we have mined the histories of GEMS, Corning, and COMM for answers, the outlines of a model of successful general managerial practice in high-tech businesses have taken form. There are a number of facets of the model, but all derive from a simple prescription: focus and lead. Build a strategic focus around the things your business does uniquely well, and then strive for total leadership in that area. Total leadership literally means striving to be best in every aspect of organizational performance: striving to be first to market—with the best-performing products, at the lowest costs, and with the highest quality—in every market segment and price tier, in every region of the globe.

Several corollaries follow. First, in markets as competitive as those examined here, total leadership is never achieved; it is a goal toward which the business must continuously strive, propelled by unrelenting competition. Second, the only possible way to approach total leadership is through a disciplined focus on the business's unique strengths. Without focus, resources are dissipated, and when this happens, leadership is lost. Third, it follows that establishing a sustainable basis of advantage must precede the formulation of the strategic focus of the business. Success in the marketplace comes first, then the strategic focus that in turn fuels subsequent success. Strategic focus without a unique and sustainable source of advantage is useless. Fourth, in high-tech global markets, the only sustainable basis for advantage is technology leadership in a particular, pre-scribed domain. Complementary assets such as strong marketing and distribution reinforce technology leadership, but they cannot substitute for it. Fifth, technology leadership grows out of a willingness and ability to pioneer both continuous and discontinuous improvements in technology. Both are necessary and neither alone is suffi-cient. One establishes and periodically renews advantage, the other sustains it. Sixth, technology leadership is built and sustained through a style of general managerial decision making that is driven by strategic imperatives and constrained by financial considerations, rather than driven by financial objectives. And finally, the relation-ship between strategic focus and technology leadership is a dynamic one. Every attempt to pioneer an entirely new business, even though it fits within the strategic focus, stretches the firm's capabilities in new directions. The result is a continuously changing and growing envelope of businesses and associated capabilities.

How common is this model of general managerial practice? It is certainly possible to find examples of U.S. firms, other than the three examined here, that appear to be pursuing total, technology-based leadership in their fields. Hewlett-Packard's printer business is the most prominent example. It is the overwhelming market leader in a highly competitive, high-tech global market. It leads in both perfor-mance and cost and has built that leadership by pioneering both continuous technological improvements (LaserJet II) and discontinu-ous improvements (the InkJet family of printers). AMP, the world's leading manufacturer of electronic connectors, appears to be another example. It controls roughly 20 percent of the worldwide market, more than three times the share of its nearest competitors. Over the past 35 years, it has grown from a $35 million to a $3 billion business, with return on equity near 20 percent. During this time, it has focused on the field of electrical and electronic connectors, emphasized both cost and performance leadership in its area of focus, and is widely considered the technology leader of the industry.

There are also U.S. firms that did not meet the standards of total leadership during the 1980s but that now appear to recognize the necessity of doing so. Intel, Xerox, and Texas Instruments are per-haps the most striking examples. Intel seems to have reached this conclusion without ever having lost its market leadership in microprocessors, Xerox after having been surpassed in important segments of its markets, and Texas Instruments in light of the painful recognition that it is no longer foremost in its field. All these firms appear in their own way to be fighting what can be described as an all-out war to achieve total leadership.

Unfortunately, in the early 1990s, these are the exceptions rather than the rule among U.S. firms. It is much more common to find U.S. firms practicing and, more significant, aspiring to a less complete form of leadership. Because of the perceived failures of U.S. firms to compete effectively in global markets, U.S. managerial practice—and conventional prescriptions for such practice—appears to have shifted from one incomplete form of leadership to an opposite but equally incomplete form. First there was the form of leadership that emphasized development of new and unique products at the expense of more disciplined, continuous improvement of existing products, and that retreated to higher ends of markets in the face of low-cost competition. In reaction to the widely criticized shortcomings of this position, the new standard emphasizes the opposite extreme—becoming cost-competitive and maintaining leadership through quality and incremental innovation. The watchwords of the day—quality, responsiveness, continuous improvement—are all critical to the maintenance of leadership. But as we have seen, maintaining leadership is only half the story. The overwhelming finding of these cases is that this more recent style of leadership is as insufficient for success in global high-tech markets as the older style it displaced. COMM, Corning, and GEMS have managed to practice the best of both eras—the ability to compete on performance and on cost; the ability to continuously improve existing product lines and to discontinuously create new lines; the ability, in short, both to sustain leadership in today's businesses and to establish leadership in tomorrow's.

Notes

1. Joseph Morone and Sherri Naughton, "Cases in Technology Transfer," unpublished paper, Rensselaer School of Management, 1990.
2. Richard S. Rosenbloom and William J. Abernathy, "The Climate for Innovation in Industry," *Research Policy*, vol. 11 (1982), p. 223.
3. See Michael E. Porter, *Competitive Strategy: Techniques for Analyzing Industries and Competitors* (New York: Free Press, 1980).
4. For a discussion of fast following and related technology strategies, see Christopher Freeman, *The Economics of Industrial Innovation* (Cambridge MA: MIT Press, 1982); Michael E. Porter, "The Technological Dimension

of Competitive Strategy," in Richard S. Rosenbloom, ed., *Research on Technological Innovation, Management and Policy* (Greenwich, CT: JAI Press, 1983), p. 10; and David J. Teece, "Profiting from Technological Innovation: Implications for Integration, Collaboration, Licensing and Public Policy," in Michael L. Tushman and William L. Moore, eds., *Readings in the Management of Innovation*, 2d ed. (Cambridge, MA: Ballinger, 1988).

5. John Schmeltzer, "Motorola Introduces Lite Phone," *Chicago Tribune*, August 7, 1991, Sect. 3, p. 3.
6. Richard Florida and Martin Kenney, *The Breakthrough Illusion* (New York: Basic Books, 1990), p. 8.
7. Joseph Morone, "GE Plastics," Working paper, Rensselaer School of Management, 1990, p. 47.

CHAPTER 6

IMPLICATIONS FOR GOVERNMENT POLICY: INDUSTRIAL COMPETITIVENESS THROUGH TECHNOLOGY LEADERSHIP

What role should the federal government play in high-tech markets? Should it protect U.S. firms competing in strategically important industries such as advanced machine tools, semiconductors, and electronic displays? Should it attempt to preserve a U.S. industrial presence in consumer electronics? Should it devise new institutions for assisting industry, such as the proposed Consumer Electronics Capital Corporation, that would offer low-cost capital to U.S. electronics companies,[1] or the proposed civilian counterpart to the Department of Defense's DARPA (Defense Advanced Research Projects Agency)?[2] As evidence of declining U.S. industrial strength in high-tech markets grows, these and similar questions are asked with increasing intensity. What was once a debate about whether the federal government should play any role at all beyond breaking down trade barriers has become a debate about the most effective forms of government intervention.

This chapter takes a somewhat unorthodox approach to that policy debate. Whereas most discussions about government competitiveness policy draw from examples of U.S. industry's failure in high-tech markets, here we draw on examples of success. We have seen that it is by no means impossible for U.S. firms to compete effectively in short-cycle-time, dynamic, investment-intensive high-tech markets. We have examined how Motorola, Corning, and GEMS built and sustained global leadership in such markets, and identified the patterns of general managerial behavior underlying that leadership. Now we consider the lessons that their success suggests for government policy.

Dimensions of the U.S. Competitiveness Problem

At an aggregate level, the problem of U.S. industrial competitiveness is nearly hidden from view.[3] U.S. industry still leads the world in the production of manufactured goods by a substantial margin. Among

OECD (Organization for Economic Cooperation and Development) member countries, it accounts for 30.6 percent of total manufacturing production, compared to 21.6 percent for Japan.[4] U.S. industry still dominates a wide range of industries, from forestry products to engineering services to computers and software to aircraft engines. And it enjoys a number of advantages that simply cannot be matched by other countries. The massive and sophisticated U.S. domestic market, for example, works to the advantage of virtually every U.S. firm in every industry. So too does the unique and still-vibrant new venture-creating community. An outstanding university research system and the continuing influence of DARPA provide the foundation for global leadership in advanced computing and software. A sophisticated health care market and billions of dollars per year of government support for R&D in life sciences contribute to the strength of the pharmaceutical industry and global leadership in biotechnology. A highly competitive industry structure, coupled with a longstanding emphasis on process engineering, underlies an equally strong chemical industry. Large investments in defense and space R&D and procurement provide the foundation for global leadership in the manufacture of weaponry, satellites, aircraft, and aircraft engines. And a rich endowment of natural resources combined with a long and successful tradition of government support for the development and diffusion of agricultural technology ensure continued global leadership in agricultural and forestry products.

Nor does the U.S. competitiveness problem become apparent when the focus narrows from aggregate production to high-technology production. The U.S. share of total OECD production in high technology is shrinking (from 40 percent in 1980 to 36 percent in 1990), while Japan's is growing (from 18 percent to 29 percent), but here again, the aggregate data show no sign of serious difficulty.[5] But this is because the government agencies that collect such data include in their definition of high-technology aircraft and parts, guided missiles and spacecraft, ordnance and accessories, drugs and medicines, and industrial inorganic chemicals—industries where, for a number of reasons, the United States faces either weak foreign competition or competition primarily from Europe. If the focus is instead on U.S. industry performance in the subset of high-technology markets where Japanese competitors have established a strong presence, the full extent of the competitiveness problem begins to reveal itself. For example, the CIA has measured the U.S. share of global exports in eight high-tech product categories: microelectronics, computers, telecommunications equipment, machine tools and robotics, scientific/precision equipment, aerospace, medicine and biologicals, and organic chemicals. Japan is a significant contender in the first five categories. In three of the five, Japanese exports surpassed those of the United States during the 1980s, and in the other two, Japanese gains have been dramatic (see Figure 6.1).

The nature of the problem is epitomized by the electronics industry. As discussed in Chapter 1, four of the top five and six of the top ten electronics producers in the world are Japanese.[6] While the United States continues to dominate the largest segments of the electronics industry—data processing and software—Japanese gains have been dramatic in a number of other important segments. In semiconductors, the U.S. share of the $50 billion (in 1988) world market shrank from 60 percent in 1980 to 30 percent in 1988, while Japan's share grew from roughly 28 percent to 35 percent. Japan's share of the memory segment of this market grew from zero in the early 1970s to 80 percent by 1988; in discrete devices, it grew from roughly 35 percent to 45 percent, while the U.S. share declined from well over 40 percent to well under 30 percent;[7] and in the fast-growing market for application-specific integrated circuits (ASICs), the top two suppliers in the world in 1988 were Fujitsu and NEC, with 15.5 percent and 15.4 percent of the world market, respectively. Overall, the U.S. share of the ASIC market declined from 90 percent in 1978 to 53 percent in 1988.[8] The only significant segment of the semiconductor industry in which U.S. firms remain clearly ahead is microprocessors, where Intel continues to dominate.

Japanese firms also achieved overall leadership in the semiconductor manufacturing equipment industry during the 1980s. Whereas in 1982, the top three semiconductor equipment suppliers were U.S.-based Perkin Elmer, Varian, and Schlumberger, the top three in 1988 were Japan-based Nikon, Tokyo Electron, and Advantest.[9] Japanese firms completely dominate in electronic displays as well. The top four producers in this important and fast-growing segment of the industry—Sharp, Toshiba, Sanyo, and Seiko Epson—controlled 89 percent of the market for liquid crystal displays in 1989.[10] U.S. firms were responsible for the important inventions in this field, but for all intents and purposes, they had exited this industry by 1990. Indeed, apart from microprocessors, the only significant electronics component segments in which the United States still maintained its lead were connectors, led by AMP, and magnetic storage devices, led by Seagate and Connor. In the case of storage devices, however, Japanese firms appeared well in the lead in the new generation of technology, optical storage.

The United States still leads the world in electronics equipment (as opposed to components) because of its overwhelming market

Figure 6.1
Percentage Share of Global Exports,
High-Technology Products

Ranking	Microelectronics 1980	Microelectronics 1989	Computers 1980	Computers 1989	Telecommunications 1980	Telecommunications 1989	Aerospace 1980	Aerospace 1989
1	United States (18.3)	Japan (22.1)	United States (38.6)	United States (24.0)	West Germany (16.7)	Japan (29.7)	United States (47.6)	United States (45.8)
2	Japan (13.2)	United States (21.9)	West Germany (11.5)	Japan (17.5)	Sweden (15.3)	West Germany (9.5)	United Kingdom (19.7)	West Germany (12.5)
3	Singapore (10.1)	Malaysia (8.9)	United Kingdom (10.4)	United Kingdom (9.0)	United States (10.9)	United States (8.8)	West Germany (9.1)	United Kingdom (10.9)
4	Malaysia (8.9)	South Korea (7.4)	France (8.6)	West Germany (6.9)	Japan (10.3)	Sweden (8.1)	France (6.0)	France (10.2)
5	West Germany (8.4)	West Germany (5.8)	Italy (6.6)	Taiwan (5.8)	Netherlands (9.3)	Hong Kong (6.3)	Canada (4.4)	Canada (4.4)

Ranking	Machine Tools and Robotics 1980	1989	Scientific/Precision 1980	1989	Medicine and Biologicals 1980	1989	Organic Chemicals 1980	1989
1	West Germany (25.8)	Japan (23.8)	United States (28.3)	United States (25.2)	West Germany (16.7)	West Germany (15.6)	West Germany (19.1)	West Germany (17.0)
2	United States (14.1)	West Germany (20.8)	West Germany (18.1)	West Germany (18.5)	Switzerland (12.5)	Switzerland (12.2)	United States (13.9)	United States (15.5)
3	Japan (11.3)	United States (12.1)	United Kingdom (9.4)	Japan (12.9)	United Kingdom (12.0)	United States (12.2)	Netherlands (10.9)	France (8.7)
4	Switzerland (9.1)	Italy (10.0)	France (8.0)	United Kingdom (9.6)	France (11.9)	United Kingdom (11.8)	France (10.7)	Netherlands (8.1)
5	Italy (8.7)	Switzerland (8.4)	Japan (7.1)	France (5.6)	United States (11.4)	France (10.3)	United Kingdom (8.4)	United Kingdom (7.2)

Source: U.S. Central Intelligence Agency, *Handbook of Economic Statistics, 1990*, CPAS 90-10001 (Washington, DC: U.S. Government Printing Office, 1990), p. 162.

share leadership in computers—by far the largest market segment in the electronics industry[11]—although even here there are familiar signs of a loss of leadership in the fast-growing low end of the market (i.e., laptop and notebook computers). In other segments of electronics equipment, the outlook is less favorable for American firms. In 1990, total production of office automation equipment in Japan equalled $11 billion, compared to $10 billion in the United States.[12] In the newest field of office automation, facsimile (fax) machines, Japanese suppliers seem far ahead, apparently building on their strong position in the low end of the copier market. The top four fax machines producers in 1988—Sharp, Murata Business Systems, Canon, and Ricoh—controlled 56 percent of the world market.[13] The largest U.S.-based supplier, Pitney Bowes, held 5.6 percent of the market, and it was sourcing its fax machines from Japanese firms. And in the consumer electronics segment of the industry, U.S. industry is notorious for its failures. Between 1970 and 1987, U.S. industry's share of the U.S. market—let alone the world market—for color TVs shrank from 90 percent to 10 percent, its share of the U.S. market for phonographic equipment shrank from 90 percent to 1 percent, audio tape recorders from 40 percent to 1 percent, and VCRs from 10 percent to 1 percent.[14]

In those high-tech markets where the Japanese have focused their efforts, then, U.S. firms have fared badly. But even this does not capture the problem completely. The Japanese have fared very well against U.S. competition in those markets on which they have focused, and they have focused on markets that are themselves the foundation of future high-tech industries. The full significance of the Japanese dominance in semiconductors, displays, and consumer electronics is not simply that they have achieved leadership in large and rapidly growing markets, but that these large and rapidly growing markets are themselves driving advances in important related markets. Semiconductors and displays are the building blocks for electronic equipment. They represent an increasingly large portion of the total value added in a growing range of high-volume, fast-growing products such as laptop computers, fax machines, compact disk players, camcorders, and portable telephones. By controlling semiconductor and display markets, Japanese firms built the foundation for dominance in these emerging electronic equipment markets. Moreover, once leadership in equipment markets is established, it drives further advances at the component level, which in turn reinforces leadership in components.

This cycle was made painfully apparent to the U.S. Department of Commerce, when in 1991, it levied a 63 percent tariff on advanced flat-panel displays imported from Japan. The action was taken on the somewhat dubious premise that Japanese firms were selling the displays in the United States below cost in an attempt to drive the handful of tiny U.S. manufacturers of displays out of business. The net effect of the action was to deny U.S. computer manufacturers access to the displays they needed for their own equipment. Not only did Japanese manufacturers of laptop computers in the United States announce they would move their operations back home in order to escape the impact of the tariff, but U.S. manufacturers such as Apple, Compaq, and IBM suggested they would be forced to do so as well![15] The point that seems to have escaped the Department of Commerce is that advanced displays, like so many of the segments of the electronics business in which Japanese firms are outperforming U.S. firms, are the building blocks for most, if not all, future electronics industries. The firms that establish leadership in these building block segments establish leverage over many other segments as well.

Precisely the same pattern seems to have occurred a decade earlier in the field of factory automation. The Japanese share of the advanced segments of the U.S. machine tool market—numerical control machine tools and machining centers—grew from roughly 5 percent in the mid-1970s to 50 percent by 1982, at which time voluntary export restraints were adopted by Japanese machine tool makers.[16] James Geier, the chairman and former CEO of Cincinnati Milacron, once a leader in machine tools and robotics and now a leader in plastic injection molding equipment, describes the Japanese strategy:

> We now know that from the beginning of the 1950s to now [1990], the Japanese government provided $11 billion in subsidies of one kind or another to its machine tool industry. . . . Why did they do that? The Brookings Institution wrote a pamphlet after World War II which pointed out that there were only about five elements that made a difference in the outcome of World War II. One of the five was U.S. leadership in machine tools. That document was read carefully in Japan. . . . They saw machine tools as a strategic industry. And it's strategic not just for military reasons. The country that has a well-developed machine tool industry has the ability to develop advanced manufacturing capabilities on multiple levels. So this was a very good industry to subsidize, because it in turn helped all of the rest of the Japanese

manufacturing. It was a good piece of strategy. Remember Japan was poor right after the war. It had to pick its spots. You see precisely the same strategy in microelectronics.[17]

Here then can be seen the full range of the competitiveness problem. On the one hand, the strongest Japanese competitors are focusing on large, fast-growing industries that are the foundation for even larger, more widespread future industries. On the other hand, when U.S. firms go head to head against their Japanese counterparts in those industries, most fare poorly. The cases in this book are the exceptions, not the rule. The real issue in competitiveness is not leadership in the aggregate, but leadership where it matters most. The cause for alarm is not the marginal decline in U.S. industry's share of overall global production, but the striking failures in specific domains of long-term strategic importance.

The Tilted Playing Field

What accounts for the relatively poor performance of U.S. industry in the high-tech markets targeted by Japan firms? Perhaps the most illuminating explanation begins with the catch phrase of the competitiveness policy debate—the level playing field. One of the most striking features of the competition for high-tech markets is how very far from level the playing field actually is. As discussed in Chapter 1, Japanese firms are larger than most of their U.S. counterparts; they are more integrated—both horizontally and vertically—and they enjoy ownership structures and financial environments that appear to be far more conducive to the investment-intensive, long-term-oriented strategies required for success in high-tech markets. Differences in U.S. and Japanese political environments reinforce these differences in industry structure and financial environment. Industry-government relations in the United States are fundamentally more adversarial than they are in Japan. The American political culture—steeped in a classic liberal tradition that emphasizes individualism and individual rights—views "big business" with suspicion. Economic populism, which propelled the tax revolt and anti-big government movement of the 1980s as well as demands to "soak the rich" in the early 1990s, has always struck a more responsive chord in the public than the state of industrial health. The regulatory environment also reflects this tradition, being far more litigious in the United States than in Japan. Garten provides a concise summary of the differences in policy orientation:

While Japan and Germany share many broad economic and social goals with America, there are important differences between the United States and its allies. Japan's main policy objective has been to protect its economy—access to raw materials abroad, access to foreign markets, and the nurturing of powerful conglomerates in industry and finance that are big enough to perform stabilizing roles in society. In America the purpose of economic policy has been different: individual choice and consumer satisfaction.[18]

The impact of these fundamental, structural differences on the competition for high-tech markets can be seen most clearly in the persistent and growing differences in the rates at which U.S. and Japanese industry invest in tangible and intangible assets. Since aggregate rates of investment are a function of a variety of economic, political, structural, and cultural factors, they are probably the single best measure of a nation's readiness to compete over the long haul. This is especially true for high-tech markets, where it is not uncommon to invest $1 or more of fixed capital for every $1 of annual sales.

Figure 6.2, from the Council on Competitiveness, shows that Japanese industry invests in plant and equipment at a significantly higher rate than U.S. industry, that this difference has persisted over decades, and that during the 1980s, it widened dramatically. Between 1985 and 1990, Japan's rate of investment as a percentage of gross domestic product (GDP) increased by 34 percent, whereas the U.S. rate remained roughly constant. As a result, by 1990, Japan was investing roughly 23.4 percent of its GDP in plant and equipment, while the United States invested 12.6 percent. In other words, although Japan's GDP is roughly half the size of that of the United States, Japanese industry is investing comparable amounts—in absolute terms—in plant and equipment.[19] And given that Japan has concentrated its efforts in strategically important industries, these aggregate statistics probably understate the difference in U.S. and Japanese investment in the high-tech industries of interest here.

Related to the rate of investment in plant and equipment is the rate of investment in R&D. Here again, the evidence points to a nation poorly prepared for the demands of competition in high-tech markets. In the aggregate, the United States invests less of its gross national product (GNP) in R&D than Japan does—2.7 percent for the United States in 1989, compared to 3 percent for Japan. Moreover, virtually all of Japan's R&D spending is for civilian purposes, whereas only 1.9 percent of U.S. GNP is. These differences became pro-

Figure 6.2
*Private Industry Expenditure
on Plant and Equipment*

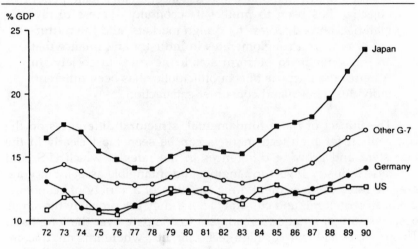

Source: U.S. Council on Competitiveness.

nounced during the 1980s, when Japan's nondefense R&D spending grew from 2.3 percent of GNP in 1981 to 3 percent of GNP in 1989, whereas U.S. nondefense R&D spending remained constant at 1.9 percent from 1983 on (see Figure 6.3).[20] A large contributor to the widening gap was the U.S. federal government, which accounts for roughly half of total R&D spending in the United States (compared to roughly 30 percent in Japan). Between 1980 and 1990, defense R&D spending grew from 47 percent of total government R&D spending to 61 percent.[21]

The picture is no more encouraging when it comes to investment in human resources. The rather limited available evidence suggests that Japanese investment in worker training far outstrips that found in the United States. A study by McDuffie and Kochan, for example, compared the amount of training both new and experienced workers received in a sample of 56 automotive assembly plants located around the world. They found that workers in the plants of U.S. firms received considerably less training than those in plants owned by Japanese and European firms. Of the 14 U.S. plants in the sample, amount of training was judged to be "moderately low" in 10 (71 percent) and "moderately high" in 4 (29 percent), whereas only one of 11 Japanese plants was judged to have "moderately low" levels, 3 (27 percent) were judged to have "moderately high" efforts, and

Figure 6.3
Nondefense R&D Expenditure

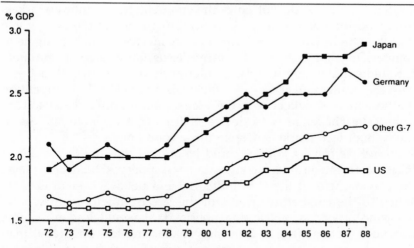

Source: U.S. Council on Competitiveness.

7 "very high."[22] This apparent underinvestment in worker training compounds the well-publicized weaknesses in the U.S. elementary and high school education system. Studies of international educational achievement in elementary and high school math and science consistently show U.S. students among the worst performers and Japanese students among the top performers.[23] U.S. workers thus appear to enter the workforce with an inferior education, and once in the workforce, receive considerably less training.

The Policy Challenge

All of these indicators of relative underinvestment point to the same underlying condition: the Japanese industrial and political system appears to be better equipped than the U.S. system for competition in high-tech markets. It is not only the differences in the ownership structure of industry in the two countries that is critical. Nor is it the larger size of Japanese firms, or their greater vertical and horizontal integration, or the higher degree of competition among Japanese firms for their domestic markets, or a government policy structure and culture in Japan that embraces the competitiveness of its firms and treats it as the primary social objective. It is the combination of all these factors that tilts the playing field for high-tech markets against

U.S. firms. For citizens of a country that enjoyed a generation of unchallenged global leadership following World War II, the possibility that their firms do not enter the competition for critical markets from a position of advantage is difficult to grasp. Yet this is precisely the situation in which U.S. firms find themselves as they struggle to compete in high-tech markets. Any discussion of steps to promote U.S. industrial strength in future high-tech markets must thus begin with the unpleasant reality of a tilted playing field. The competition for these markets will be waged under conditions unfavorable to U.S. firms. The challenge is to devise policies that promote success in future high-tech markets despite those conditions.

Level the playing field? It could be argued that the first order of business for government competitiveness policy should be to level the playing field. If the U.S. industrial and political system is badly suited to the competitive rigors of the late twentieth century, why not concentrate on developing policies that would lead to a more beneficial system? If U.S. firms are smaller and less integrated than their Japanese counterparts, why not pursue ideas like the National Advisory Committee on Semiconductors' Consumer Electronics Capital Corporation,[24] Ferguson's proposal for a "Euro-American Keiretsu,"[25] and the abortive attempt in 1989 to create U.S. Memories, a consortium to produce advanced semiconductor memory devices?[26]

The likelihood of any such changes in the foreseeable future is remote. There is no national consensus that U.S. industrial competitiveness should be a policy priority, let alone that significant structural change should be promoted. Even if it there were, it is not clear how the system can best be changed. Those aspects of the U.S. system that leave U.S. industry at a disadvantage are threads of a larger fabric; they cannot be isolated and replaced. The financial environment in the United States that focuses attention on short-term earnings, the political environment that resists making industrial competitiveness a national priority, and the industry structure that is much less integrated than Japan's and much more resistant to cooperation among firms are all integral components of a larger system. They are as deeply rooted in U.S. culture, history, and economic structure as the features of the Japanese system that benefit Japan's firms are in theirs.[27]

To be sure, some structural change is taking place and will continue to do so, but it is modest in scope. During the 1980s, the Department of Commerce's National Bureau of Standards evolved into the National Institute for Standards and Technology—the only agency in the federal R&D system with the explicit mission of supporting industrial technology. Its total budget for 1990 was $170 million, less than two-tenths of 1 percent of U.S. R&D spending. The National Science Foundation instituted Engineering Research Centers, designed to support university research groups oriented toward industrial R&D. Their total budget for 1990 was less than $50 million. Antitrust laws were modified to allow for collaboration among firms in so-called "pre-competitive R&D," and the Department of Commerce actively promoted the formation of R&D alliances and consortia. But even Sematech, a $200 million per year R&D consortium funded by industry and government to support R&D on semiconductor manufacturing technology, and by far the most prominent of such consortia, will not significantly affect the competitive balance in the semiconductor industry. Two hundred million dollars in cooperative R&D is almost irrelevant in an industry where the leading Japanese manufacturers spend twice as much on R&D and capital equipment as the leading U.S. manufacturers, and by virtue of their vertical integration and fundamentally different ownership structures, are better able to sustain significant, long-term losses in the all-important battle for market share.

Whatever structural evolution is occurring in the United States is thus happening slowly in a mostly incremental, trial-and-error fashion. The context for government competitiveness policy over the next generation will continue to be a tilted playing field in the competition for high-tech markets, caused by structural differences in the economic and political systems of Japan and the United States that work to the disadvantage of U.S. firms. For the foreseeable future, the challenge for government policy makers is to devise measures that increase the likelihood of success in the face of structural disadvantage.

The Lessons of Success—Implications for Competitiveness Policy

This brings us back to GEMS, Motorola, and Corning. For if the policy challenge is to increase the likelihood of success in high-tech markets, despite the tilted playing field, here are three firms that have done precisely that—succeeded in short-cycle-time, investment-intensive high-tech markets against strong Japanese competitors in the face of structural disadvantages that tilt the playing field against U.S. firms. What do these cases teach us about what government can do to help other U.S. firms compete in such markets?

Lesson #1: Build Advantage Through Technology Leadership

The markets pursued by GEMS, COMM, and Corning were attacked by the same vertically and horizontally integrated Japanese electron-

ics giants that overwhelmed the U.S. consumer electronics and semiconductor industries. But unlike their counterparts in consumer electronics and semiconductors, GEMS, COMM, and Corning have
managed to stay ahead technologically. They have built and sustained global market leadership by building and sustaining technological leadership. Their general management, it is accurate to say,
was obsessed with leadership in their areas of focus, and they believed that the primary means to such leadership was better technology. With better technology, GEMS, COMM, and Corning were able
to offset the structural advantages of their competitors. This is what
Dave Duke meant when he argued, "If we tie, we lose." He knew
Corning was facing competitors—both U.S. and Japanese—with
vastly superior resources and therefore, if Corning could not outinno-
vate them, it would rapidly fall behind.

The first lesson of these cases, then, is that given enduring structural disadvantages, the objective for U.S. policy makers should be
to help U.S. firms build and maintain technology leadership, which
provides compensating advantage and offsets the tilted playing field.
If there is a guiding principle for policy makers concerned about U.S.
industrial competitiveness in these cases, it is Dave Duke's admonition: if we tie, we lose.

While the guiding principle for policy is clear, so too is evidence
that the United States is dissipating its ability to build technology
leadership. A growing number of independent assessments of the
relative strength of U.S. and Japanese technology find the same underlying pattern: in some fields of high technology—most notably
electronic components and manufacturing technology—Japan has
not only caught up to the United States but has surpassed it. In other
fields—like chemicals, pharmaceuticals, and computers and software—the United States remains ahead. But in almost all fields, the
U.S. position is deteriorating, and nowhere is it getting stronger.
Figures 6.4 and 6.5 summarize the results of two representative studies, one by the U.S. Department of Commerce, the other by the
Council on Competitiveness.

It is noteworthy that the United States is still ahead technologically in areas in which U.S. industry continues to enjoy significant
structural advantages. But where the structural conditions are
skewed against U.S. industry—in electronics-related, consumer-
oriented, short-cycle-time high-tech markets—U.S. technology leadership has deteriorated badly and in many instances has already been
lost. So while these cases of success may offer a clear guiding principle for government policy—build market leadership on technology
leadership—a new question remains: Assuming it is not already too

Figure 6.4
Assessment of Technology Strength—U.S. Status Relative to Japan's

	Present	Future
Behind	Advanced Materials Adv. Semiconductor Devices Digital Imaging Technology High-Density Data Storage Optoelectronics	Advanced Materials Biotechnology Digital Imaging Technology Superconductors Adv. Semiconductor Devices High-Density Data Storage High-Performance Computing Medical Devices and Diagnostics Optoelectronics Sensor Technology
Even	Superconductors	Artificial Intelligence Flexible Computer- Integrated Manufacturing
Ahead	Artificial Intelligence Biotechnology Flexible Computer- Integrated Manufacturing High-Performance Computing Medical Devices and Diagnostic Sensor Technology	

Source: Adapted from National Science Board, *The Competitive Strength of U.S Industrial Science and Technology*, Figures 1-17, 1-18 (Washington, DC: U.S. Government Printing Office, 1992).

late, how should government lay the foundation for industrial technology leadership?

Lesson #2: Technology Leadership Is Driven by General Management, Not Government Management

A second lesson from these cases centers on the critical role general management plays in building technology leadership. Technology leadership derives from general managerial practice; it is shaped by the strategic focus that general management displays, by the consistency with which it applies that focus, by its pursuit of total rather than just high-end leadership, by its willingness and ability to pioneer both continuous and discontinuous improvements in technology, and by a style of decision making characterized by a willingness to learn by doing in the face of uncertainty and driven by the imperative to stay ahead rather than by financial objectives.

Figure 6.5
Assessment of U.S. Technology Strength

Technology	Strong	Competitive	Weak	Losing Badly or Lost
Materials/ Materials Process	Bioactive/Biocompatible Materials Bioprocessing Drug Discovery Techniques Emissions Reduction Genetic Engineering Recycling/Waste Processing	Catalysts Chemical Synthesis Magnetic Materials Metal Matrix Composites Net Shape Forming Optical Materials Photoresists Polymers Polymer Matrix Composites Process Controls Superconductors	Advanced Metals Membranes Precision Coating	Display Materials Electronic Ceramics Electronic Packaging Materials Gallium Arsenide Silicon Structural Ceramics
Engineering & Production	Computer-Aided Engineering Systems Engineering	Advanced Welding Computer-Integrated Manufacturing Human Factors Engineering Joining & Fastening Technologies Measurement Techniques Structural Dynamics	Design for Manufacturing Design for Manufacturing Processes Flexible Manufacturing High-Speed Machining Integration of Research, Design, and Manufacturing Leading-Edge Scientific Instruments Precision Bearings Precision Matching & Forming Total Quality Management	Integrated Circuit Fabrication and Test Equipment Robotics and Automated Equipment

Electronic Components	Magnetic Information Storage Microprocessors	Logic Chips Sensors Submicron	Actuators Electro Photography Electrostatics Laser Devices Photonics	Electroluminescent Displays Liquid Crystal Displays Memory Chips Multichips Packaging Systems Optical Information Storage Plasma and Vacuum Fluorescent Displays Printed Circuit Board Technology
Information	Animation & Full Motion Video Applications Software Artificial Intelligence Computer Modeling & Simulation Data Representation Data Retrieval & Update Expert Systems Graphics Hardware & Software Handwriting & Speech Recognition High-Level Software Languages Natural Language Neural Networks Operating Systems Optical Character Recognition Processor Architecture Semantic Modeling & Interpretation Software Engineering Transmitters & Receivers	Broadband Switching Digital Infrastructure Digital Signal Processing Fiber Optic Systems Hardware Integration Multiplexing Spectrum Technologies		
Powertrain & Propulsion	Airbreathing Propulsion Low-Emission Engines Rocket Propulsion	Alternative Fuel Engines Electrical Storage Technologies Electric Motors & Drives	High Fuel Economy/Power Density Engines	

Source: National Science Board, *The Competitive Strength of U.S. Industrial Science and Technology*, Appendix Table 1-20 (Washington, DC: U.S. Government Printing Office, 1992).

Figure 6.6
General Managerial Environments

		Decision-Making Style	
		financially driven	*strategically driven*
	impatient		
FINANCIAL ENVIRONMENT			
	patient		

Since technology leadership is shaped by general management, is there anything government can do to promote technology leadership in more firms? There appear to be a number of possibilities, which, at the risk of oversimplifying, can be illustrated by the two by two matrix shown in Figure 6.6. The matrix describes four idealized classes of general managerial environments. They are defined by two dimensions, the first of which refers to general managerial decision-making style. Decision making can be divided into the two broad classes discussed in Chapter 1—the more conventional, analytically oriented, financially driven style sometimes referred to as "management by the numbers"; and the less conventional, experience-based, strategically driven style found in the three cases. The goal of both kinds of management is an attractive return on investment. But the first treats a new business opportunity as a potential vehicle for financial investment and asks how the projected return compares to alternative investment candidates, whereas the other treats a new business opportunity as the means to pursuing strategic objectives and asks whether the opportunity represents a step in the right direction and if so, how the opportunity can be pursued in a way that is affordable.

The second dimension refers to the financial environment in which general managers operate. A large and growing body of evidence suggests that the Japanese financial environment is more conducive than the U.S. environment to the long-term investment-intensive strategies required to succeed in high-technology markets. The most striking difference—although it is only one of several—is the nature of corporate ownership structures. In Japan, they are dominated by stable shareholders, and in the United States, by financial investors, many driven to maximize return in the near term. There

Figure 6.7
General Managerial Environments

		Decision-Making Style	
		financially driven	*strategically driven*
FINANCIAL ENVIRONMENT	*impatient*	many U.S. firms	U.S.- based successes
	patient		many Japanese firms

seem to be two idealized types of financial environment—a less patient environment, concerned with short-term profit maximizing, and a more patient environment, which places greater emphasis on longer-term strategic well-being.

The problem of U.S. industrial competitiveness in high-tech industries can be characterized in terms of this matrix. Many U.S. firms operate in the upper left cell—in an impatient financial environment with managers who, not surprisingly given their environment, exhibit a financially driven style of decision making. Meanwhile, many Japanese firms function in the lower right cell. Given a very different financial environment, their management seems to place less emphasis on quarterly returns and more on long-term survival and growth.[28] The U.S. firms examined in this book—firms that have built market leadership through technology leadership—operate in the upper right cell. They face the impatient financial environment of their U.S. counterparts, but they exhibit a more strategic style of decision making. They manage the way they do *despite* their environment (see Figure 6.7).

This is the challenge when devising policies that promote managerial behavior that is conducive to building technology leadership. Government must promote a style of decision making that is incompatible with the larger financial environment. There are two logically distinct approaches to attacking this conundrum, which can also be shown on the matrix. First, government could take measures to nudge the U.S. system farther down the vertical axis—measures intended to alter the environment in which management operates. Second, government could take measures to nudge the U.S. system farther along the horizontal axis—measures intended to alter the actual patterns of managerial behavior, independent of any changes in the environment. Needless to say, both approaches are problematic. The concrete forms they might take are far from clear, likely to be controversial, and in all probability would lead to very gradual change at best.

Changing the financial environment. The cases in this book offer a clear and consistent message: sustained success in high-tech markets requires the ability to grow and periodically renew businesses by pioneering radical and generational innovations. This ability requires general management that is willing and able to persist during the long, pre-emergent phase of low or negative returns coupled with high investment. Any policy proposals designed to improve the financial environment for technology leadership should be measured against this basic finding.

This does not mean that continuous incremental innovation within existing businesses is unimportant. On the contrary, we have seen that it is essential for maintaining leadership. But leadership cannot be maintained if it is not first established and then periodically renewed, and it is this process that requires the type of managerial decision making most clearly in conflict with the U.S. financial environment. The problem is not a lack of R&D or new product development by itself, but rather a lack of R&D and new product development aimed at the risky, uncertain creation of new businesses and product lines. The U.S. financial environment rewards the manager who focuses on maintaining leadership in existing lines of business, since important measures like shortening customer response time and enhancing quality can quickly lead to improvements in the bottom line. But the financial environment is as likely to penalize as it is to reward the manager who, in addition to taking these steps, invests in the development of new businesses and product lines that may (or may not) prove profitable in five to ten years.

The ideal policy change would therefore lead investors to pressure managers for evidence that while they are taking steps to improve today's profitability, they are also laying the foundations for tomorrow's. The historical success of the U.S. venture-capital community suggests that this kind of orientation is compatible with the U.S. institutional structure. The problem is not so much to create investor interest in long-term growth as it is to enhance the value investors attach to it relative to near-term results. At the same time, any policy designed to promote technology leadership must be politically feasible. Above all, it should be simple, incremental, and reversible. The more elaborate the proposed policy change, the more complicated its effects; the more widespread its impact on groups that might be negatively influenced, the greater the political resistance to the proposed change. For similar reasons, proposals for change should avoid penalizing short-term-oriented actions and, instead, aim at rewarding the desired behavior. Penalizing actions that are a natural and inherent part of the overall institutional structure—such as short-term trading—is the step most likely to generate political opposition while at the same time spawning new practices that result in the same overall effect.

Are there any simple, reversible policy steps that reward patience among investors without penalizing impatience? Of the many changes that have been proposed to lengthen the time horizons of U.S. business,[29] significantly reducing the capital gains tax on investments held for an extended period of time—five to seven years—most clearly moves in this direction. To have an impact on investor behavior, the tax rate on long-term gains would have to be significantly (on the order of 50 percent) lower than the rate on ordinary capital gains. In effect, a change of this kind lowers the cost of capital for investors with long time horizons. If the reduction is large enough, or more precisely, if the difference between the tax rate on normal and long-term capital gains is large enough, shareholder stability should increase, which in turn ought to lead to a greater demand by shareholders for evidence that the firm's management is tending to the growth of new lines of business. To be sure, this would not eliminate the emphasis on quarterly returns, but it should bring some balance to how performance is judged in financial markets. Moreover, this kind of policy change seems politically feasible. It would be less vulnerable to the criticism that it exacerbates the deficit than reducing the overall tax rate on capital gains since it would apply to a much smaller base. It would not benefit only the rich since homeowners would be among the most direct beneficiaries; nor would it interfere with the workings of the marketplace because it is compatible with the existing structure of financial markets and does not penalize short-term transactions.

There may be other policy measures that would bring about the same end; there may even be some that would do so more efficiently than a reduction in the tax on gains from long-term holdings. The important point is that the priority should be to increase shareholder interest in and concern about actions being taken today that will affect the bottom line in the future.

Changing managerial practices directly. A different but complementary approach to promoting the style of management required for technology leadership entails a move along the horizontal dimension of our matrix—through policies that would change managerial behavior directly, rather than indirectly, through changes in the financial environment. R&D and investment tax credits, along with accelerated depreciation, are the most obvious options. But to be effective, they must have a significant impact on cash flow. A measure like the 25 percent tax credit on increases in R&D spending that was instituted in 1981 has too small an effect on cash flow to significantly alter managerial behavior.[30] Unfortunately, there is no way of knowing in advance how large the credit must be in order to have the desired effect; and of course, the larger the credit the more intransigent the problems of political feasibility. More to the point, even if a larger R&D tax credit were instituted, it still might not induce the kind of long-term-oriented action required to build technology leadership. In their current form, R&D tax credits can just as easily be used to subsidize minor modifications of existing products—which are important but far from sufficient for building technology leadership.

Perhaps the solution is not to expand the existing R&D tax credit or to resurrect the old investment tax credit, but to develop more targeted versions. For example, a substantial tax credit for investment in certain intangible assets—such as worker training—might result in significant benefits. Even more intriguing is a substantial tax credit for investment and R&D spending associated with the pre-emergent stage of new businesses and product lines during the period of negative cash flow, when bottom line pressures are most severe. If it were possible to devise accounting rules for identifying "pre-emergent" investment and spending, tax credits could then be targeted specifically at these activities, rather than at more general investment and spending. The drain on the tax roles would be far smaller than a more generalized tax credit, yet if the credits were significant, the impact on management's orientation toward such activities would be far greater.

An entirely different path to altering managerial behavior—more speculative and requiring more time to take effect—is to develop new approaches to management education. These cases of success suggest that conventional American management training, with its emphasis on analysis rather than experience and its treatment of new business opportunities as potential vehicles for financial investment rather than as potential strategic forays, is inappropriate for teaching how to create market leadership through technology leadership. One potential role for government is to encourage experiments in management education that lead to a greater synthesis than now exists between the traditional management functions (marketing, finance, and so forth) and the traditional engineering functions (design, manufacturing, and so forth). Federal support for experiments in the integration of management and technology represent a natural extension of the National Science Foundation's mission and would have a negligible budgetary impact.

Lesson #3: Technology Leadership Is Built Within a Strategic Context

Another theme that runs through these cases is closely related to the integral role general management plays in building technology leadership: successful technology development occurs within specific strategic contexts. It is woven into the overall strategic fabric of the firm—building on experience and unique capabilities, and enhancing them in return.

This raises questions about the wisdom of government-sponsored development of commercial technology. As evidence of U.S. industrial decline in high-tech markets has grown, so too has the clamor for a more active government role in commercial technology development. Among the most common policy proposals are the establishment of a civilian DARPA that would fund commercial technology development; expansion of the Department of Commerce's NIST, which would itself develop commercial technology; use of the federal government's national labs—which account for one-sixth of the entire nation's R&D capacity—for commercial technology development; and government sponsorship and funding of cooperative industrial and university R&D on generic, precompetitive technology.[31] The potential difficulty with all these ideas is that they result in R&D projects that are isolated from the specific strategic contexts of specific firms competing in specific industries on the basis of specific sets of competencies and historical experiences. In the absence of a strategic context, how is project selection and development to be guided? What performance and cost levels should be targeted? What motivation is there to persist in development once the inevitable difficulties arise? What motivation is there to suffer through the pain of the pre-emergent state? Indeed, what standards are to be used to judge success and failure?

The underlying problem with many of the proposals for government sponsorship of commercial technology is that they assume technology development is an essentially linear process: first comes the underlying science and engineering, then the generic technology development, and then the product-specific technology development.[32] This is especially true of what had become by the early 1990s the most popular approach to a more active role for government in commercial technology development—government sponsorship and funding of precompetitive, generic-technology development projects. This approach stems from the widely held belief that the decline in U.S. industrial technology stems not from a decline in fundamental research—where the United States, largely on the basis of its outstanding university research system, is still pre-eminent—but from a failure to effectively translate that research into leadership products and processes. This failure, it is often argued, is caused by an institutional gap between university research labs and industrial labs. The former do not push their research far enough into development to reach a state where it can become useful for product-oriented industrial labs, while the latter do not reach back far enough into fundamental research to translate the fruits of university research into new products and processes. The way to bridge this technology transfer gap, according to this argument, is for government to promote and fund collaborative R&D projects involving industry, universities, and government laboratories that would develop technology to the point where it can be taken up by individual firms. In what looks very much like a technological relay race, universities conduct the underlying science and engineering research, hand it off to the precompetitive generic technology consortia, which in turn advance the academic research and then pass the resulting generic technology baton to individual firms, which race each other to develop new products and processes.

Yet as the histories of GEMS, COMM, and Corning make clear, the development process in firms that have been especially successful at bringing technology to market is anything but linear. Basic research is often essential to the process, but it is hardly ever the starting point. Successful technology development grows out of a context shaped by the strategic focus of the firm, past experiences in related markets, and past technology development, both successful and unsuccessful. Motorola's development of portable cellular telephones was part of a long stream of experiences that left the company with a set of competencies, background, and strategic interests in portable communications that was absolutely unique. Corning's efforts to develop optical fibers, for all the outstanding fundamental research that went into it, grew out of decades of experience with glass lasers, optical glasses, and fused silica.

Corning's history also points to other difficulties with this notion of generic, precompetitive R&D. In the early 1970s, a large number of firms were carrying out what might be viewed today as redundant programs to develop generic technology for drawing optical fibers. This would seem to have been an ideal candidate for cooperative generic, precompetitive technology development. But when exactly was Corning's lengthy effort to develop the fibers in the "precompetitive stage"? Corning achieved its position of advantage in optical fibers precisely because it had established an early lead in the generic process technology. And it had this early lead because this was an opportunity that built on its historical areas of competence. What would have been the basis for advantage had it not established and then rapidly capitalized on this early lead? Or consider the LCD glass case. Corning developed a proprietary process for making high-performance glass, and it is this process that is now the basis for its competitive advantage. Is the process generic technology? Yes, in the sense that all its competitors are now striving to develop a process for drawing high-performance glass that can compete with it. But would Corning have won its leadership position if it had been jointly developing this process? In a world where technology development is highly integrated into the strategic context of the firm, the dividing line between the precompetitive and competitive stages of research may be impossible to draw. Moreover, it may well be that collaborating in the early stages of technology development has the effect of equalizing the technological starting point, which is the reverse of what is needed if the key to success on an unlevel playing field is technology leadership.

How is the gap between scientific and engineering research and industrial products and processes to be filled if not by cooperative, generic technology development? The answer offered by these cases is that the best mechanism for bridging this gap is industry R&D, shaped by a consistent strategic focus and the drive for total leadership within that focus. If the gap is not being bridged by firms in this fashion, then the problem is not a lack of gap-filling R&D, but rather a lack of the strategic management that creates the demand and environment for this kind of R&D. Without it, government-sponsored development of generic technology, no matter how excellent the R&D, is unlikely to result in leadership products and processes. To build advantage on the basis of technology, technology development must be driven by general management and shaped by the strategic context of the firm. Technology push, funded by government, is no substitute for strategy pull.

In short, the gap between science and product in this country stems from the failure of U.S. firms to take the steps necessary to pull science and engineering into the industrial technology context. The answer is not to perform more R&D outside the strategic context of firms, but to change the behavior of management so that there is a greater demand for this kind of R&D within firms. The answer, in other words, are policies that lead to the changes in managerial practices discussed above.

*Lesson # 4. Technology Leadership Begins with Radical
and Generational Innovation*

GEMS, COMM, and Corning all established and periodically renewed their leadership through radical and generational innovations.
Motorola attained its position in communications by pioneering mobile radios, portable radios, pagers, mobile and portable cellular
phones, portable data, and global portable cellular phones. Throughout its history, Corning built its market strength on major innovations, from PYROCERAM and spin-cast TV bulbs to optical fibers,
cellular ceramics, and fusion glass for LCDs. And even though GEMS
did not pioneer CT and MR, it established its dominance only when
it introduced fundamentally different and better approaches to these
products.

The primary argument of this book has been that the process of
building competitive advantage through discontinuous innovation is
driven by general management. The right kind of strategic management is a necessary condition for building technology leadership. But
it is not sufficient. Technology leadership still rests ultimately on
acts of individual creativity—on the ideas and activities of talented
scientists and engineers. Motorola's strategic management shaped
the focus on mobile and portable products, and provided the persistence and continuity required to bring such products to market, as
did Corning's strategic management with glass and ceramics and
GEMS' with diagnostic imaging. But focus, persistence, and continuity would have not have amounted to much without the creative
efforts of people like Marty Cooper, Red Redington, Robert Maurer,
and their associates. While outstanding R&D is usually wasted in the
absence of the right kind of strategic management, the reverse is
equally true: the right kind of strategic management cannot build
competitive advantage on the basis of technology without the right
individuals in R&D, engineering, and manufacturing.

These individuals are the product of a university-based system
of research and education that is by any measure the strongest in the
world. Traditionally, the federal government has had the primary
responsibility for supporting university science and engineering.
Support has come mostly in the form of R&D grants and contracts
from a variety of federal government agencies. Although industry
support of university R&D nearly tripled in constant dollars during
the 1980s (reaching $1.1 billion in 1990), industry still accounted for
only 7 percent of total funding of university-based science and engineering research in 1990, compared with 58 percent from the federal
government.[33] This, then, is an area in which U.S. industry's compet-

itiveness in high-tech markets clearly depends on the actions of the federal government.

Unfortunately, the federal R&D system is structured in such a way that industry's need for scientific and engineering talent and fundamental knowledge receives low priority. The federal R&D system is a hodge-podge of government mission agencies that took shape haphazardly in the years immediately following World War II. The primary R&D funding agencies are Department of Defense (DoD), National Aeronautics and Space Administration (NASA), Department of Energy (DOE), Health and Human Services (HHS), Department of Agriculture (DOA), Environmental Protection Agency (EPA), Department of Transportation (DOT), Department of Commerce (DOC), and the National Science Foundation (NSF). In 1990, the total federal R&D budget was roughly $65 billion. Of this total, 65 percent was directed toward defense by DoD and DOE. Another 26 percent was allocated to health, energy, and space by HHS, DOE, and NASA. The rest was divided among a number of smaller agencies, including NSF which accounts for about 2.5 percent of the total R&D budget.[34] The overall result is a fragmented, decentralized, and largely uncoordinated system for funding science and engineering research, driven primarily by the goals of these government mission agencies.[35] When the federal government has supported research in areas of science and engineering of importance to industry, it has usually done so as a by-product of mission agency objectives. Even when the federal government directly supports industrial R&D—and more than one-third of the total R&D performed by U.S. industry is funded by the federal government (compared to 2 percent in Japan)—it is R&D directed at government missions, particularly defense and space.

When the technology needs of industry and government coincide, this approach to federal R&D works to the advantage of U.S. industry. Much of the life sciences R&D funded by the National Institutes of Health, roughly $6 billion in 1990, contributes directly to the talent and knowledge pool from which the strong U.S. pharmaceutical and biotechnology industries draw. Likewise, in the decades immediately following the war, computer, semiconductor, and aircraft engine businesses in the United States received enormous headstarts from DoD and NASA R&D funding and procurement. But the days when industry's technology needs coincided with DoD's and when DoD procurement tended to drive industrial technology development are long gone. The performance needs of military and space systems have for the most part diverged from those of industry, and as a result, the spill-over benefits to industry from government mission-oriented R&D are far weaker than they used to be.[36]

The structure of the federal R&D system, while it was well suited to the industrial world of the 1950s and 1960s, thus has the unfortunate effect of skewing R&D spending priorities away from the needs of today's industry. One of the clearest indications can be seen in the pattern of government support for academic R&D during the 1980s. In the competition for high-tech markets, the one responsibility that most unambiguously belongs to government is maintaining an outstanding, university-based talent and knowledge pool. Yet even as U.S. industry was losing its leadership in one high-tech market after another, federal support of academic R&D as a percentage of GNP was declining. Between 1980 and 1989, total federal R&D spending grew from 1.12 percent of GNP to 1.19 percent, roughly a 6 percent increase. But federal support of academic R&D fell from .19 percent of GNP to .13 percent, a decline of 32 percent; and if increases in life sciences funding from NIH are excluded, federal support of academic R&D as a percentage of GNP actually declined by 40 percent. What were the priorities for federal R&D spending during this period? R&D spending by DoD grew from $14 billion to $37.5 billion, or from .5 percent of GNP to .74 percent; NIH R&D spending grew from $3.2 billion to $6.2 billion, a slightly faster rate than GNP growth; and NASA R&D spending grew from $3.2 billion to $5.4 billion, slightly less than the GNP growth rate.[37]

Priorities for future R&D spending continue to reflect the mission agency orientation. The largest government R&D projects planned for the 1990s—excluding DoD's, which are undergoing dramatic re-evaluation—are NASA's space station, projected at $37 billion spread over 16 years, and DOE's superconducting super collider, expected to cost $8.6 billion over 11 years.[38] Even in areas of technology that are more clearly relevant to industry's needs, this agency orientation is evident. In manufacturing technology, for example, most of the $150 million that the federal government spent on robotics-related R&D in 1990 was oriented toward defense and space missions. Two-thirds was directed at developing a robotic arm for the space station. A 1988 survey of American manufacturers conducted by the Robot Industries Association found that "many of the DoD- and NASA-funded efforts in robotics deal with mobility and navigation, the areas deemed least important" by the survey respondents.[39] Similarly, 90 percent of the $118 million in federal R&D funding for advanced imaging was oriented toward defense. In advanced computing, 62 percent of the $448 million was for defense, space, or energy missions, although here it might be argued that there is still a significant potential for important spin-off benefits. Funding in the field of high-temperature superconductivity displays a similar pattern. Of the total federal R&D funding of $228 million in 1990, DoD and DOE accounted for $188 million.[40] In late 1988, a presidential advisory panel formed to assess the nation's capability in the field concluded:

> While there is a high level of activity in U.S. industry today, much of it is scattered and in monitoring groups and is unlikely to survive in what we believe will be a long-distance race. And while there is a high level of activity by the U.S. government today both in government labs and in support of universities, the work is primarily structured around government rather than commercial applications. In contrast, the Japanese government laboratories have a long tradition of materials work done closely with industry, and the Japanese government has put in place . . . a structure that will support, coordinate, and sustain the various individual industrial efforts in Japan as the Japanese companies work their way through the early stages of this new technology and look for applications.[41]

There is no question that the government's mission-oriented investment in R&D has produced enormous spin-off benefits over the course of the past half-century, not the least of which is an outstanding university research system. But the pertinent issue for competitiveness policy in the early 1990s is whether the priorities implicit in the structure of the federal R&D system should be adjusted in light of the dramatic changes in the world of industrial technology that have occurred since the late 1940s. Given the importance of technology leadership to U.S. industry and of outstanding science and engineering talent and knowledge to the ability of U.S. industry to build technology leadership, and given that the primary responsibility for maintaining the strength of the nation's universities that produce this talent and knowledge belongs to the federal government, it makes no sense to continue to treat support of this talent and knowledge base as a secondary benefit of funding government missions. Nor does it make any sense as U.S. strength in critical areas of commercial high technology declines that the primary nondefense initiatives of the federal R&D system are the superconducting super collider and the space station. Supporters of both have attempted to justify these projects in part on the basis of the contribution they might make to industrial competitiveness, but the arguments are tortured, and few industry leaders concur. It would surely make more sense to redirect some of the energy and resources now devoted to mission agency megaprojects to research and education programs that would be of more direct benefit to industry. For example, the single most important initiative of the 1980s aimed at strengthening the research and education base in areas of technology of direct relevance to industry is the NSF's Engineering Research Centers program (ERC). The ERCs, introduced in 1984, were designed to be a new kind of university-based activity that would "improve engineering research so that U.S. engineers will be better prepared to contribute to engineering practice and to assist U.S. industry in becoming more competitive in world markets."[42] The original objective was to establish 25 of these centers, each with steady-state federal funding of about $5 million (1983 dollars). The program has received enthusiastic ratings from industry and an independent review panel formed by the National Academy of Engineering. Yet reflecting the relative lack of importance attached to industrial competitiveness within the U.S. R&D system, funding for the program had grown to only $41 million in 1989.[43]

Compare the relative impacts of the following two policy alternatives on the nation's long-term competitiveness in high-tech markets: the roughly $2 billion per year in R&D that will be spent on NASA's space station, or $200 million per year in new NSF spending for a spectrum of university-based activities—from new ERCs to more support of individual investigators to new curricula—targeted at areas of science and engineering of importance to industry. The following assessment of a sample of ERCs by the review panel of the National Academy of Engineering describes the multiplier effect of the second approach:

> One ERC has begun, at its industrial partners' request, a new master's degree in systems engineering. Another has established a coherent graduate program in interfacial engineering. A third has now involved 168 undergraduates from nine departments in research on biotechnology process engineering, along with 53 graduate students, 16 postdoctoral students, 7 visiting faculty members and 9 industry personnel. A fourth has developed a new generation of courses and texts in telecommunications. In general, larger numbers of graduate students are being drawn into the ERCs' fields, and students from a variety of disciplines are now becoming involved with, as one of them put it, "real problems" that give them a grasp of the use of their work in ways that clearly excite them.[44]

While the Engineering Research Centers highlight how inappropriate the federal R&D priorities of the 1950s are to the needs of the 1990s, they also show that relatively small amounts of federal R&D funds can make a big difference. It should be possible for the federal government to meet its responsibility to maintain an outstanding talent and knowledge base at universities through incremental changes in the distribution of funding among federal agencies. The most direct solution would be to allocate a greater percentage of the federal R&D budget to the one agency that already defines the strength of university-based science and engineering as its primary mission. If the NSF represented 4 percent of the federal R&D budget, rather than its current 2.5 percent, the opportunities for improvement would be enormous.[45] With an additional $1 billion reallocated from other mission-directed R&D, NSF could support major new university-based science and engineering research and education in areas of importance to industry. This would serve two mutually supporting objectives: to strengthen the university science and engineering base and to turn it away from government missions and toward technology of commercial significance. And these two objectives would be served without an increase in the federal deficit.

Lesson #5: Once Established, Technology Leadership Is Maintained Through Continuous Improvements in Both Performance and Cost

The ability of GEMS, COMM, and Corning to build and renew leadership through radical and generational innovations is matched by their ability to maintain leadership through continuous improvements in both the performance and cost of their products and processes. Here, finally, is an aspect of the process of building advantage on the basis of technology that is relatively compatible with the U.S. financial environment. Continuous improvements in cost and performance, if vigorously pursued, can lead to relatively quick financial returns with a relatively high degree of certainty and low levels of investment. This suggests that the problem of promoting such continuous improvement among U.S. firms poses less of a challenge to policy making than the problem of promoting the more discontinuous aspects of technology leadership. In fact, one simple and inexpensive government policy already seems to have produced significant benefits. For both Motorola and Corning, pursuit of total quality was one of senior management's primary vehicles for continuously improving both the performance and cost of existing products and processes. The Department of Commerce's Malcolm Baldrige Quality Award has increased awareness among U.S. firms of the value of such efforts by holding up as role models firms that have achieved high levels of total quality. Perhaps most important, it has offered a concrete and highly visible target for catalyzing companywide campaigns for assessing and improving quality.[46]

If there remains a serious obstacle in the United States to continuous improvement in cost and performance, it lies not in the financial environment or the managerial practices reinforced by that environment, but in the government mission-oriented culture that still predominates in U.S. research institutions. We have seen that the federal mission agencies dominate federal R&D funding. Unfortunately, the culture of technology development and engineering found in funding agencies like DoD and NASA is fundamentally different from the culture required for technology leadership in commercial high-technology markets. The defense and aerospace culture emphasizes "one-of-a-kind," high-performance systems that require customized, and often manual, manufacturing—precisely the reverse of the demands placed on high-tech firms competing head to head with Japanese firms. The culture of a funding agency like NSF, on the other hand, is dominated by the rigid divisions of the traditional academic disciplines. While this makes it totally different from the defense and aerospace culture, it is no less distant from the world of commercial technology. With federal R&D funding the primary source of support for universities, the science and engineering talent in this country is therefore being educated into, and assimilating the values of, a culture that is 20 years out of date from the perspective of industrial competitiveness. When young scientists and engineers move from universities to industry, they may actually be contaminating the commercial sector with values and practices that are fundamentally inappropriate for the competitive, short-cycle-time, cost- and performance-oriented world of high technology.

Fortunately, once again the solution is simple: more interactions between industry and universities, and fewer between universities and the government agency culture. The more university-based science and engineering are oriented to problems of importance to industry, the more likely it is that students will be exposed to the need to balance high performance with low cost and elegant design with manufacturability. The more faculty and students interact with industrial scientists and engineers rather than government agency program officers, the more opportunities there will be to break down the cultural barriers against the attitudes and practices required for total, as opposed to just high-end, leadership. The same policy measures that would help develop the talent necessary for radical and generational innovation—for example, $200 million a year for more industry-oriented research and education in universities rather than $2 billion a year for a space station—would also help create the kind of attitudes and values needed to recognize that cost and performance leadership go hand in hand.

Lesson #6. Technology Leadership Is Driven by Competition

In each case, pursuit of technology leadership was motivated by the threat of competition. GEMS did not take CT or MR seriously until its position was directly threatened. COMM's total leadership philosophy evolved in response to the growing strength of Japanese competitors. And the most striking difference between Corning's TV bulb business and its new generation of businesses is that lack of competition led to complacency in the TV bulb business, whereas now, the constant threat of competition drives the ambitious pursuit of cost and performance leadership. The specifics vary from case to case, but the underlying lesson does not: there is nothing quite like competition to spur the often painful and always expensive pursuit of technology leadership.

The lesson for government policy could not be clearer. Measures that reduce exposure to competition are counterproductive. Protectionism is fundamentally incompatible with technology leadership. The only exception is the rare case in which there is strong domestic competition; then it may be possible to protect domestic firms from foreign competition, while still enjoying the benefits of competition. This appears to have happened in Japan, where competition within Japanese markets among Japanese firms is particularly intense.[47] But the more likely scenario for the United States is one in which policies are devised to protect a declining domestic industry unable to keep up with its foreign competitors. Under these circumstances, protectionism is unlikely to do more than delay the inevitable.

It is sometimes maintained that temporary protection from competition can provide firms with the breathing space they need to reestablish their positions. But this also is incompatible with our findings. If the primary source of competitive advantage for U.S. companies in high-tech markets is technology leadership, and if competition spurs the pursuit of this leadership, it is difficult to see how a reduction in competitive pressure increases the likelihood of long-term success. Even for firms that have fallen behind, direct incentives and perhaps even subsidies for the kinds of activities that lead to development of new generations of technology and businesses (see lessons 2 and 3 above) would be more effective than protection from competition.

That competition drives the pursuit of technology leadership is incompatible with another policy idea popular in the late 1980s and early 1990s: cooperative R&D among firms, focused on the precompetitive stage of technology development. It is one thing for firms that have fallen behind to form an alliance as part of the effort to catch up. U.S. semiconductor manufacturers, for example, are increasingly dependent on Japanese suppliers of semiconductor manufacturing equipment. Sematech is an attempt by these firms to reduce their dependence on foreign suppliers by jointly funding development of new generations of equipment. But it is quite a different matter for a leader, or a firm that aspires to be a leader, to engage in cooperation. In the semiconductor industry, Intel has never suggested that U.S. industry should cooperate in the development of new generations of microprocessors, or new generations of design technology, which is the source of much of Intel's advantage. Cooperation is proposed only in those areas where Intel and its counterparts have fallen behind—or perhaps more accurately, where their equipment suppliers have fallen behind. Leadership, as should be clear from all of these cases, is driven by an obsession with winning—an obsession with getting there first and then staying ahead. This determination is fueled by the threat of competition, not the promise of cooperation. In principle, the pursuit of technology leadership is as incompatible with cooperative R&D as it is with protectionism.

Leaders do engage in cooperative arrangements, as we have seen in these cases—most notably Corning with its optical fiber joint ventures and GEMS with YMS. But in each instance, the joint ventures were established to enhance leadership that had already been won, rather than to create the leadership in the first place. Corning's were primarily intended to ensure market access; and market access was an issue only when Corning had reached a leadership position in optical fiber technology. YMS served precisely the same function for GEMS—an important vehicle for entry into low-end and foreign markets once GEMS had already achieved its dominant position in CT and MR.

Lesson #7: Government Policies Influence Pursuit of Leadership in Diverse Ways

One other policy-related theme that threads its way through these cases is that the pursuit of technology leadership is influenced by many government policies and regulations, only some of which are considered relevant to industrial competitiveness. Regulations designed to curb health costs, for example, led to a collapse of the market for CT at the very time GEMS was in its most vulnerable position. Hospitals began to postpone their CT orders, and this gave GEMS the time it needed to develop an improved product and with it, market leadership. The same regulatory effect occurred during the development of MR, although in this instance the collapse of demand badly damaged GEMS' profitability just as the need to invest in MR was at its peak.

Motorola's pursuit of leadership was influenced by two entirely different sets of policies. FCC regulation of the frequency spectrum was a constant concern. One of the reasons COMM explored low-frequency paging in the 1950s was because the low-frequency spectrum was unregulated. Twenty years later, the need for regulatory approval significantly slowed COMM's attempts to create a portable and mobile cellular telephone business. It was ready to introduce its first products five years before FCC licenses were finally granted. And now in the 1990s, one of the most significant obstacles to creating Iridium is government regulation of airwaves, not just in the United States, but in every country served by the system. Trade policy also played a critical role in Motorola's history. Motorola's attempt to break into the Japanese market for paging, which had such a fundamental effect on its thinking about quality, would have been impossible without the intervention of the U.S. Special Trade Representative and an interested congressional delegation. Similarly, it made effective use of antidumping regulations in its response to attacks on the low end of the paging market.

The government policy that affected Corning's pursuit of leadership most dramatically was the divestiture of AT&T. Prior to the divestiture, Corning's fiber optics business faced the unhappy prospect of competing with its largest potential customer. The breakup of AT&T opened the market to new competitors like MCI and GTE, which were the first significant customers for Corning's fiber. Patents and regulations protecting patents also played an important role in the history of Corning's success. A willingness to prosecute violators of its intellectual property rights was an integral part of Corning's larger campaign to build and maintain technology leadership.

Two general types of policy influences on the pursuit of leadership are apparent in these cases. First, there are the influences of policies that bear directly on the problem of competitiveness. Trade policy and patent protection are examples. What is most interesting here is the relationship of these policies to the pursuit of technology leadership. They become especially useful to U.S. firms in high-tech markets once those firms have established technology leadership.

The efforts of the U.S. Special Trade Representative in Motorola's case were useful only because Motorola was able to meet NTT's performance requirements and compete with Japanese pager manufacturers. Also, laws protecting intellectual property rights were important to Corning only because it had established a leadership position in optical fibers. In the absence of technology leadership, trade and patent policy are blunt instruments in a government's efforts to build competitiveness in high-tech markets. They can further the interests of U.S. firms that have established leadership, but they cannot compensate for the absence of leadership.

These cases also highlight a second class of policy influences on the pursuit of technology leadership. These spring from policies that tend to be driven by goals other than competitiveness. The clearest examples are federal regulation of the airwaves and health care cost reimbursement. Both played a significant role in our cases, yet neither was shaped by a concern with industrial competitiveness. Health care cost reimbursement regulations, for example, arose from a need for cost containment. Given the diversity of this second class of policies, there is no single or overarching prescription for managing the myriad ways in which they can influence the pursuit of competitiveness in high-tech markets. It is possible to increase the likelihood that the effects of such policies on competitiveness are taken into account during policy deliberations, which is the intended function of the notorious White House Cabinet Council on Competitiveness, established during the Bush administration and chaired by Vice President Quayle. But beyond ensuring a certain consideration, there does not appear to be any additional generic measure that can be taken. It would be impossible in the U.S. political system to mandate that concerns about competitiveness be given priority in policy debates about health care cost containment, regulating the airwaves, and the like. The best that can be achieved is for competitiveness to become one of the values that is weighed in the push and pull of policy debates. In some instances—the FCC's treatment of the standards for high-definition TV transmissions is a good example—competitiveness will receive a high priority.[48] In others—the debate over health care cost containment—it will probably continue to be subordinated to other policy objectives.

If there is one generalization that can be made about the effect on competitiveness of this second class of policies, it is that, like those in the first class, they cannot improve the competitiveness of U.S. firms in high-tech markets in the absence of technology leadership. They cannot compensate for the absence of the managerial practices that shape technology leadership. They can further the interests of firms that have already laid the foundation for leadership (as the divestiture of AT&T seemed to have done for Corning); unhappily, they can also hamper such firms (as the FCC may have done in the past in Motorola's case). But one thing they cannot do is make noncompetitive firms competitive. They cannot make leaders out of firms that have not taken the painstaking measures required to build and sustain competitive advantage in high-tech markets.

Conclusion

Any serious consideration of policies designed to promote the competitiveness of U.S. firms in high-tech markets must begin with the reality of the tilted playing field. U.S. firms tend to be smaller and less integrated than their Japanese counterparts, their ownership structures are more oriented toward near-term financial return, and they operate in a political environment where the extent of the challenge posed by global competition in the post-cold war era has not yet been fully grasped. The path of least resistance is to retreat to arenas in which the terms of competition are more favorable, just as U.S. makers of autos, consumer electronics, and machine tools moved to the high ends of their markets in the 1970s. This appears to be the course that the United States is pursuing in effect, although not in intent. In such industries as pharmaceuticals, agricultural and forest products, aerospace and defense, and nonfinancial services and entertainment, the United States enjoys significant structural advantages—the playing field is tilted in favor of the United States. Unfortunately, the path of least resistance is a costly one. The markets from which the United States is retreating are fundamental to long-term economic growth. Electronics, advanced materials, and automation are literally strategic industries. They are the foundations on which much of the world's future industrial capability will be based. This is well illustrated by the computer industry—one of the few short-cycle-time high-tech industries in which U.S. firms still hold a clear lead. Increasingly, the value added by this industry lies in the basic components that make up the computer—memory chips and microprocessors, mass storage devices, and displays. Leadership in two of these basic components is now controlled by Japanese electronics companies. The result is that in the fastest-growing segments of the computer industry, U.S. leadership is already lost.

The alternative to retreating to the more favorable playing fields is to follow the path blazed by GEMS, Motorola, and Corning: compete in the face of structural disadvantages by building advantage on the basis of technology leadership. What can government do to promote the ability of U.S. firms to compete on the basis of technology? First and foremost, it must base its actions on the recognition that technology leadership is built by the right kind of strategic management, the absence of which simply cannot be compensated for by government, trade, or technology policy. The first priority in competitiveness policy must be to promote the right kinds of managerial practices. Second, the right kind of strategic management can only build technology leadership if it has the right kind of talent. It is here that competitiveness policy and technology policy meet. The second priority must be to maintain the strength of the university talent and knowledge pool. To do so, the federal R&D system must shed its postwar priorities and confront the harsh truths about the nature of high-tech competition in the 1990s. Finally, government policy must resist the allure of protectionism, for one of the clearest lessons from these cases is that competition spurs the pursuit of technology leadership. U.S. firms must be forced to realize that in order to succeed in high-tech markets, they must fully accept Dave Duke's dictum: if we tie, we lose. And the only way to avoid a tie is to lead technologically.

Notes

1. See National Advisory Committee on Semiconductors, *A Strategic Industry at Risk, A Report to the President and Congress,* Arlington, VA, November 1989.

2. See Joseph Morone, "The Structure of the Federal R&D System and the Need for Change," *The Bridge,* National Academy of Engineering, Fall 1989.

3. Reich and others argue that as corporations become global enterprises, concerns about competitiveness of a nation's firms become obsolete. A firm's contribution to the U.S. economy becomes far more important than the nationality of its ownership or the physical location of its headquarters. This argument, however, rests on an assumption of doubtful empirical validity. While today's market leaders are global companies in the markets they serve and in the range of countries in which they have operations, most still have a clearly identifiable home base—that is, a nation that serves as the physical center for their strategic thinking, advanced technology, and new product and process development. And if a home base can be identified for most prominent multinational firms, there remains good reason to be concerned about the competitiveness of a nation's industries. Since the home base is the locus of activities requiring the most advanced skills, then it is by definition the locus of activities that contribute most to national productivity and standard of living. It follows that if one nation becomes the home base for the leaders of a

disproportionately large number of important industries, its people should benefit relative to those of the nations that have lost leadership in those industries. From a national policy-making perspective, what matters is not the nationality of a firm's ownership or management, but the geographic location of its home base and the high-value activities associated with its home base. That Corning and Motorola are owned by primarily U.S. investors is of far less policy relevance than that they are industry leaders with home bases in the United States. That NEC and Sony are owned primarily by Japanese investors is of far less policy relevance than that they are industry leaders with home bases in Japan. The important distinction is not between American and Japanese firms, but between U.S.-based and Japanese-based firms.

    See Robert B. Reich, "Who Is Us?," *Harvard Business Review*, vol. 68 (January–February 1990), pp. 53–64; for a discussion of the concept of a home base, see Michael E. Porter, *The Competitive Advantage of Nations* (New York: Free Press, 1990), p. 19.

4. The OECD accounts for three-quarters of total world exports of manufactured goods.

    While the U.S. share of OECD production declined from 33.5 percent in 1980, and Japan's share grew from 18.7 percent, U.S. industry is still the clear leader in aggregate production. See National Science Board, *Science & Engineering Indicators—1991*, NSB 91-1 (Washington, DC: U.S. Government Printing Office), pp. 136, 401.

5. Ibid.

6. "Business Roundup," *IEEE Spectrum*, vol. 28 (January 1991), p. 80.

7. National Advisory Committee on Semiconductors, *A Strategic Industry at Risk*, pp. 9–11.

8. Arsen J. Darnay, ed., *Market Share Reporter, 1991* (New York: Gale Research, 1991), pp. 2, 313.

9. National Advisory Committee on Semiconductors, *A Strategic Industry at Risk*, p. 12.

10. Darnay, *Market Share Reporter*, p. 283.

11. "Business Roundup," p. 81.

12. Ibid.

13. Darnay, *Market Share Reporter*, p. 300.

14. Council on Competitiveness, *Picking Up the Pace: The Commercial Challenge to American Innovation*, Washington, DC, 1989, p. 15.

15. David Sanger, "U.S. Tariff Appears to Backfire," *New York Times*, September 26, 1991, p. D1.

16. Ravi Sarathy, "The Interplay of Industrial Policy and International Strategy: Japan's Machine Tool Industry," *California Management Review*, vol. 31 (Spring 1989), pp. 132–133.

17. Interview with James Geier, chairman, Cincinnati Milacron, July 10, 1990.

18. Jeffrey E. Garten, "Japan and Germany: American Concerns," *Foreign Affairs*, vol. 68 (Winter 1989/1990), p. 86.

19. Council on Competitiveness, *Competitiveness Index 1991*, Washington, DC, July 1991, p. 8.

20. National Science Board, Committee on Industrial Support for R&D, *The Competitive Strength of U.S. Industrial Science and Technology: Strategic Issues*, 1992, Appendix table 1–10.

21. Council on Competitiveness, *Competitiveness Index*, p. 8; National Science Board, *Science & Engineering Indicators*, 1991, p. 342.

22. Cited in Thomas Kochan and Paul Osterman, "Human Resource Development and Utilization: Is There Too Little in the U.S.?," Draft, MIT Sloan School of Management, December 1990, p. 68.

23. See, for example, National Science Board, *Science & Engineering Indicators—1989*, NSB 89-1 (Washington, DC: U.S. Government Printing Office, 1989), pp. 27–31.

24. National Advisory Committee on Semiconductors, *A Strategic Industry at Risk*, p. 23.

25. Charles H. Ferguson, "Computers and the Coming of the U.S. Keiretsu," *Harvard Business Review*, vol. 68 (July–August 1990), pp. 55–70.

26. "Kane Reflects on Demise of U.S. Memories," *Challenges*, vol. 3 (March 1990), p. 1.

27. This is a lesson that U.S. policy makers seem incapable of learning when it applies to Japan. During the post–World War II occupation, the U.S. government outlawed Japan's zaibatsu. Within ten years, they had re-emerged as keiretsu. Forty years later, U.S. trade representatives began complaining about the "structural impediments to trade," suggesting that in the interests of fair trade, perhaps Japan should modify its keiretsu structure. For a comprehensive review of developments in trade policy, see Laura Tyson, *Who's Bashing Whom: Trade Conflicts in High-Technology Industries* (Washington, DC: Institute for International Economics, 1992).

28. For a useful review of the literature on this issue, see Gerald H. Anderson, "Why U.S. Managers Might Be More Short-run Oriented Than the Japanese," *Economic Commentary*, Federal Reserve Bank of Cleveland, November 1, 1991.

29. Among the most common are reinstating the investment tax credit, reducing taxes on capital gains, accelerating depreciation schedules, restraining leveraged buyouts and corporate raiding, taxing short-term turnover of securities, eliminating the prohibitions against holding both debt and equity, changing the regulations and practices regarding boards of directors, and protecting boards from shareholder suits. These proposals are often accompanied by calls for reducing the federal deficit and increasing incentives for personal savings.

    For an analysis of the problem of short U.S. time horizons, see National Academy of Engineering, Committee on Time Horizons and Technology Investment, *Time Horizons and Technology Investment* (Washington, DC: National Academy Press, 1992).

30. The 1981 Tax Act introduced a credit on 25 percent of the increase in R&D expenditures over the average of the preceding three years. The Tax Act of 1986 narrowed the definition of the activities qualifying for the credit and reduced the credit to 20 percent. See United States General

Accounting Office, *Tax Policy and Administration*, GAO/GGD-89-114, September 1989.

31. See, for example, The Carnegie Commission on Science, Technology and Government, *Technology and Economic Performance: Organizing the Executive Branch for a Stronger National Technology Base*, New York, September 1991.

32. See Stephen J. Kline, "Innovation Is Not a Linear Process," *Research Management*, vol. XXVIII (July–August 1985), pp. 36–45.

33. National Science Board, *The Competitive Strength of U.S. Industrial Science and Technology*, Appendix table 1–2.

34. National Science Board, *Science & Engineering Indicators*, 1991, pp. 83–100.

35. For a more complete discussion, see Morone, "The Structure of the Federal R&D System and the Need for Change."

36. See Jean C. Derian, *America's Struggle for Leadership in Technology* (Cambridge, MA: MIT Press, 1990).

37. National Science Board, *Science & Engineering Indicators*, pp. 274, 300.

38. U.S. Congress, Office of Technology Assessment, *Federally Funded Research: Decisions for a Decade*, OTA-SET-490 (Washington, DC: Government Printing Office, 1991), p. 162.

39. Leo E. Hanifin, "The Paradox of American Manufacturing," in National Academy of Engineering, *The Challenge to Manufacturing: A Proposal for a National Forum*, Washington, DC, 1988, p. 19.

40. Council on Competitiveness, *Gaining New Ground: Technology Priorities for America's Future*, Washington, DC, February 1991, p. 40.

41. The Committee to Advise the President on High-Temperature Superconductivity, *High-Temperature Superconductivity: Perseverance and Cooperation*, Executive Office of the President, Office of Science and Technology Policy, 1988, p. 8.

42. National Academy of Engineering, *Guidelines for Engineering Research Centers*, Washington, DC, 1983, p. 3.

43. National Academy of Engineering, *Assessment of the National Science Foundation's Engineering Research Centers Program*, Washington, DC, 1989, p. 12.

44. Ibid.

45. In 1990, the Bush administration did endorse a recommendation to double the size of NSF in five years, but actual funding has lagged behind the pace required for such growth.

46. See David A. Garvin, "How the Baldrige Award Really Works," *Harvard Business Review*, vol. 69 (November–December 1991), pp. 80–95.

47. "See, for example, Michael Porter, "The Competitive Advantage of Nations," *Harvard Business Review*, vol. 68 (March–April 1990), p. 82.

48. For an interesting discussion, see George Gilder, "Now or Never," *Forbes*, October 14, 1991, pp. 188–198.

INDEX

279

About the Author

Joseph Morone is an associate professor at the RPI School of Management. He holds the Andersen Consulting Professorship of Management and is director of the Center for Science and Technology Policy. Before joining the faculty at RPI, he worked at General Electric Company's Corporate Research and Development, the White House Office of Science and Technology Policy, and the Keyworth Company, a consulting firm that specialized in technology management.

Dr. Morone holds a Ph.D from Yale University in political science. He has written on various aspects of the management of technology—for example, "The Cost of Capital—The Managerial Perspective," which appeared in the summer 1991 issue of *California Management Review*. He also has interests in science and technology policy and co-authored (with Edward J. Woodhouse) *The Demise of Nuclear Power?: Lessons for Democratic Control of Technology* (Yale University Press), and *Averting Catastrophe: Strategies for Regulating Risky Technologies* (University of California Press).